EARLY CHRISTIANITY IN THE FIRST CENTURY

Jesus' Witnesses to the Ends of the Earth

Edward D. Andrews

EARLY CHRISTIANITY IN THE FIRST CENTURY

Jesus' Witnesses to the Ends of the Earth

Edward D. Andrews

EARLY CHRISTIANITY IN THE FIRST CENTURY

Jesus' Witnesses to the Ends of the Earth

Edward D. Andrews

ISBN-13: 978-1-945757-50-1

ISBN-10: 1-945757-50-7

Christian Publishing House

Cambridge, Ohio

EARLY CHRISTIANITY IN THE FIRST CENTURY: Jesus' Witnesses to the Ends of the Earth © 2017 by Christian Publishing House

support@christianpublishers.org

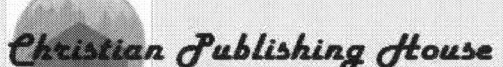

Professional Christian Publishing of the Good News

EARLY CHRISTIANS INTRODUCTION
First Century Christianity

Acts 11:26 English Standard Version (ESV)

26 and when he had found him, he brought him to Antioch. For a whole year they met with the church and taught a great many people. And in Antioch **the disciples were first called Christians**.

The Latinized Greek term *Christianos* (Christian) appears only in Acts 11:26; 26:28, and 1 Pet. 4:16 in the Greek New Testament, which was a designation by the Gentles for those who followed Jesus Christ, to make a distinction between them and the Jews, as they were not Grecian Jews. Of course, the Jews used the Greek term Χριστος [*Christos*, Messiah] because they believed in the coming of the Messiah, so they would have never referred to the followers of Jesus as *Christianos*. The Jews referred to the followers of Jesus as the *Galileans* or *Nazarenes*. *Young's Literal Translation* (YLT) reads, "The disciples also were **divinely** **called** first in Antioch Christians." This suggests that God had something to do with their being called *Christianos* (Christian). However, when we look at over fifty others translations, we find "first called" not "divinely called." Why do we find such a difference? The Greek verb *chrematisai* in this text is generally rendered simply as "were called."

Young's Literal Translation (YLT) was published in 1862. When we look at older literature, we can see how YLT came to their rendering, "The disciples also were divinely called first in Antioch Christians." Strong's *Exhaustive Concordance of the Bible*, in its Greek dictionary (1890, p. 78), defines *chrematisai* as "to utter an oracle . . . i.e. divinely intimate." Edward Robinson's *Greek and English Lexicon* (1885, p. 786) says it means, "Spoken in respect to a divine response, oracle, declaration, to give response, to speak as an oracle, to warn from God." Thayer's *Greek-English Lexicon of the New Testament* (1889, p. 671): "to give a divine command or admonition, to teach from heaven ... to be divinely commanded, admonished, instructed ... to be the mouthpiece of divine revelations, to promulge the commands of God." Thomas Scott in his *Explanatory Notes* on this text (1832, Vol. III, p. 419) says: "The word implies that this was done by divine revelation: for it has generally this signification in the New Testament, and is rendered 'warned from God' or 'warned of God,' even when there is no word for GOD in the Greek." Concerning Acts 11:26, Clarke's *Commentary* says: "The word [*chrematisai*] in our common text, which we translate *were called*, signifies in the New Testament, to *appoint, warn,* or *nominate,* by *Divine direction.* In this sense, the word is used, Matt. ii. 12 . . . If, therefore, the name was given by *Divine appointment*, it is most likely that Saul and Barnabas were directed to give it; and that, therefore, the name *Christian* is from God."

A lexicon is simply a dictionary that alphabetically lists words and their meanings, e.g. of an ancient language, i.e., Hebrew-English or Greek-English. When the BDAG (*A Greek-English Lexicon of the New Testament and other Early Christian Literature*), contains Greek words, it give us all of the meanings as to the words use at that time (early Christianity). Looking at our English word "hand," it has over 20 different meanings, depending on the context. "Hand" can mean what we have at the end of our arm, a pointer on a clock, the cards dealt to a player in a card game (a losing hand) and a round of applause (a big hand for our next contestant). It can also mean power (your future is in your own hands), a member of the crew of a vessel (Attention, all hands!), as well as about another twenty meanings. The word "hand" standing alone has no meaning, as it lacks context. Yes, we would have to assume the primary meaning if we lacked context, namely, what we have at the end of our arm, the human hand.

The same holds true with the Greek verb *chrematisai* in our Greek-English Lexicon BDAG (p. 1090, 3rd edition). It contains two means (1) **impart a divine message, make known a divine injunction/warning** (Active Heb. 12:25; Passive Matt 2:22) and (2) **to take/bear a name/title** (as so and so), **to go under the name of,** act., but freq. rendered as pass. in Engl. tr.: ***be called/named, be identified as*** ... (Rom 7:3; Ac 11:26) The question is, what is our context?

Excursion: John B. Polhill

In all three instances [*Christianos*] is a term used by outsiders to designate Christians. Evidently the term was not originally used by Christians of themselves. They preferred terms like "believers, disciples, brothers." The first extensive usage by a Christian writer to designate fellow believers was by Ignatius, bishop of Antioch, around the turn of the second century. The term (*Christianoi*) consists of the Greek word for Christ/Messiah (*Christos*) with the *Latin* ending *ianus*, meaning *belonging to, identified by*. Examples of similar formations are *Herodianoi*, partisans of Herod, and *Augustianoi*, the zealotic followers of Nero.[1] The term was often used by Roman writers to designate

---

[1] Most commentators are in agreement that the term was first applied to Christians by outsiders. For an opposing view, which sees it as first used by Christians as a self-designation, see H. B. Mattingly, "The Origin of the Name Christiani," *JTS* 9 (1958): 26–37; E. J. Bickerman, "The Name of Christians," *HTR* 42 (1949): 109–24; C. Spicq, "Ce que signifie le titre de Chretien," *ST* 15 (1961): 68–78.

followers of Christ.[2] The early usage in Antioch is perhaps indicative of two things. For one, it is the sort of term Gentiles would have used and perhaps reflects the success of Antioch's Gentile mission. Gentiles were dubbing their fellow Gentiles who became followers of Christ "Christians." Second, it reflects that Christianity was beginning to have an identity of its own and no longer was viewed as a totally Jewish entity. Again, the success among Gentiles would have hastened this process in Antioch. (Polhill 2001, 274)

The Christians actually referred to themselves as *disciples* (a learner, a pupil, Acts 6:1), *believers* (Ac 2:44), *brothers* (Ac 10:23), *holy ones* (Ac 9:13), and *the Way* (Ac 9:2). They also referred to themselves as the *chosen ones* (Col 3:12), *slaves to God* and *slaves of Christ Jesus* (Rom. 6:22; Phil 1:1) the *church of God* and *those who call upon the Lord*. (Ac 20:28; 1 Cor. 1:2; 2 Tim. 2:22. These designations carried with them doctrinal meaning and were used within the Christian congregations. Those outside of Christianity mainly referred to them as *the Way* (Ac 9:2; 19:9, 23; 22:4), and enemies of the church called them *the sect of the Nazarenes* or simply as *this sect*. (Ac 24:5; 28:22) The name *Christianos* was used as early as 44 C.E., just eleven years after the death, resurrection and ascension of Christ. We see it again around 58 C.E., in the city of Caesarea, being used by King Herod Agrippa II himself, who said to Paul, "In a short time you will persuade me to become a Christian."—Ac 26:28.

Paul said of the Corinthian Christian congregation,[3] "For I am jealous for you with a godly jealousy; for I betrothed you to one husband, so that to Christ I might present you as a pure virgin." (2 Cor. 11:2) All Christians should have an intense or strong desire to do everything within their power to assist fellow Christians to remain exclusive in their faith to God and obedient to Christ. Paul was comparing the spiritual brothers to a virgin (pure and clean) to Christ, as his potential bride. Paul was jealously protecting them so that they may remain pure for Christ. Paul demonstrated his zeal for them by way of his many lengthy letters to them and other first century Christians and congregations. Paul also said to the Ephesian Christians, "the husband is the head of the wife as Christ is the head of the church. He is the Savior of the body." (Eph. 5:23) The

---

[2] Cf. Josephus, *Antiquities* 18.64; Tacitus, *Annals* 15.44; Pliny, *Epistles* 10.96–97; Lucian, *Alexander* 25.38.

[3] In the Greek New Testament, the Greek word *ecclesia* is rendered as "congregation" throughout this publication. In almost all Bibles, it is rendered "church," but its actual meaning is "congregation." This does not mean that we will not use the more common term of "church." Ecclesia is generally used in a collective sense (1 Cor. 12:28), and at other times it refers to a specific group in some city or home.—Acts 8:1; Romans 8:5

only wife that Jesus Christ has is his relationship with the Christian congregation. Christ is the head of the church, which obligates him to care for its members with the decisions that he makes for them.

Galatians 3:26-28 New American Standard Bible (NASB)	Colossians 3:11 New American Standard Bible (NASB)
26 For you are all sons of God through faith in Christ Jesus. 27 For all of you who were baptized into Christ have clothed yourselves with Christ. 28 There is neither Jew nor Greek, there is neither slave nor free man, there is neither male nor female; for you are all one in Christ Jesus.	11 a renewal in which there is no distinction between Greek and Jew, circumcised and uncircumcised, barbarian, Scythian, slave and freeman, but Christ is all, and in all.

As to being "one in Christ Jesus," Max Anders writes, "Having explained the vertical change that grace brought, now Paul shows its horizontal effect when he states **you are all one in Christ**. In Christ, human distinctions lose their significance. Regardless of race, profession, or gender, all who come to Christ must come the same way—through faith and repentance. As a result, with all distinctions erased, all believers are united in Christ. This does not mean that all distinctions are erased on the human level. A slave was still a slave in the eyes of Rome, but not in the eyes of God."[4]

First-Century Christians

Acts 1:8 English Standard Version (ESV)

8 But you will receive power when the Holy Spirit has come upon you, and you will be my witnesses in Jerusalem and in all Judea and Samaria, and to the end of the earth."

Before Jesus ascended back to heaven, he appointed his disciples to be witnesses. However, who were these witnesses, and who were they to be witnessing for? The account says, "you will be my witnesses." Did Jesus mean that God's people, no longer natural Israel, but the Christian congregation was no longer to be witnesses of the Father? Remember the words of Isaiah to Israel about the Father, "you are my witnesses, said Jehovah, and my servant whom I have chosen; that you may know and

---

[4] (Anders, Holman New Testament Commentary: vol. 8, Galatians, Ephesians, Philippians, Colossians 1999, 40)

believe me, and understand that I am he: before me there was no God formed, neither shall there be after me." (Isa. 43:10, ASV)

Transition from the nation of Israel to the Christian congregation meant that the new witnesses would be both witnesses of the Father and the Son. Therefore, the first Christians were going to witness about the role that Jesus would be playing in the sanctification of his Father's name, as well as the sovereignty issue and the coming Kingdom of God. (Rom. 16:25-27; Phil. 2:9-11) They bore witnesses that the long awaited seed, the long awaited Messiah, the Son of God, who came to be known as Jesus Christ had been sent by his Father, to "**not** to be served **but to** serve, and to give his life as a ransom for many." (Matt. 20:28) They bore witness to the one 'whom the people of Israel crucified, whom God raised from the dead." (Ac 4:10) The disciples of Jesus Christ in the first century were given one primary responsibility, which every Christian has had since, including us.

Matthew 24:14; 28:19-20; Acts 1:8 English Standard Version (ESV)

¹⁴ And this gospel of the kingdom will be **proclaim**ed throughout **the whole world** as a testimony to all nations, and then the end will come. ¹⁹ Go therefore and **make disciples** of **all nations** ... **teaching** them to observe all that I have commanded you. And behold, I am with you always, to the end of the age." "But you will receive power when the Holy Spirit has come upon you, and you will be **my witnesses** in Jerusalem and in all Judea and Samaria, and **to the end of the earth**."

We will cover this more fully below, under the heading, The Christian Evangelist. However, for now, let us briefly consider the importance and seriousness of this assignment. Jesus said, "Go," but to whom? The assignment is to 'proclaim, teach and make disciples to all nations, to the most distant parts of the earth.' Initially, when this was given there were only Jewish believers. It was especially demanding for them. (See Acts 10:9-16, 28.) Why? For the past 2,000 years the descendants of Abraham, Isaac and Jacob, were the only true way to God. There was no need to go out and find followers because they were born into the pure worship of God. If a Gentile wanted to become a part of the one true way to God, he came to the nation of Israel. (1 Ki. 8:41-43) Initially, when Jesus sent out his twelve disciples, he said, "go, preach, saying" ..., but it was specifically "to the lost sheep of the house of Israel." (Matt. 10:1, 6-7) Now, things were to be different, they were to go to people of 'all nations, to the most distant parts of the earth.' Why were theses Christians and us being commissioned?

Jesus said to "make disciples." Yes, the disciples were to make more disciples, of all who had a receptive heart, and accepted the biblical truths. What was specifically involved? According to *A Dictionary of Biblical Languages*, the Greek word rendered "disciple" (*mathetes*) a **follower**, often a disciple who is a believer and close follower, though other less committed relationships are indicated (Mt 8:21; 10:1; 12:49; Lk 14:27; A 6:1; **2**. LN 27.16 **pupil**, student, one tutored, implying a closer relationship than mere information (Mt 10:24, 25)."[5] The Greek word *mathetes* means one who is a "learner," "a taught one." This is not just a pupil, but also includes the sense of one who adheres to someone, i.e., one who follows, obeys, observes, sticks to, stands by this one, which is Jesus Christ for the Christian disciple.

The Christian Evangelist

Why do Christians desire to talk about their beliefs? Jesus said, "And this gospel of the kingdom will be proclaimed in the whole inhabited earth for a testimony to all the nations, and then the end will come." (Matt. 24:14) This is the assignment that all Christians are obligated to be a part of, to the best of their abilities, based on their gifts and talents. Jesus also said, "You shall love your neighbor as yourself." (Matt. 22:39) Jesus commanded that we "go therefore and make disciples of all nations, baptizing them" and "teaching them to observe all that I have commanded you." (Matt. 28:19-20) All true Christians[6] have a

---

[5] Swanson, James. *A Dictionary of Biblical Languages: Greek*, Washington: Logos Research Systems, 1997, Greek GK #3412

[6] As of the early 21st century, Christianity has around 2.2 billion adherents, out of about 7 billion people. Of these 2.2 billion, there are true Christians and there are false Christians. We are going to use one doctrine herein (inerrancy of Scripture), in establishing who is a true Christian, as opposed to who is a false Christian. You are **not** a true Christian if you do not accept **full inerrancy** of Scripture. This means that a true Christian would agree with the entire short statement below.

1. God, who is Himself Truth and speaks truth only, has inspired Holy Scripture in order thereby to reveal Himself to lost mankind through Jesus Christ as Creator and Lord, Redeemer and Judge. Holy Scripture is God's witness to Himself.

2. Holy Scripture, being God's own Word, written by men prepared and superintended by His Spirit, **is of infallible divine authority in all matters upon which it touches**: it is to be believed, as God's instruction, in all that it affirms, obeyed, as God's command, in all that it requires; embraced, as God's pledge, in all that it promises.

3. The Holy Spirit, Scripture's divine Author, both authenticates it to us by His inward witness and opens our minds to understand its meaning.

4. Being wholly and verbally God-given, **Scripture is without error or fault in all its teaching**, no less in what it states about God's acts in creation, about the events of world history, and about its own literary origins under God, than in its witness to God's saving grace in individual lives.

determination to imitate God, which moves us to persist in reflecting his glory through our sharing of the Good News with others.

Within the heart of each true Christian, is the desire that he 'love the Lord his God with all his heart and with all his soul and with all his mind.' (Matt. 22:37) If this is the case, we to would be patient, not wishing that any should perish, but that all should reach repentance.' (2 Pet 3:9) For the true Christian, "for out of the abundance of the heart his mouth speaks." (Luke 6:45) The apostle Paul helps see the importance of the work that lies ahead,

Romans 10:14 English Standard Version (ESV)

¹⁴ How then will they call on him in whom they have not believed? And how are they to believe in him of whom they have never heard? And how are they to hear without someone preaching?

Every Christian should realize that effective communication would be one of the determining factors in whether the unbeliever will accept the truth. Some may feel that the message will get through to the unbeliever, if he is receptive to the Good News regardless of communication skills. While that may be true on occasion, it is not the rule it is the exception. Moreover, it needs to be realized that our communicating skills are to be used to affect the hearts and minds of both the receptive and unreceptive. With the **unreceptive**, our skills must be stronger, as we are reasoning from the Scriptures, to overturn whatever has made this one unreceptive to the truth. It might be best if I were to put it this way, effective communication skills do not guarantee that one will accept the truth of God's Word, but a lack of communication skills means that it is far less likely that they will accept the truth of God's word.

As a firefighter and a police officer, a Christian evangelist is on the job 24/7, as an opportunity to share a biblical message may occur at any time. Moreover, our conduct is always on display, and it is a form of witnessing to others. (1 Pet. 2:12) Whether we realize it or not we are always sending and receiving messages consciously and subconsciously with others by our tone, our demeanor, our body language, and so on. Again, our ability to communicate with clearness and precision, resolution and assurance is usually the difference between being successful and unsuccessful in our efforts to reach the hearts and minds of prospective (i.e., future) Christian disciples.

---

5. The authority of Scripture is inescapably impaired if this total divine inerrancy is in any way limited or disregarded, or made relative to a view of truth contrary to the Bible's own; and such lapses bring serious loss to both the individual and the Church.—http://bible-translation.net/page/chicago-statement-on-biblical-inerrancy-icbi

All Christians are Expected to Carry Out the Work of An Evangelist

Before delving into our book on Evangelism, let us take a moment to listen to one of the world's leading authorities on Spiritual disciplines for our Christian life by Donald S. Whitney, who covers our obligation to evangelize very well,

> Most of those reading this book will not need convincing that evangelism is expected of every Christian. All Christians are not expected to use the same methods of evangelism, but all Christians are expected to evangelize.

> Before we go further, let's define our terms. What is evangelism? If we want to define it thoroughly, we could say that evangelism is to present Jesus Christ in the power of the Holy Spirit to sinful people, in order that they may come to put their trust in God through Him, to receive Him as their Savior, and serve Him as their King in the fellowship of His Church.[7] If we want to define it simply, we could say that New Testament evangelism is communicating the gospel. Anyone who faithfully relates the essential elements of God's salvation through Jesus Christ is evangelizing. This is true whether your words are spoken, written, or recorded, and whether they are delivered to one person or to a crowd.

Why is evangelism expected of us? The Lord Jesus Christ Himself has commanded us to witness. Consider His authority in the following:

> "Therefore go and make disciples of all nations, baptizing them in the name of the Father and of the Son and of the Holy Spirit, and teaching them to obey everything I have commanded you. And surely I will be with you always, to the very end of the age" (Matt. 28: 19-20).

> "He said to them, 'Go into all the world and preach the good news to all creation'" (Mark 16: 15).

> "And repentance and forgiveness of sins will be preached in his name to all nations, beginning at Jerusalem" (Luke 24: 47).

> "Again Jesus said, 'Peace be with you! As the Father has sent me, I am sending you'" (John 20: 21).

---

[7] See J. I. Packer, Evangelism and the Sovereignty of God (Downers Grove, IL: InterVarsity Press, 1979), pages 37-57.

"But you will receive power when the Holy Spirit comes on you; and you will be my witnesses in Jerusalem, and in all Judea and Samaria, and to the ends of the earth" (Acts 1: 8).

These commands weren't given to the apostles only. For example, the apostles never came to this nation. For the command of Jesus to be fulfilled and for America to hear about Christ, the gospel had to come here by other Christians. And the apostles will never come to your home, your neighborhood, or to the place where you work. For the Great Commission to be fulfilled there, for Christ to have a witness in that "remote part" of the earth, a Christian like you must discipline yourself to do it.

Some Christians believe that evangelism is a gift and the responsibility of only those with that gift. They appeal to Ephesians 4:11 for support: "It was he who gave some to be apostles, some to be prophets, some to be evangelists, and some to be pastors and teachers." While it is true that God gifts some for ministry as evangelists, He calls all believers to be His witnesses and provides them with both the power to witness and a powerful message. Every evangelist is called to be a witness, but only a few witnesses are called to the vocational ministry of an evangelist. Just as each Christian, regardless of spiritual gift or ministry, is to love others, so each believer is to evangelize whether or not his or her gift is that of evangelist.

Think of our responsibility for personal evangelism from the perspective of 1 Peter 2:9: "But you are a chosen people, a royal priesthood, a holy nation, a people belonging to God." Many Christians who are familiar with this part of the verse don't have a clue how the rest of it goes. It goes on to say that these privileges are yours, Christian, "that you may declare the praises of him who called you out of darkness into his wonderful light." We normally think of this verse as establishing the doctrine of the priesthood of all believers. But it is equally appropriate to say that it also exhorts us to a kind of prophet hood of all believers. God expects each of us to "declare the praises" of Jesus Christ.[8]

While this author agrees with Whitney's every word in the above, I would emphasize that we are to evangelize, so as to make disciples, which is more involved that simply sharing the Gospel. Paul summarizes

---

[8] Whitney, Donald S. (2012-01-05). Spiritual Disciplines for the Christian Life with Bonus Content (Pilgrimage Growth Guide) (p. 100-101). Navpress.

the most basic elements of the gospel message, that is, the death, burial, resurrection, and appearances of the resurrected Christ. (1 Cor. 18:1-8) Therefore, the Gospel explained in detail or simply stated as Paul has put it, will not be enough to convert many unbelievers to the faith. Therefore, it is best to understand our responsibility as evangelist, in the sense of being able to proclaim or explain our Christian teachings both offensively and defensively: to **(1)** defend God's Word, **(2)** defend the faith, **(3)** pull some who doubt back from the fire, and **(4)** most importantly, to help the lost find salvation.

All Christians are to be Evangelizers

Evangelism is the work of a Christian evangelist, of which all true Christians are obligated to partake to some extent, which seeks to persuade other people to become Christian, especially by sharing the basics of the Gospel, but also the deeper message of biblical truths. Today the Gospel is almost an unknown, so what does the Christian evangelist do? **Preevangelism** is laying a foundation for those who have no knowledge of the Gospel, giving them background information, so that they are able to grasp what they are hearing. The Christian evangelist is preparing their mind and heart so that they will be receptive to the biblical truths. In many ways, this is known as apologetics.

Christian apologetics [Greek: *apologia*, "verbal defense, speech in defense"] is a field of **Christian theology** which endeavors to offer a reasonable and sensible basis for the **Christian faith**, defending the faith against objections. It is reasoning from the Scriptures, explaining and proving, as one instructs in sound doctrine, many times having to overturn false reasoning before he can plant the seeds of truth. It can also be earnestly contending for the faith and saving one from losing their faith, as they have begun to doubt. Moreover, it can involve rebuking those who contradict the truth. It is being prepared to make a defense to anyone who asks the Christian evangelist for a reason for the hope that is in him or her. – Jude 1.3, 21-23; 1 Pet 3.15; Acts 17:2-3; Titus 1:9.

What do we mean by **obligated** and what we mean by **evangelism** are at the heart of the matter and are indeed related to each other?

EVANGELISM: An evangelist is a proclaimer of the gospel or good news, as well as all biblical truths. There are levels of evangelism, which is pictured in first-century Christianity. All Christians evangelized in the first century, but a select few fit the role of a full-time evangelist (Ephesians 4:8, 11-12), as was true of Philip and Timothy.

15

Both Philip and Timothy are specifically mentioned as evangelizers. (Ac 21:8; 2 Tim. 4:5) Philip was a full-time evangelist after Pentecost, who was sent to the city of Samaria, having great success. An angel even directed Philip to an Ethiopian Eunuch, to share the good news about Christ with him. Because of the Eunuch's already having knowledge of God by way of the Old Testament, Philip was able to help him understand that the Hebrew Scriptures pointed to Christ as the long-awaited Messiah. In the end, Philip baptized the Eunuch. After that, the Spirit again sent Philip on a mission, this time to Azotus and all the cities on the way to Caesarea. (Ac 8:5, 12, 14, 26-40) Paul evangelized in many lands, setting up one congregation after another. (2 Cor. 10:13-16) Timothy was an evangelizer or missionary, and Paul placed distinct importance on evangelizing when he gave his parting encouragement to Timothy. – 2 Timothy 4:5; 1 Timothy 1:3.

The office of apostle and evangelist seem to overlap in some areas, but could be distinguished in that apostles traveled and set up congregations, which took evangelizing skills, but also developed the congregations after they were established. The evangelists were more of a missionary, being stationed in certain areas to grow and develop congregations. In addition, if we look at all of the apostles and the evangelists, plus Paul's more than one hundred traveling companions, it seems very unlikely that they could have had Christianity at over one million by the 125 C.E. This was accomplished because all Christians were obligated to carry out some level of evangelism.

OBLIGATED: In the broadest sense of the term for evangelizer, all Christians are obligated to play some role as an evangelist.

• *Basic Evangelism* is planting seeds of truth and watering any seeds that have been planted. [In the basic sense of this word (euaggelistes), this would involve all Christians.] In some cases, it may be that one Christian planted the seed, which were initially rejected, so he was left in a good way because the planter did not try to force the truth down his throat. However, later he faces something in life that moves him to reconsider those seeds and another Christian waters what had already been planted by the first Christian. This evangelism can be carried out in all of the methods that are available: informal, house-to-house, street, phone, the internet, and the like. What amount of time is invested in the evangelism work is up to each Christian to decide for themselves?

• *Making Disciples* is having any role in the process of getting an unbeliever from his unbelief state to the point of accepting Christ as his Savior and being baptized. Once the unbeliever has become a believer, he is still developed until he has become strong. Any Christian could potentially carry this one person through all of the developmental stages.

On the other hand, it may be that several have some part. It is like a person that specializes in a certain aspect of a job, but all are aware of the other aspects, in case they are called on to carry out that phase. Again, each Christian must decide for themselves what role they are to have, and how much of a role, but should be prepared to fill any role if needed.

• *Part-Time or Full-Time Evangelist* is one who sees this as their calling and chooses to be very involved as an evangelist in their local church and community. They may work part-time to supplement their work as an evangelist. They may be married with children, but they realize their gift is in the field of evangelism. If it were the wife, the husband would work toward supporting her work as an evangelist and vice-versa. If it were a single person, he or she would supplement their work by being employed part-time, but also the church would help as well. This person is well trained in every aspect of bringing one to Christ.

• *Congregation Evangelists* should be very involved in evangelizing their communities and helping the church members play their role at the basic levels of evangelism. There is nothing to say that one church could not have many within, who take on part-time or full-time evangelism within the congregation, which would and should be cultivated.

We live in a world today where Genesis 6:5 and 8:21 is magnified a thousand fold.

Genesis 6:5 Updated American Standard Version (UASV)

⁵ Jehovah saw that the wickedness of man was great in the earth, and that every inclination of the thoughts of his heart was only evil continually.

Genesis 8:21 Updated American Standard Version (UASV)

²¹ And when Jehovah smelled the pleasing aroma, and Jehovah said in his heart, "I will never again curse the ground because of man, for the inclination of man's heart is evil from his youth. Neither will I ever again strike down every living thing as I have done.

Matthew 24:14 English Standard Version (ESV)

¹⁴ And this gospel [good news] of the kingdom will be proclaimed throughout the whole world as a testimony to all nations, and then the end will come.

With much of what people see today, one wonders what the Goods News could be.

Isaiah 52:7 English Standard Version (ESV)

⁷ How beautiful upon the mountains are the feet of him who brings good news, who publishes peace, who brings good news of happiness, who publishes salvation, who says to Zion, "Your God reigns."

Nahum 1:15 English Standard Version (ESV)

¹⁵ Behold, upon the mountains, the feet of him
who brings good news,
who publishes peace!
Keep your feasts, O Judah;
fulfill your vows,
for never again shall the worthless pass through you;
he is utterly cut off.

Romans 10:15 English Standard Version (ESV)

¹⁵ And how are they to preach unless they are sent? As it is written, "How beautiful are the feet of those who preach the good news!"[9]

Christianity today, has sadly, fallen away from the evangelism that they had been assigned, the proclaiming and teaching of the good news, the making of disciples. (Matt. 24:14; 28:19-20) The first-century Christians were very zealous when it came to sharing the good news and biblical truths with others. In fact, the new believers were taught the basics of the faith before they were baptized. Once they were baptized, they were immediately involved in spreading these same biblical truths to others. This is why just seventy years after the sacrificial death of Jesus Christ; there were more than a million Christians spread all throughout the then known world of the Roman Empire. Christians today, should have this same zeal because Jesus gave only one command that was to be carried out after his departure, the making of disciples.

The good news is that this current evil age that we live in is not all that we have to look forward to, as all have the opportunity of gaining eternal life. Yes, the way of salvation is open to all. Therefore, Christians today should be in the work of being used by God to help as many as possible to find the path of salvation, before Christ's second coming.

John 3:16 English Standard Version (ESV)

¹⁶ "For God so loved the world, that he gave his only Son, that whoever believes in him should not perish but have eternal life.

---

[9] Romans 10:15 : Cited from Isa. 52:7; [Nah. 1:15; Eph. 6:15]

John 3:36 English Standard Version (ESV)

³⁶ Whoever believes in the Son has eternal life; whoever does not obey the Son shall not see life, but the wrath of God remains on him.

Revelation 21:3-4 English Standard Version (ESV)

³ And I heard a loud voice from the throne saying, "Behold, the dwelling place of God is with man. He will dwell with them, and they will be his people, and God himself will be with them as their God. ⁴ He will wipe away every tear from their eyes, and death shall be no more, neither shall there be mourning, nor crying, nor pain anymore, for the former things have passed away."

Jesus Set the Example

Christians today should be seeking to walk in the steps of their exemplar, Jesus Christ. Yes, we have been called, so that we might follow in Jesus' steps.

1 Peter 2:21 English Standard Version (ESV)

²¹ For to this you have been called, because Christ also suffered for you, leaving you an example, so that you might follow in his steps.

Luke 4:17-21 English Standard Version (ESV)

¹⁷ And the scroll of the prophet Isaiah was given to him. He unrolled the scroll and found the place where it was written,

¹⁸ "The Spirit of the Lord is upon me,
because he has anointed me
to proclaim good news to the poor.
He has sent me **to proclaim liberty** to the captives
and recovering of sight to the blind,
to set at liberty those who are oppressed,
¹⁹ **to proclaim** the year of the Lord's favor."

²⁰ And he rolled up the scroll and gave it back to the attendant and sat down. And the eyes of all in the synagogue were fixed on him. ²¹ And he began to say to them, "Today this Scripture has been fulfilled in your hearing."

A survey of the Gospels indicates that Jesus' publishing program—via his traveling throughout Galilee and Judea and proclaiming the good news of the kingdom—was extensive and effective. Thousands and thousands of people heard the word from Jesus himself. In ancient times, the method of oral publication was far more effective than written publication.

Books were expensive to make, and many people did not read. Most relied on oral proclamation and aural reception to receive messages. Indeed, most education was based upon oral delivery and aural reception/memorization to transmit texts. Thus, Jesus taught his disciples orally, and they committed his teachings to memory. When it came time, several years later, for the disciples to put these teachings into writing, they were aided by the Holy Spirit, who would remind the disciples of all that Jesus had taught them (John 14:26). Jesus' disciples, commissioned by him, continued the same publishing work after Jesus' death and resurrection. This publishing is known as the *kerygma* (Greek for "proclamation"). The word *kerygma* is taken straight from a well-known practice in ancient times. A king publicized his decrees throughout his empire by means of a *kerux* (a town crier or herald). This person, who often served as a close confidant of the king, would travel throughout the realm, announcing to the people whatever the king wished to make known. In English, we known him as a herald. Each New Testament disciple considered himself or herself to be like the *kerux*, a herald and publisher of the Good News.[10]

Yes, Jesus was an evangelizer, and he trained hundreds of evangelizers throughout his three and half years of ministry. "He went throughout all Galilee, teaching in their synagogues and proclaiming the gospel of the kingdom." (Matthew 4:23) Then, he said to his disciples, "The harvest is plentiful, but the laborers are few; 38, therefore, pray earnestly to the Lord of the harvest to send out laborers into his harvest." (Matt. 9:37-38) The apostles set up Christian congregations, with every Christian following the footsteps of Christ, to be an evangelizer.

There is nothing, wrong with helping our neighbor deal with the social ills of the world, or taking some time to support a political candidate whom we hope will implement laws that will allow for the greater work of evangelizing. However, some segments of Christianity has become a social institution, working night and day to save the world of humankind that is alienated from God. This has diverted them from the lifesaving work of being an evangelist. In the days of the Cold War between the United States and the former Soviet Union, a citizen of the United States would consider it treason if another citizen spent time promoting communism from the former Soviet Bloc. While we are citizens of this world and the country that we live in, our true Kingdom is the Kingdom of God in the person of Jesus Christ. Below we will quote

---

[10] Philip Comfort, *Encountering the Manuscripts: An Introduction to New Testament Paleography & Textual Criticism* (Nashville, TN: Broadman & Holman, 2005), 2.

the *Holman Illustrate Bible Dictionary* at length, to understand and appreciate what the Kingdom of God is.

The Kingdom of God

In the NT the fullest revelation of God's divine rule is in the person of Jesus Christ. His birth was heralded as the birth of a king (Luke 1:32–33). The ministry of John the Baptist prepared for the coming of God's kingdom (Matt. 3:2). The crucifixion was perceived as the death of a king (Mark 15:26–32).

Jesus preached that God's kingdom was at hand (Matt. 11:12). His miracles, preaching, forgiving sins, and resurrection are an in-breaking of God's sovereign rule in this dark, evil age.

God's kingdom was manifested in the church. Jesus commissioned the making of disciples on the basis of His kingly authority (Matt. 28:18–20). Peter's sermon at Pentecost underscored that a descendant of David would occupy David's throne forever, a promise fulfilled in the resurrection of Christ (Acts 2:30–32). Believers are transferred from the dominion of darkness into the kingdom of the Son of God (Col. 1:13).

God's kingdom may be understood in terms of "reign" or "realm." Reign conveys the fact that God exerts His divine authority over His subjects/kingdom. Realm suggests location, and God's realm is universal. God's reign extends over all things. He is universally sovereign over the nations, humankind, the angels, the dominion of darkness and its inhabitants, and even the cosmos, individual believers, and the church.

In the OT the kingdom of God encompasses the past, present, and future. The kingdom of God had implications in the theocratic state. The kingdom of God is "already" present but "not yet" fully completed, both a present and future reality. The kingdom was inaugurated in the incarnation, life, ministry, death, and resurrection of Jesus. God's kingdom blessings are in some measure possessed now. People presently find and enter God's kingdom. God is now manifesting His authoritative rule in the lives of His people. God's kingdom, however, awaits its complete realization. His people still endure sufferings and tribulations. When fully consummated, hardships will cease. Kingdom citizens currently dwell alongside inhabitants of the kingdom of darkness. God will eventually dispel all darkness. The final inheritance of the citizens of God's kingdom is yet to be fully realized. The resurrection body for life in the eschatological kingdom is a blessing awaiting culmination.

God's kingdom is soteriological in nature, expressed in the redemption of fallen persons. The reign of Christ instituted the destruction of all evil powers hostile to the will of God. Satan, the "god of this age," along with his demonic horde, seeks to hold the hearts of people captive in darkness. Christ has defeated Satan and the powers of darkness and delivers believers. Although Satan still is active in this present darkness, his ultimate conquest and destruction are assured through Christ's sacrificial death and resurrection. Sinners enter Christ's kingdom through regeneration.

Many of Jesus' parables emphasize the mysterious nature of God's kingdom. For example, an insignificant mustard seed will grow a tree, as God's kingdom will grow far beyond its inception (Matt. 13:31–32). The kingdom of God is like seed scattered on the ground. Some seed will fall on good soil, take root, and grow. Other seed, however, will fall on hard, rocky ground and will not grow. Likewise, the kingdom will take root in the hearts of some but will be rejected and unfruitful in others (Matt. 13:3–8). As wheat and tares grow side by side, indistinguishable from each other, so also the sons of the kingdom of God and the sons of the kingdom of darkness grow together in the world until ultimately separated by God (Matt. 13:24–30, 36–43).

Although closely related, the kingdom and the church are distinct. George Eldon Ladd identified four elements in the relationship of the kingdom of God to the church. The kingdom of God creates the church. God's redemptive rule is manifested over and through the church. The church is a "custodian" of the kingdom. The church also witnesses to God's divine rule.

The kingdom of God is the work of God, not produced by human ingenuity. God brought it into the world through Jesus Christ, and it presently works through the church. The church preaches the kingdom of God and anticipates the eventual consummation.[11]

The last sentence of our quote says in part, "the church preaches kingdom of God." This has not been the case for almost 2,000 years.

---

[11] Stan Norman with Gentry Peter, "Kingdom of God," ed. Chad Brand, *Holman Illustrated Bible Dictionary* (Nashville, TN: Holman Bible Publishers, 2003), 988–989.

Today, the church sends out missionaries to foreign lands and preaches from the pulpit to those who are already Christian, as well as those, who happen into the church.

Romans 10:13-17 English Standard Version (ESV)

[13] For "everyone who calls on [through worship and prayer] the name of the Lord will be saved."

[14] How then will they call on him in whom they have not believed? And how are they to believe in him of whom they have never heard? And **how are they to hear without someone preaching**? [15] And how are they to preach unless **they are sent**? As it is written, "How beautiful are **the feet of those who preach** the good news!" [16] But they have not all obeyed the gospel. For Isaiah says, "Lord, who has believed what he has heard from us?" [17] So **faith comes from hearing**, and **hearing through the word of Christ**.

> **10:14b**. Faith requires hearing. **And how can they believe in the one of whom they have not heard?** More than anything else, this question is the crux of all missiological activity since the first century. God has ordained that people must hear (or read, or otherwise understand the content of) the word of God in order to be saved. One who knows the gospel must communicate it to one who does not know it.[12]

Yes, missionaries have been sent out throughout the last few centuries, but this is not the first-century way, it is the way of the last few centuries. However, over the last few decades, many trained in missions have come to realize the error of their ways. They have tried to grow the church by going outside of their community, to grow it back to their community. This was mistake number one. The other alternative was to grow from your community out to the rest of the world. Their second mistake was to use just a select few (missionaries), believing they were going to get the Great Commission accomplished. Of late, we hear much about having missionary churches that evangelize their own community, with their own members. While this belief is best and correct, I am unaware of any that are doing it as it should be done, and most are not doing it at all.

> **10:14c**. Hearing requires preaching. **And how can they hear without someone preaching to them?** Since no other media except the human voice was of practical value in spreading the gospel in the first century, **preaching** is Paul's

---

[12] Kenneth Boa and William Kruidenier, *Romans*, vol. 6, Holman New Testament Commentary (Nashville, TN: Broadman & Holman Publishers, 2000), 314.

method of choice. And yet, in the media-rich day in which we minister, has anything replaced preaching as the most effective way to communicate the gospel? We thank God for the printed page, and even for cutting-edge presentations of the gospel circling the globe on the internet. But it is still the human voice that cracks with passion, the human eye that wells with tears of gratitude, and the human frame that shuffles to the podium, bent from a lifetime of service to the gospel, which reaches the needy human heart most readily. Hearing may not *require* **preaching** in person today, but it always benefits from it.[13]

I agree with the Holman Commentary that modern technology is great, but there is but one-way to reach "the whole world as a testimony to all nations" (Matt. 24:14). Yes, it is the human voice, but not as the Holman Commentary suggests with one man walking to a podium to preach, but for hundreds of millions to take to their communities, trained to preach (herald, proclaim) the message, and to teach what they had been taught "to one who does not know it."

First-Century Christians Evangelized

[Jesus] reminded them in John 20:20 of his crucifixion: "He showed them his hands and side. The disciples were overjoyed when they saw the Lord." Then he reminded them again about his peace in verse 21. Jesus said, "Peace be with you!" Jesus proclaimed peace, reminded them of his crucifixion, pronounced peace again, and then told them, "As the Father has sent me, I am sending you" (John 20: 21). With that one command, Jesus announced two thousand years of direction for the church, still in effect for the churches of today, even your church. He proclaimed that we are sent. The church is, and you are individually, God's missionary to the world. Your church is God's instrument to reach the world, and it includes reaching your community. We are sent on mission by God. We are to be a missions-centered church by calling, nature, and choice. We are called to be on mission in our community. We have been sent to be on mission in our context, and we must accept that call, that directive to be on mission where God has placed us, not five, not fifty, not five hundred years ago and not thirty miles away, not three hundred miles away, not three thousand miles away. We are exhorted to be on mission where God has

---

[13] Ibid., 314.

placed us now, and our job is to [evangelize] wherever we are.[14]

Yes, the Great Commission was an assignment given to all Christians, which starts right in your own backyard. You can effectively evangelize the world, if you do it one community at a time, starting with your community.

Matthew 28:19-20 English Standard Version (ESV)

[19] Go therefore and make disciples of **all nations**, ... teaching them ... I am with you always, to the end of the age."

> In the Greek, the words for "all nations" are *panta ta ethnē*. We get our English word ethnic from the Greek word *ethnē*. When we hear (or read) Jesus' command to "go to all nations," we think countries. But when Jesus spoke those words, there were no countries as we understand them today. The nation-state is an invention of the modern era. In Jesus' day there were groups of people, and there were empires. Jesus' instructions mean that we must go to all the people groups in the world. The Jewish disciples of that day knew that Jesus was speaking about the Gentiles. The gospel was to go beyond the Jewish nation. But they also thought of Phoenicians, Macedonians, Greeks, Romans, and others Jesus did not use the word for empires like the Roman Empire, the Persian, or the Greek. Jesus used the word for peoples, and the Jews knew this meant all the different kinds of Gentiles. It meant to go to all the different kinds of people that existed. This is still God's plan today. In today's world, we have to remember that we are still sent ... to all different kinds of peoples. The word peoples represents every ethno-linguistic people group around the world, all the different ethnicities present in our cities, and even the different generations that live in our communities.[15]

Who were all involved in the evangelism work of the first-century? The evidence is all too clear that all Christians were evangelizing their communities, with a select few, taking the message everywhere.

---

[14] Putman, David; Ed Stetzer (2006-05-01). Breaking the Missional Code: Your Church Can Become a Missionary in Your Community (pp. 30-31). B&H Publishing. Kindle Edition.

[15] Putman, David; Ed Stetzer (2006-05-01). Breaking the Missional Code: Your Church Can Become a Missionary in Your Community (p. 34). B&H Publishing. Kindle Edition

Acts 1:14 English Standard Version (ESV)

¹⁴ All these with one accord were devoting themselves to prayer, together with the women and Mary the mother of Jesus, and his brothers.

Acts 2:1, 4 English Standard Version (ESV)

¹ When the day of Pentecost arrived, they were all together in one place. ⁴ And they were all [men and women] filled with the Holy Spirit and began to speak in other tongues as the Spirit gave them utterance.

Acts 2:17 English Standard Version (ESV)

¹⁷ "'And in the last days it shall be, God declares,
that I will pour out my Spirit on all flesh,
and your **sons** and your **daughters** shall prophesy,*
  and your young men shall see visions,
  and your old men shall dream dreams; (See Joel 2:28-29)

* The Greek behind the word "prophecy" here does not carry the meaning of "prediction," or "foretelling," (Gr., *propheteuo*), but literally means "a speaker out [Gr., pro, "before" or "in front of," and *phemi*, "say"]" and thus describes a proclaimer, one who proclaims messages of God. That is, namely "**to proclaim an inspired revelation, prophesy** ... **Acts 2:17f; John 3:1; 19:6; 21:9; 1 Cor, 11:4f ...; 13:9; 14:1, 3–5, 24, 31, 39; Rev. 11:3** ..."[16]

Matthew 24:14 English Standard Version (ESV)

¹⁴ And this gospel of the kingdom will be **proclaimed throughout the whole world** as a testimony to all nations, and then the end will come.

Acts 1:8 English Standard Version (ESV)

⁸ But you will receive power when the Holy Spirit has come upon you, and you will be my witnesses **in Jerusalem** and **in all Judea** and **Samaria**, and **to the end of the earth.**"

The prophecy of Jesus that the Good News would be "**proclaimed throughout the [then known] whole world** to all the nations [peoples], and then the end will come," was applicable to them, and was carried out. The "nations" (Gr., *ethnē*), means the same as it does at Matthew 28:19, where we are commanded to "make disciples of **all nations.**" The first-century Christians made disciples of **all nations** (the

---

[16] William Arndt, Frederick W. Danker, and Walter Bauer, *A Greek-English Lexicon of the New Testament and Other Early Christian Literature* (Chicago: University of Chicago Press, 2000), 890.

peoples), in all of **the then known world,**[17] before **the end came** for the natural nation of Israel, as the Romans destroyed Jerusalem in 70 C.E.,[18] killing over a million Jews, and taking hundreds of thousands captive. The apostle Paul wrote the Christians in Colossae about ten years earlier, 60 C.E, commenting on the spread of Christianity

Colossians 1:23 English Standard Version (ESV)

[23] if indeed you continue in the faith, stable and steadfast, not shifting from the hope of the gospel that you heard, **which has been proclaimed in all creation under heaven,** and of which I, Paul, became a minister.

First-Century Christian Worship and the Truth

The early Christians met in congregations, which for many of them, were private homes, to take in the truth. (Rom. 16:3-5) The book of Hebrews tells us some of what took place at these meetings. They were there, in part, to "consider how to stir up one another to love and good works, not neglecting to meet together, as is the habit of some, but encouraging one another, and all the more as you see the Day drawing near." (Heb. 10:24-25) Tertullian of the late second, early third century (c.155–after 220 C.E.), wrote, "We meet to read the books of God ... In any case, with those holy words we feed our faith, we lift up our hope, we confirm our confidence."[19] In order to become a Christian, certain requirements had to be met, as we can see from the *Zondervan Handbook to the History of Christianity*,

As before, people who converted to Christianity were baptized. First, however, the new believer would be properly instructed in the beliefs and practices of Christianity. These 'beginner' Christians were the 'catechumens' (from the Greek meaning 'oral handing down', that is, teaching by word of

---

[17] Christianity had spread from Jerusalem to Rome, Macedonia, Greece, Asia, Bithynia, Pontus, Galatia, Cappadocia, Pamphylia, Syria, Cyprus, Crete, Babylon, Persian Gulf, Spain, Italy, Malta, Illyricum, Media, Parthia, Elam Arabia, Cyrene, Libya, Egypt, and Ethiopia.

[18] Dates of events before the Common Era (Also known as AD) are marked by the abbreviation B.C.E. Dates of events during the Common Era are marked by the abbreviation C.E.

[19] Thomas C. Oden, Ministry Through Word and Sacrament, Classic Pastoral Care, 59 (New York: Crossroad, 1989).

mouth) and the way in which they were instructed developed as time went on. In the First Apology, published in the middle of the second century, the Christian writer Justin Martyr (c. 100-165) gives us a valuable insight into how people were admitted into the church in Rome:[20]

> As many as are persuaded and believe that what we teach and say is true, and undertake to be able to live accordingly, are instructed to pray and to entreat God with fasting, for the remission of their sins that are past, we praying and fasting with them. Then they are brought by us where there is water, and are regenerated in the same manner in which we were ourselves regenerated. For, in the name of God, the Father and Lord of the universe, and of our Saviour Jesus Christ, and of the Holy Spirit, they then receive the washing with water.[21]

Thus, there were explicit requirements before someone could be baptized: education of basic doctrinal beliefs, praying, fasting, and a commitment to live a moral life and an understanding of Christian beliefs. These new believers were discovered by taking the message into the community. Then, they were taught to become a disciple of Jesus Christ. They were then organized into Christian congregations. These same disciples (learners) were trained to make more disciples in the same way, preaching the Good News, and sharing the basic doctrinal beliefs.

Acts 5:42 English Standard Version (ESV)

[42] And every day, in the temple and from house to house, they did not cease teaching and preaching that the Christ is Jesus.

Acts 14:21-23 English Standard Version (ESV)

[21] When they had preached the gospel to that city and had made many disciples, they returned to Lystra and to Iconium and to Antioch, [22] strengthening the souls of the disciples, encouraging them to continue in the faith, and saying that through many tribulations we must enter the kingdom of God. [23] And when they had appointed elders for them in every church, with prayer and fasting they committed them to the Lord in whom they had believed.

---

[20] Jonathan Hill, *Zondervan Handbook to the History of Christianity*, 46 (Grand Rapids: Zondervan, 2006).

[21] Justin Martyr, "The First Apology of Justin", in The Ante-Nicene Fathers, Volume I: The Apostolic Fathers With Justin Martyr and Irenaeus, ed. Alexander Roberts, James Donaldson and A. Cleveland Coxe, 183 (Buffalo, NY: Christian Literature Company, 1885).

Acts 20:20 English Standard Version (ESV)

²⁰ how I did not shrink from declaring to you anything that was profitable, and teaching you in public and from house to house,

The Ends of the Earth

Jesus had just recently given his disciples The Great Commission, to 'go and make disciples of all nations ... teaching them ... you will receive power when the Holy Spirit has come on you, and you will be my witnesses in Jerusalem, in all Judea and Samaria, and to the ends of the earth. (Matt. 28:18-20, Ac 1:8) Now, "he was lifted up while they were looking on, and a cloud received him out of their sight." (Ac 1:9) Jesus was taken back to heaven, to be with the Father. It was just ten short days later that this making disciples and teaching began, Pentecost 33 C.E. As Jesus had promised, when he said, "I am sending the promise of my Father upon you," for they were to "be baptized with the Holy Spirit." (Ac 2:1-4; compare Lu 24:49 and Ac 1:4-5.) They were then filled with a zeal and strength that they had never felt before, and so they preached, they taught about the death and resurrection of Jesus Christ, as well as his return in Kingdom power and authority.

The disciples followed Jesus' instruction and began their preaching, teaching and making disciples; just he had laid it out, saying, "you will be my witnesses in Jerusalem, in all Judea and Samaria, and to the ends of the earth." They began bearing witness about the Father and the Son right there in Jerusalem. 'They were all filled with the Holy Spirit and began to speak in other tongues as the Spirit gave them utterance. Dwelling in Jerusalem Jews, devout men from every nation under heaven and they were bewildered because each one was hearing them speak in his own language.' (Acts 2:5-11, 40) "But many of those who had heard the word believed, and the number of the men came to about five thousand." "And the word of God continued to increase, and the number of the disciples multiplied greatly in Jerusalem, and a great many of the priests became obedient to the faith." (Acts 4:4; 6:7) Later, 'Philip followed Jesus' course direction by preaching the good news about the kingdom of God and the name of Jesus Christ' to the Samaritans.—Acts 8:12.

For seven years, only the Jews and proselytes were brought into the Christian congregation. However, in 36 C.E., Peter aided in the conversion of the first Gentile Cornelius, taking the good news to the Gentiles, i.e., non-Jewish people. (Acts 10) With the travels of Paul, Christianity grew so quick; Paul could write about 60 C.E. that the gospel "has been proclaimed in all creation under heaven." (Col. 1:23) We find that by the begging of the second century, Jesus disciples had taken the good news all throughout the Roman Empire, Asia, Europe, and Africa, with Christians numbering more than one million.

This offers us hope. If the Christian disciples of just 120 could grow to such numbers, in such far-reaching places, in just 70-years, with no modern day technologies, what could be accomplished today? Jesus had asked, "When the Son of Man comes, will he find faith on earth?" (Lu 18:8) At present, this is a troublesome question, because the one Christianity that Jesus founded and the disciples grew, it has become 41,000 different varieties, with over eighty percent being liberal, who have failed to carry out the Great Commission as commanded. Nevertheless, in our day, with our technology, things could change directions very quickly, and grow at tremendous speed. Moreover, Jesus made it very clear that most would reject him and that there would be false, imitation Christians, with a remnant being faithful followers.

Structure and Functioning on a Large Scale

From the days of Moses Exodus from Egypt, the Israelite nation was working and functioning on a large scale under the direction of God and involving the systematic coordination of many different considerations. Israel had its elders and heads, its judges and officers, who were organized by God himself, by way of the Mosaic Law. (Josh. 23:1-2) However, the Israelites lost their favored position because of 1,500 years of on again off again false worship (e.g. immoral sexual relations, sacrificing their children to the god of Molech, and leaders abusing and oppressing their people), culminating into their rejecting and having executed the Son of God. (Matt. 21:42, 43; 23:37, 38; Acts 4:24-28) Therefore, the Christian congregation that Jesus founded and the apostles grew replaced the nation of Israel on Pentecost 33 C.E.

How was that first-century Christian congregation structured to function to the point of growing from 120 to over one million in just 70 plus years? We are fortunate that Luke offers us, in the book of Acts, a summary report of how the Christian congregation was doing. "Here we have the first. In it our author describes what a biblical church really looks like, not only in the first century, but in every century from the Lord's ascension until his second coming ... A biblical church is marked by teaching. Thousands of new converts needed to understand precisely how Peter linked Old Testament text with the ministry of Jesus." (K. O. Gangel 1998, 31) From the very beginning we are told that they "they devoted themselves to the apostles' teaching." (Ac 2:42) Moreover, we are also told that were 'attending the temple together, day by day' (Ac 2:46) The proclaiming, teaching and making disciples spread, to the point of forming one congregation right after another, inside and outside of

Jerusalem. (Acts 8:1; 9:31; 11:19-21; 14:21-23) These early Christians assembled together (Greek *homothumadon*, translated **together** 1:14; 2:46; 4:24; 5:12), as well as in private homes.—Acts 19:8, 9; Rom. 16:3, 5; Col. 4:15

Today, we have 41,000 different denominations that call themselves Christians. How did the first-century Christian congregation stay one in Christ? They had one leader. From the beginning, the Father gave Jesus, who was both Lord and Christ (anointed one) as head over all things to the church.' (Acts 2:34-36; Eph. 1:22) After his ascension back to heaven, Jesus Christ sent the Holy Spirit, and he led the Christian congregation as a unit. He did this through the Holy Spirit and angels.—Acts 2:33; compare Acts 5:19, 20; 8:26; 1 Pet. 3:22

However, Jesus has one other thing that he used to maintain the oneness of the Christian congregation. He had the apostles, faithful men, who were appointed to serve in different capacities, traveling apostles with authority to affect change in any church, and the apostles and older men (i.e., elders) in Jerusalem. This group was initially the apostles (including Paul) and ones such as James, the half-brother of Jesus. Eventually, it came to include elders within the Jerusalem congregation as well. Persons such as Paul, Barnabas, Philip (not the apostle) and Peter were sent out to visit congregations, to establish new congregations, to pen letters, offering counsel, giving direction. These early Christians recognized that Jesus Christ was using Jerusalem's elders, to lead and direct the whole of the church. (Acts 2:42; 6:1-6; 8:14-17; 11:22; 15:1-31) What was the result? Luke sums it up nicely,

Acts 16:4-5 English Standard Version (ESV)

⁴ As they went on their way through the cities, they delivered to them for observance the decisions that had been reached by the apostles and elders who were in Jerusalem. ⁵ So the churches were strengthened in the faith, and they increased in numbers daily.

These "apostles and elders who were in Jerusalem," appointed those who would travel to set up and visit the congregations, appointing elders and servants within the congregations. There were qualifications for these overseers and servants. (1 Tim. 3:1-13; Titus 1:5-9; 1 Pet. 5:1-3) The overseers were expected to be obedient to the Scriptures, which included the Old Testament and any letters that they received from the Holy Spirit appoint apostles and elders in Jerusalem, and the visiting apostles. (Acts 20:28; Titus 1:9) The congregation members were expected to 'obey their leaders and submit to them, for they are keeping watch over their souls, as those who will have to give an account.' (Heb. 13:17) There was **no local church autonomy**, which was **not bound** to the apostles and elders in Jerusalem, as well as the visiting apostles. What do we mean by **autonomy**?

Autonomy means freedom, independence, i.e. that each church, selects its leadership, determines its form of worship, decides financial matters and directs other church-related affairs outside of any outside influences. In other words, there is no body of elders, no organizational head, which has any authority over an **autonomous** church, even if it is a denomination of tens of thousands of churches. The Baptist denomination is of this structure. This is not a biblical concept and is a twisting of Scriptures, to get the desired outcome. Let us just offer one example of taking the Scriptures out of context.

Some cite Acts 6:3-6, and say that the churches of the New Testament were allowed to select individuals from their church to care for their needs. First, this is in the very beginning, before the church grew into tens of thousands of congregations. Second, the congregations were directed to do it this way, it was not something that they came up with on their own, but rather it was in the direction of the apostles and elders in Jerusalem. Third, see how it is worded, 'churches of the New Testament were allowed to select persons from their own church.' This is wrong on two fronts. If one were allowed to do something, it would mean that there was a higher authority that could just as easily disallow it. Moreover, it was not that they were allowed, but that this is the way, they were told to do it. Notice verse 3, which says what the apostles told to do, "Therefore, brothers, pick out from among you seven men." (Ac 6:3) Now, look at verse 6, which says, "These they set before the apostles, and they prayed and laid their hands on them." Therefore, it actually went like this,

(1) there was a disagreement over the dispensing of food,

(2) the apostles and elders **told the congregations** to appoint "seven men of good repute, full of the Spirit and of wisdom" (**criteria set by** apostles and elders),

(3) which was **followed by** the congregations, and

(4) **approved by** the apostles and elders, i.e., Holy Spirit, because they laid hands on them.

What we see in the first-century Christian congregation was Jesus Christ being their leader. We further see the Holy Spirit appointing apostles and elders, who were then guided to send out apostles. The apostle who was sent out was then guided to appoint congregation overseers and servants. Finally, we see that the congregation members were obligated to obey the ones taking the lead, and all obeying the

Scriptures and the apostles and elders. Moreover, Knute Larson commenting on Titus 1:9, a letter from Paul to a person, Titus, he has assigned to appointing overseers in the congregations (Tit 1:4-5), "Having described the personal qualities of a person fit for church leadership, Paul finished with one more necessity. The leader **must hold firmly to the trustworthy message as it has been taught.** Those who presume to lead must embrace the traditional teachings which came through Christ and the apostles." (Larson 2000, 345)

Early Christians had Love for One Another

We know that the first-century Christians presented a sacrifice of praise as believers acknowledged God's goodness, greatness, and mercy. (Ps. 51:15–17) However, being Christian was about discipleship as well, which shaped the entire life of those who committed themselves to Christ. The beliefs of the early Christians transformed their lives, and they proclaimed them to all who would listen.

The early Christians removed the old person with its practices and put on a new person,

Colossians 3:5-10 English Standard Version (ESV)

5 Put to death therefore what is earthly in you: sexual immorality, impurity, passion, evil desire, and covetousness, which is idolatry. 6 On account of these the wrath of God is coming. 7 In these you too once walked, when you were living in them. 8 But now you must put them all away: anger, wrath, malice, slander, and obscene talk from your mouth. 9 Do not lie to one another, seeing that you have put off the old self with its practices 10 and have put on the new self, which is being renewed in knowledge after the image of its creator.

The early Christians were truthful, honest, hardworking, and trustworthy,

Ephesians 4:25, 28 English Standard Version (ESV)

25 Therefore, having put away falsehood, let each one of you speak the truth with his neighbor, for we are members one of another. 28 Let the thief no longer steal, but rather let him labor, doing honest work with his own hands, so that he may have something to share with anyone in need.

The early Christians were morally clean, and became known as the Way,

Galatians 5:19-21 English Standard Version (ESV)

¹⁹ Now the works of the flesh are evident: sexual immorality, impurity, sensuality, ²⁰ idolatry, sorcery, enmity, strife, jealousy, fits of anger, rivalries, dissensions, divisions, ²¹ envy, drunkenness, orgies, and things like these. I warn you, as I warned you before, that those who do such things will not inherit the kingdom of God.

The early Christians possessed the greatest quality of all,

John 13:35	**Romans 15:26**	**Galatians 2:10**
³⁵ By this all people will know that you are my disciples, if you have love for one another."	²⁶ For Macedonia and Achaia have been pleased to make some contribution for the poor among the saints at Jerusalem.	¹⁰ Only, they asked us to remember the poor, the very thing I was eager to do.

The early Christians were willing to die for one another,

Philippians 2:25-30 English Standard Version (ESV)

²⁵ I have thought it necessary to send to you Epaphroditus my brother and fellow worker and fellow soldier, and your messenger and minister to my need, ²⁶ for he has been longing for you all and has been distressed because you heard that he was ill. ²⁷ Indeed he was ill, near to death. But God had mercy on him, and not only on him but on me also, lest I should have sorrow upon sorrow. ²⁸ I am the more eager to send him, therefore, that you may rejoice at seeing him again, and that I may be less anxious. ²⁹ So receive him in the Lord with all joy, and honor such men, ³⁰ for he nearly died for the work of Christ, risking his life to complete what was lacking in your service to me.

The early Christians clearly followed through on Jesus' command,

John 13:34-35 English Standard Version (ESV)

³⁴ A new commandment I give to you, that you love one another: just as I have loved you, you also are to love one another. ³⁵ By this all people will know that you are my disciples, if you have love for one another."

The early Christians passed on the knowledge and love that Jesus had exemplified,

Matthew 28:20 English Standard Version (ESV)

²⁰ teaching them to observe all that I have commanded you. And behold, I am with you always, to the end of the age."

Early Christians were not of the World

We keep asking, how the first Christians went from 120 disciples at Pentecost 33 C.E. to more than a million shortly after the death of the apostle John. The answer is given to us by their obedience of Jesus command they proclaim the good news; they teach biblical truths and make disciples. They took this great commission seriously. In fact, they were able to be more active and efficient because they heeded Jesus us words that they were 'not to be of this world.' Jesus had told Pilate, "My kingdom **is not of this world**. If my kingdom were of this world, my servants would have been fighting, that I might not be delivered over to the Jews. But my kingdom is not from the world." A very short time earlier, he had said to his disciples, "If you were of the world, the world would love you as its own; but because you are not of the world, but I chose you out of the world, therefore the world hates you." (John 15:19) What did it mean to be "not of this world"?

Paul made a similar statement that helps shed more light on what Jesus meant. He writes about "those who deal with the world as though they had no dealings with it. For the present form of this world is passing away." Paul's words may seem to be absurd or contradictory (those who deal with the world as though they had no dealings), but in fact, they are correct. This world is a reference to the condition of humanity in this world. In other words, it is a reference to the world of humankind in our imperfect, fallen state, living under the rulership of the god of this world, Satan the Devil. We are all in this imperfect, fallen world, with its immoral pleasure, pain and suffering, and responsibilities that must be met for our survival. However, while Christians have to have dealings in Satan's world, they can live as though they have no dealings, by not using the things of the world entirely. The apostle John and James, Jesus' half-brother, shed some more light.

Do Not Love the World

1 John 2:15-17 English Standard Version (ESV)

[15] Do not love the world or **the things in the world**. If anyone loves the world, the love of the Father is not in him. [16] For all that is in the world—**the desires of the flesh** and **the desires of the eyes** and **pride of life**—is not from the Father but is from the world.[17] And **the world** is passing away along with **its desires**, but whoever does the will of God abides forever.

Jesus is not asking that we are taken out of the world. He says in prayer to the Father, "I do not ask that you take them out of the world, but that you keep them from the evil one." (John 17.15) Satan is the evil one, whom Paul calls, "the god of this world." (2 Cor. 4:3-4) Throughout these last 6,000 plus years of human history, Satan has used the world to cater to our fallen flesh, our natural desires toward bad. James, Jesus half-brother, writes,

James 1:13-15 Updated American Standard Version (UASV)

13 Let no one say when he is tempted, "I am being tempted by God," for God cannot be tempted[22] with evil,[23] and he himself tempts no one. 14 But each one is tempted when he is carried away and enticed by his own desire.[24] 15 Then the desire when it has conceived gives birth to sin, and sin when it is fully grown brings forth death.

The apostle Paul says,

Romans 5:12 English Standard Version (ESV)

12 Therefore, just as **sin came into the world** through one man, and death through sin, and so death spread to all men because all sinned

In addition, Moses had already inform us that,

Genesis 6:5 The American Translation (AT)

5 When the LORD saw that the wickedness of man on the earth was great, and that the **whole bent of his thinking was never anything but evil**, the LORD regretted that he had ever made man on the earth.

Genesis 8:21 The American Translation (AT)

21 I will never again curse the soil, though the **bent of man's mind** may be **evil from his very youth**; nor ever again will I ever again destroy all life creature as I have just done.

Jeremiah informs us that,

Jeremiah 17:9 English Standard Version (ESV)

9 The **heart is deceitful** above all things,
  and **desperately sick**;
who can understand it?

The apostle Paul writes,

---

22 Lit untempted

23 That is evil persons, or evil things

24 Or own lust

Romans 7:21-24 English Standard Version (ESV)

²¹ So I find it to be a law that when I want to do right, evil lies close at hand. ²² For I delight in **the law of God**, in my inner being, ²³ but I see in my members another law waging war against **the law of my mind** and making me captive to the **law of sin** that dwells in my members. ²⁴ Wretched man that I am! Who will deliver me from this body of death?

Notice in the above that Paul references "the law of [his] mind." For a person who has a strong faith that **law of his mind** is ruled by a phenomenon that he delights in, namely "**the law of God.**" Certainly, we see that "**the law of sin**" is waging a war against the law of the mind. Nevertheless, the Christian can conquer 'the law of sin' with the help of God. Paul goes on to say in verse 25, "Thanks be to God through Jesus Christ our Lord! So then, I myself serve the law of God with my mind, but with my flesh I serve the law of sin."

However, not all is lost, because Paul also tells us that we can 'be renewed in the spirit of our minds.' (Eph. 4:23) We can 'put off the old person with its practices and have put on the new self. We will then be renewed in knowledge according to the image of our Creator.' We will be transformed by the renewing of our mind, so that you may discern what is the good, pleasing, and perfect will of God.'—Colossians 3:9-10; Romans 12:2

Satan has designed the world that is under his rulership, to corrupt our 'deceitful hearts,' which John identifies three areas for us: **(1)** the desires of the flesh, [Gen. 3:1-6; Lu 4:1-3] **(2)** the desire of the eyes [Gen 3:6; Lu 4:5-6], and **(3)** pride of life [Gen. 2:17; 3:5; Lu 4:9-12]. If we entertain and cultivate these desires of the fallen flesh, we will sin, with sin potentially leading to death, if we do not repent.

James 1:27 English Standard Version (ESV)
²⁷ Religion that is pure and undefiled before God, the Father, is this: to visit orphans and widows in their affliction, and to **keep oneself unstained from <u>the world</u>**.

James 4:4 English Standard Version (ESV)
⁴ You adulterous people! Do you not know that **friendship with the world** is **enmity with God**? Therefore whoever wishes to be **a friend of the world** makes himself **an enemy of God**.

What did James mean by his words, "keep oneself unstained from the world"? It is these types of verses that help us appreciate that "the "world is being used in a metaphorical sense, meaning humankind. Our parents did not want us spending time with a certain type of younger ones, because they did not share our values, and were apt to get in trouble with all forms of authority. The world's entertainment is mostly immoral and graphically violent. Therefore, under Paul's words "those who deal with the world" [with its entirety of entertainment], do so "as though they had no dealings" [limited entertainment]. We can suffer two different kinds of pains by using the world fully: **(1)** be carried away and enticed by our own desire; then, the desire when it has conceived will give birth to sin, and sin when it is fully grown brings forth death. **(2)** We can be so distracted with trying to save the world (humankind) that John tells us is "passing away, along with **its desires.**"

What did James mean by his words, warning against forming a "friendship with the world"? We see it is the same thing we have been talking about, using the things in Satan's world more fully than is necessary. Christians are still imperfect, and they will stumble at times, being 'stained" by the world of humanity that is alienated from God. However, following the Bible's counsel of repenting, they make a course correction and desist from the worldly contacts and the like that led down that path. Nevertheless, some will willfully take on the mental disposition of humankind that is alienated from God, and they ignore all of the above warnings and commands. Jesus said,

Luke 12:29-31 English Standard Version (ESV) ²⁹ And do not seek what you are to eat and what you are to drink, nor be worried. ³⁰ For all the nations of the world seek after these things, and your Father knows that you need them. ³¹ Instead, seek his kingdom, and these things will be added to you.	Do Jesus' words mean that we do not go out and get a job to provide our family with food, water, clothes, and a roof over our head? No, "seeking," means, "to pursue," "to chase after" it, to the exclusion of the kingdom work of preaching, teaching, as well as making disciples.
Matthew 6:33 English Standard Version (ESV) ³³ But seek first the kingdom of God and his righteousness, and all these things will be added to you.	Notice that we are instead, to be seeking the Kingdom, i.e. "to pursue," "to chase after" it, to the exclusion of the world

Yes, in other words, we are **not of this world**, nor are we using it fully because we are **not** setting aside our commission from Jesus, by choosing the desires of this world over him. In other words, our number one priority in life is the work Jesus assigned, not using and saving a world [wicked humanity] that is passing away. Paul offers us a summary statement of all that we have just discussed.

Romans 12:2 English Standard Version (ESV)

² Do not be conformed to this world, but be transformed by the renewal of your mind, that by testing you may discern what is the will of God, what is good and acceptable and perfect.

Jesus likewise offers us a warning,

Matthew 7:21-23 English Standard Version (ESV)

²¹ "Not everyone who says to me, 'Lord, Lord,' will enter the kingdom of heaven, but **the one** who does **the will of my Father** who is in heaven. ²² On that day many will say to me, 'Lord, Lord, did we not prophesy in your name, and cast out demons in your name, and do many mighty works in your name?' ²³ And then will I declare to them, 'I never knew you; depart from me, you workers of lawlessness.

The apostle Peter comments on this as well,

1 Peter 4:3-4 English Standard Version (ESV)

³ For the time that is past suffices for doing what the Gentiles want to do, living in sensuality, passions, drunkenness, orgies, drinking parties, and lawless idolatry. ⁴ With respect to this they are surprised when you do not join them in the same flood of debauchery, and they malign you;

Because the first century Christians was not of this world, by not fully sharing in its desires, they were persecuted by the Roman Empire for what seemed like seditious behavior. They **did not** visit the bathhouses, where immoral acts took place (homosexual activity, fornication and adultery). They **did not** go to the games at the coliseum where graphic violence took place. They **did not** run for public office as a politician. They **did not** volunteer for military service. They **did not** throw incense on the statues of gods that they passed on the streets, so they were believed to be involved and encouraged rebellion against the Roman government. This brings us into our next section, being persecuted because of their righteous standing before God.

Persecution from the Start

Jesus said,

John 15:20 English Standard Version (ESV)

²⁰ Remember the word that I said to you: 'A servant is not greater than his master.' If they persecuted me, they will also persecute you. If they kept my word, they will also keep yours.

Jesus was actually the first human to suffer persecution and martyrdom. (Matt. 26:67; 27:26-31, 38-44) Jesus' words came true almost immediately, "If they persecuted me, they will also persecute you." (Matt. 10:22-23; Ac 4:13-17; 5:17-21) Why such hatred for one's who paid their taxes and obeyed Roman and Jewish laws?

They were the best citizens that the Roman Empire could have ever asked for, but they stood out for other reasons. Yes, they possessed Christian values, morality, and integrity. However, they had a zeal for sharing the good news with others, converting many other citizens of the Roman Empire. Yet, one would think, here are great citizens developing other great citizens, what is the problem. Well, Christians did not involve themselves in pagan worship, they did not worship the emperor, nor were they involved in the affairs of the Roman Empire, they did not socialize at the bath houses, or go to the coliseums. The Roman government viewed this as treasonous. Moreover, they were converting hundreds of thousands of other Roman citizens, i.e., stealing people from the Roman ways of life. In addition, they were taking many thousands from the Jewish religion of the day, Judaism. Remember that the first seven years after Jesus baptism, only Jews became Christians. Even after Gentiles started coming in, it was mostly Jewish converts for some time. It was the religious leaders, who pointed these things out to the authorities, misinforming the political rulers of the day. (Acts 12:1-5; 13:45, 50; 14:1-7; 16:19-24) Of course, a far more powerful person behind the scenes, Satan the Devil, was simply using all of the persecutors. (Gen 3:15; John 8:44; 12:31; 16:11; 2 Cor. 4:3-4; Rev. 12:9; 12:12, 17) What was Satan's initial objective? Initially, he wanted to stumble Jesus by temptations and persecution. (Matt. 4:1-11) When that failed, his objective was to destroy Christianity in its infancy, to put a stop to their witnessing about Jesus. Once that failed, he realized, if one cannot remove the waters of truth, the next best thing is to water the truths down with misinformation. There will be more on this below.

As we have already made clear, Christianity grew like a wildfire in the first century, and persecution was like throwing fuel on the first, because it contributed to an even faster growth. The Christian body followed in the footsteps of Jesus, Stephen, James, Peter and Paul, they continued to proclaim the Word of God with great zeal, as Peter said, "We must obey God rather than men." (Acts 4:19-20, 29; 5:27-32) They received strength from the Holy Spirit, knowing that something greater was coming to those that endured, as Jesus said, "the one who endures to the end will be saved."—Matthew 5:10; 24:13; Romans 8:35-39; 15:5

Jewish Historian Josephus, about 93 C.E., 60 years after Jesus execution, writes, "Now, there was about this time Jesus, a wise man, if it be lawful to call him a man, for he was a doer of wonderful works—a teacher of such men as receive the truth with pleasure. He drew over to him both many of the Jews, and many of the Gentiles. He was [the] Christ; (64) and when Pilate, at the suggestion of the principal men amongst us, had condemned him to the cross,[25] those that loved him at the first did not forsake him, for he appeared to them alive again the third day,[26] as the divine prophets had foretold these and ten thousand other wonderful things concerning him; and the tribe of Christians, so named from him, **are not extinct at this day**.—*Antiquities of the Jews* 18.62-64 (Bold and underline mine)

What have we learned, thus far, about the first century Christians? They zealously and boldly carried out the great commission that Jesus had assigned them: proclaim the Word, teach, and make disciples witnessing about the Father and the Son "in Jerusalem and in all Judea and Samaria, and to the end of the earth." (Matt. 24:14; 28:19-20; Ac 1:8) We also learned that they did not go about this in some unorganized way. They were organized with a body of older men and apostles from Jerusalem, who sent out other apostles to establish congregations, care for congregations once established, and to appoint elders and servants to care for these congregations. They were instructed, helped in their doctrinal decisions by the older men and apostles in Jerusalem, along with the apostles that visited them. They possessed Christian values, morality, and integrity. They loved one another. They followed Jesus, Paul James and John's counsel 'to not be of this world,' "keep oneself unstained from the world," not forming a "friendship with the world," and not "loving the world or the things in the world." Because of these things and more, they were "persecuted for righteousness' sake." (Matt 5:10)

In order to become a Christian in early Christianity, before they could be baptized, a few things had to take place. We can see these from the *Zondervan Handbook to the History of Christianity*,

> As before, people who converted to Christianity were baptized. First, however, the new believer would be properly instructed in the beliefs and practices of Christianity. These 'beginner' Christians were the 'catechumens' (from the Greek meaning 'oral handing down', that is, teaching by word of mouth) and the way in which they were instructed developed as time went on. In the First Apology, published in the middle of the second century, the Christian writer Justin Martyr (c. 100-

---

[25] a.d. 33, April 3.

[26] April 5.

165) gives us a valuable insight into how people were admitted into the church in Rome:[27]

> As many as are persuaded and believe that what we teach and say is true, and undertake to be able to live accordingly, are instructed to pray and to entreat God with fasting, for the remission of their sins that are past, we praying and fasting with them. Then they are brought by us where there is water, and are regenerated in the same manner in which we were ourselves regenerated. For, in the name of God, the Father and Lord of the universe, and of our Saviour Jesus Christ, and of the Holy Spirit, they then receive the washing with water.[28]

Thus, there were definite requirements before someone could be baptized: the education of basic doctrinal beliefs, praying, fasting, and a commitment to live a moral life and an understanding of Christian beliefs. These new believers were discovered by taking the message into the community. Then, they were taught to become a disciple of Jesus Christ. They were then organized into Christian congregations. These same disciples (learners) were trained to make more disciples, in the same way, preaching the Good News, and sharing the basic doctrinal beliefs.

Acts 5:42 English Standard Version (ESV)

[42] And every day, in the temple and from house to house, they did not cease teaching and preaching that the Christ is Jesus.

Acts 14:21-23 English Standard Version (ESV)

[21] When they had preached the gospel to that city and had made many disciples, they returned to Lystra and to Iconium and to Antioch, [22] strengthening the souls of the disciples, encouraging them to continue in the faith, and saying that through many tribulations we must enter the kingdom of God. [23] And when they had appointed elders for them in every church, with prayer and fasting they committed them to the Lord in whom they had believed.

Acts 20:20 English Standard Version (ESV)

[20] how I did not shrink from declaring to you anything that was profitable, and teaching you in public and from house to house,

---

[27] Jonathan Hill, *Zondervan Handbook to the History of Christianity*, 46 (Grand Rapids: Zondervan, 2006).

[28] Justin Martyr, "The First Apology of Justin", in The Ante-Nicene Fathers, Volume I: The Apostolic Fathers With Justin Martyr and Irenaeus, ed. Alexander Roberts, James Donaldson and A. Cleveland Coxe, 183 (Buffalo, NY: Christian Literature Company, 1885).

This organized approach is what contributed to their unity, to one Christian denomination, and to their rapid growth. However, remember Satan had a new plan for this young Christianity, for he had failed to defeat them in infancy. As they closed out, the first century and entered the second century, they were endangered by a serious and sinister, treacherous, crafty new danger. John died about 98-100 C.E., and by 140 C.E., divisions were already apparent among the early Christians. Will Durant states, "Celsus [second-century opponent of Christianity] himself had sarcastically observed that Christians were 'split up into ever so many factions, each individual desiring to have his own party.' About 187 [C.E.] Irenaeus listed twenty varieties of Christianity; about 384 [C.E.] Epiphanius counted eighty."—*The Story of Civilization: Part III—Caesar and Christ.* Today, we actually have over 41,000 different denominations. How did this come about? We must return to the first century.

The Great Apostasy

2 Thessalonians 2:1a, 3 New American Standard Bible (NASB)

[1] Now we request you, brethren, with regard to the coming of our Lord Jesus Christ … [3] Let no one in any way deceive you, for it will not come unless **the apostasy comes first**, and the man of lawlessness is revealed, the son of destruction,

On this text, New Testament scholar Knute Larson writes, "Before that great day comes, Paul declared, the rebellion must occur. The word used here is *apostasia* or apostasy. Before the day of the Lord, there will be a great denial, a deliberate turning away by those who profess to belong to Christ. It will be a rebellion. Having once allied themselves with Christ, they will abandon him. Within the recognized church there will come a time when people will forsake their faith. Throughout history, there have been defections from the faith. But the apostasy about which he wrote to the Thessalonians would be of greater magnitude and would signal the coming of the end." (Larson 2000, 105)

The apostle Paul says to the Ephesian elders; there is but "one Lord, one faith, one baptism." (Eph. 4:5) Paul penned those words about 60 C.E., and he was informing them that there was but one Christian faith. Yet, today we see more varieties of Christian faith than we care to count, all claiming that they are the truth and the way. Whenever a brave soul dares to be truthful and bring up that there are doctrinal differences, different doctrinal position, and different standards of conduct, he is shouted down as an alarmist. They claim that most of these denominations are the same on the essential doctrines, i.e., the salvation doctrines. Well, this actually is not true and is an attempt at hiding the truth, because even the salvation doctrines have anywhere from three to five different interpretations. Regardless, we must concern ourselves with a crucial question from Jesus Christ, "when the Son of Man comes, will he find faith on earth?" (Lu 18:8) This is a whole other discussion. We concern ourselves with how these divisions came about in the first place.

As has already been stated, but bears repeating, the blame lies with Satan. He attempted to have Jesus killed as a baby, he tempted Jesus in the wilderness after his baptism, and he attempted persecution right from the start. Peter wrote, "Be sober-minded; be watchful. Your adversary, the devil, prowls around like a roaring lion, seeking someone to devour." (1 Pet. 5:8) Initially, the persecution to this young Christian body came from Jewish religious leaders, and then from the Roman Empire itself. With "all authority in heaven" (Matt. 28:20) Jesus watched on, as the Holy Spirit guided and directed them, this infancy Christian congregation endured the best that Satan and his henchman had to offer. (See Rev. 1:9; 2:3, 19) As we know from Scripture, Satan is not one to give up, so he devised a new plan, divide and conquer. Yes, he would cause divisions within the Christian congregation. Satan broke out the ultimate weapon— **the apostasy.**[29] We need not believe that all of a sudden the apostasy came into the Christian congregation. No, Jesus was watching from heaven, and he made sure that he warned them while he was here on earth of what was to come, and he made the young Christian congregation aware of what was coming and when it was getting started.—Colossians 1:18

"[Jesus] Be Aware of False Prophets . . .

[Peter] There Will Be False Teachers Among You."

Matthew 7:15 English Standard Version (ESV)

[15] "Beware of false prophets, who come to you in sheep's clothing but inwardly are ravenous wolves.

Jesus was well aware of what Satan would try to accomplish step-by-step, and that divisions through those from within were on the list. New Testament scholar Stuart K. Weber says, "Jesus had an important reason for inserting the wolf metaphor (Acts 20:27–31)—to alert his listeners to the danger of a false prophet. If the false prophets were thought of as a source of bad fruit, then the disciples might think it was enough simply to

---

[29] In the Greek New Testament, the noun "apostasy" (Gr., *apostasia*) has the sense of "desertion, abandonment or rebellion." (Acts 21:21, ftn.) There it predominantly is alluding to abandonment; a drawing away from or abandoning of pure worship.

recognize and ignore the false prophet, refusing to consume his bad fruit, and awaiting God's judgment on him. But the wolf metaphor attributes a more active and malicious motive to the false prophet. He is actually an enemy of the sheep, and, if not confronted, will get his way by destroying the sheep." (Weber 2000, 101)

Weber mentions Acts 20:28-30, where Paul, about **56 C.E.**, warned the Ephesian elders,

Acts 20:28-30 Revised Standard Version (RSV)

²⁸ Take heed to yourselves and to all the flock, in which the Holy Spirit has made you overseers, to care for the church of God which he obtained with the blood of his own Son. ²⁹ I know that after my departure fierce wolves will come in among you, not sparing the flock; ³⁰ and **from among your own selves** will arise men **speaking perverse things, to draw away the disciples after them**.

Yes, these, who standoff from the Truth and the Way, would not be seeking their own disciples, but rather they would be seeking, "to draw away the disciples after them." i.e., the disciples of Christ. Jesus was well aware that the easiest way to defeat any group is to divide them, and so was Satan, who had been watching humanity for over 4,000 years, and especially the Israelites (Isaac and Ishmael / Jacob and Esau / Israel and Judah), as "Satan disguises himself as an angel of light. So it is no surprise if his servants, also, disguise themselves as servants of righteousness." (2 Cor. 11:14-15)

The apostle Peter also spoke of these things about **64 C.E.**, "there will be false teachers among you, who will secretly bring in destructive heresies . . . in their greed they will exploit you with false words.." (2 Pet. 2:1, 3) These abandoned the faithful words, became false teachers, rising within the Christian congregation, sharing their corrupting influence, intending to hide, disguise, or mislead.

These dire warnings by Jesus and the New Testament Authors had their beginnings in the first century C.E. Yes, they began small, but burst forth on the scene in the second century.

"[Paul says it] Is Already at Work"

About **51 C.E.**, some 18-years after Jesus' death, resurrection and ascension, division was already starting to creep into the faith, "the mystery of lawlessness is already at work." (2 Thess. 2:7) Yes, the power of **the man of lawlessness** was already present, which is the power of Satan, the god of this world (2 Cor. 4:3-4), and his tens of millions of demons, are hard at work behind the scenes.

There was even some divisions beginning as early as **49 C.E.**, when the elders wrote a letter to the Gentile believers, saying,

> Since we have heard that some persons have gone out from us and troubled you with words, unsettling your minds, although we gave them no instructions (Ac 15:24)

Here we see that some *within* were being very vocal about their opposition to the direction the faith was heading. Here, it was over whether the Gentiles needed to be circumcised, suggesting that they needed to be obedient to the Mosaic Law. (Ac 15:1, 5)

As the years progressed throughout the first-century, this divisive "talk [would] spread like gangrene." (2 Tim. 2:17, c. **65 C.E.**) About **51 C.E.**, They had some in Thessalonica, at worst, going ahead of, or at best, misunderstanding Paul, and wrongly stating by word and a bogus letter "that the day of the Lord has come." (2 Thess. 2:1-2) In Corinth, about **55 C.E.**, "some of [were saying] that there is no resurrection of the dead. (1 Cor. 15:12) About **65 C.E.**, some were "saying that the resurrection has already happened. They [were] upsetting the faith of some." (2 Tim 2:16-18)

Throughout the next three decades, no inspired books were written. However, by the time of the Apostle John's letter writing days of 96-98 C.E., he tells us "Now many antichrists have come. Therefore we know that it is the last hour." (1 John 2:18) These are ones, "who denies that Jesus is the Christ" and ones who not confess "Jesus Christ has come in the flesh is from God." (1 John 2:22; 4:2-3)

From 33 C.E. to 100 C.E., the apostles served Christ as a restraint against "the apostasy" that was coming. Paul stated at 2 Thessalonians 2:7, "For the mystery of lawlessness is already at work. Only he [Apostle by Christ] who now restrains it [the apostasy] will do so until he **[apostles]** is out of the way." 2 Thessalonians 2:3 said, "Let no one deceive you in any way **[misinterpretation or false teachers of Paul's first letter]**. For that day **[presence, parousia (second coming) of Christ]** will not come, unless the apostasy comes first, and the man of lawlessness **[likely one person, or maybe an organization / movement, empowered by Satan]** is revealed, the son of destruction."

We must keep in mind that the meaning of any given text is what the author meant by the words that he used, as should have been understood by his audience, and had some relevance/meaning for his audience. The rebellion [apostasy] began slowly in the first century and would break forth after the death of the last apostle, i.e., John. As a historian, Ariel Durant informed us earlier, by 187 C.E., there were 20 varieties of Christianity, and by 384 C.E., there were 80 varieties of

Christianity. Christianity would become one again, a universal religion, i.e., Catholicism.

Gnostic Belief

Marcion (85-c.160) was a semi-Gnostic, who believed that the teachings of Jesus were irreconcilable with the actions of the God of the Old Testament. He viewed the God of the Old Testament, Jehovah, to be vicious, violent and cruel, an oppressor who gave out material rewards to those worshiping him. In contrast, Marcion described the New Testament God, Jesus Christ, as a perfect God, the God of unadulterated love and compassion, of kindness and quick to forgive.

Montanus (late second century) was a "prophet" from Asia Minor, who believed that their revelation came directly from the Holy Spirit, which superseded the authority of Jesus, Paul, Peter, John, James, anyone really. They believed in the imminent return of Christ and the setting up of the New Jerusalem in Pepuza. He was more concerned about Christian conduct than he was Christian doctrine, wanting to get back to the Christian values of the first century. However, he took this to the extreme, just as John Calvin would some 1,300 years later in the 16th century. Montanism was a movement focused around prophecy, especially the founder's views, being seen as the light for their time. They believed that the apostle and prophets had the power to forgive sin.

Valentinus (c.100-c.160) was a Greek poet, who founded his school in Rome, and most prominent early Christian gnostic theologian. He claimed that though Jesus' heavenly (spiritual) body was of Mary, he was not actually born from her. This belief came about because Gnostics viewed all matter as evil. Therefore, if Jesus had really been a real human person with a physical body, he would have been evil. Another form of Gnosticism was Docetism, which claimed that Jesus Christ was not a real person, i.e., it was mere appearance and illusion, which would have included his death and resurrection.

Manes (c. 216-274) was the prophet and the founder of Manichaeism, a gnostic religion. He sought to combine elements of Christianity, Buddhism, and Zoroastrianism, based on a rigid dualism of good and evil, locked in an eternal struggle. He believed that salvation is possible through education, self-denial, fasting, and chastity. He also believed that he was an "apostle of Jesus Christ," (Ramsey 2006, 272) although, strictly speaking, his religion was not a movement of Christian Gnosticism in the earlier approach.

Beginning with the Council of Nicaea in 325 C.E., Emperor Constantine legalized Christianity in an attempt at reunited the empire.

He fully understood that religious division was a threat to the continuation of the Roman Empire. However, it was Emperor Theodosius I (347 – 395 C.E.), who banned paganism and imposed Christianity as the State religion of the Roman Empire. The Roman Catholic Church can trace its existence back to the council of Nicaea in 325 C.E. at best. Protestantism had its beginnings in the Reformation of the 16th century. However, there were dissensions in within Catholicism for a thousand years.

Outline of Christian Divisions

Start of Apostasy - 2nd Century

Roman Catholic Church

- 4th Century   (Constantine)
- 5th Century   Coptic
  - Jacobite
- 1054 C.E.   Eastern Orthodox
  - Russian
  - Greek
  - Romanian and others
- 16th Century Reformation
  - Lutheran
  - German
  - Swedish
  - American and others
  - Anglican
  - Episcopal
  - Methodist
  - Salvation Army
  - Baptist
  - Pentecostal
  - Congregational
  - Calvinism

- Presbyterian
- Reformed Churches

Pre-Reformation

- **Bishop Agobard** of Lyons, France (779-840), was against image worship, churches dedicated to saints and church liturgy that was contrary to Scripture.

- **Bishop Claudius** (d. between 827 and 839 C.E.)

- **Archdeacon Bérenger**, or Berengarius, of Tours, France (11th century C.E.), excommunicated as a heretic in 1050

- **Peter of Bruys** (1117-c. 1131), left the church because he disagreed with infant baptism, transubstantiation, prayers for the dead, worship of the cross and the need for church buildings.

- **Henry of Lausanne** (died imprisoned around 1148), spoke out against church liturgy, the corrupt clergy and the religious hierarchy.

- **Peter Waldo** (c. 1140–c. 1218) and the Waldenses, rejected purgatory, Masses for the dead, papal pardons and indulgences, and the worship of Mary and the saints.

- **John Wycliffe** (c. 1330-1384) preached against corruption in the monastic orders, papal taxation, the doctrine of transubstantiation (doctrine that the bread and wine of Communion become, in substance, but not appearance, the body and blood of Jesus Christ at consecration), the confession, and church involvement in temporal affairs.

- **Jan Hus** (c. 1369-1415) preached against the corruption of the Roman Church and stressed the importance of reading the Bible. This swiftly fetched the anger of the hierarchy upon him. In 1403, the church leaders ordered him to stop preaching the antipapal notions of Wycliffe, whose books they had openly burned. Hus, nevertheless, went on to pen some of the most hurtful impeachments against the Church and their practices, such as the sale of indulgences. He was condemned and excommunicated in 1410.

Reformation

- **Girolamo Savonarola** (1452-98) was of the San Marcos monastery in Florence, Italy, spoke out against the corruption in the Church.

- **Martin Luther** (1483-1546) was a monk-scholar, was also a doctor of theology and a professor of Biblical studies at the University of Wittenberg. He took issue with papal indulgences, power, purgatory, plenary remission of all penalties of the pope, among many other issues.

- **Ulrich Zwingli** (1484-1531) was a Catholic priest, who agreed with Luther in many doctrinal areas, in addition to the removal of all vestiges of the Roman Church: images, crucifixes, clerical garb, and even liturgical music. However, he disagreed with Luther's literal interpretation of the Eucharist, or Mass (Communion), as he said it "must be taken figuratively or metaphorically; 'This is my body,' means, 'The bread signifies my body,' or 'is a figure of my body.'" This one issues caused the them to part ways.

- **Anabaptists** (i.e., rejected infant baptism, so rebaptized adults, *ana* meaning "again" in Greek), **Mennonites** (Dutch Reformer Menno Simons), and **Hutterites** (Tyrolean Jacob Hutter), felt that the Reformers did not go far enough in rejecting the failings of the Catholic Church.

- **John Calvin** (1509-64) published *Institutes of the Christian Religion*, in which he summarized the ideas of the early church fathers and medieval theologians, as well as those of Luther and Zwingli. His theological views would take too much space. John Calvin had Michael Servetus burned to death as a heretic. Calvin defended his actions in these words: "When the papists are so harsh and violent in defense of their superstitions that they rage cruelly to shed innocent blood, are not Christian magistrates shamed to show themselves less ardent in defense of the sure truth?" Calvin's religious extremism and personal hatred made him unwilling to see and understand the radicalness of his judgments and choked out and Christian principles.

- **William Tyndale** (1494-1536) had to flee from England, published his New Testament in 1526, and completed most of the Old Testament after his betrayal and arrest, in a dungeon. He would be strangled at the stake, and his body was burned. The 1611 King James Version was actually 97 percent Tyndale's translation. He denounced the practice of prayer to saints. He taught justification by faith, the return of Christ, and mortality of the soul.

- **Jacobus Arminius** (1560-1609), graduated from Holland's Leiden University, after which he spent six years in Switzerland, studying theology under Théodore de Bèze, the successor to Protestant Reformer John Calvin. Rather than support Calvinism, he went against it, especially the doctrine of predestination, which was at the core of Calvinism.

Catholicism Summary

Roman Catholicism has tainted itself with its history of immorality and bloodshed, as well as Its pagan-tainted religious ideas and practices. The centuries-long oppression, torture, rape, pillage, and murder of tens of millions of men, women, and children cannot come from true Christianity. They were the biggest offenders of the apostasy that Paul said had to come before the return of Christ.

Protestantism Summary

The Reformation gave us a return to the Bible in the common man's languages, which the Catholic Church had locked up in the dead language of Latin for 500-years. The Reformers brought the common folk freedom from papal authority but also from many erroneous Bible doctrines and dogmas that had gone on for a thousand years. However, the Protestant denominations have found themselves so fragmented and divided; one can only wonder where the truth and the Way lie.

Over eighty percent of Protestant Christianity is liberal-progressive as to their biblical and social beliefs, which began in the late 18th century up until the present. This covers too much area for a summary, but to mention just a few, they treat the Bible as being from man, not inspired and fully inerrant. They prefer to explain away the Bible accounts of miracles as myths, legends, or folk tales. They do not believe in the historicity of Bible characters such as Adam and Job. They say that Moses did not write the first five books of the Bible but that they were written by several writers from the tenth to the fifth centuries B.C.E., and were compiled after that. They say Isaiah did not author the book bearing his name in the early eighth century B.C.E., but that two or three writers penned it, centuries later. They claim that Daniel did not pen his book in the sixth century B.C.E., but rather it was written in the second century B.C.E. They claim that the Bible is full of errors, mistakes, and contradictions, as to the history, science, and geography. Higher criticism has opened Pandora's Box to an overflow of pseudo-scholarly works whose result has been to weaken, challenge and destabilize people's assurance in the trustworthiness of the Bible. Who needs enemies like agnostics and atheists, when we have liberal Bible scholars? We have not even delved into their unbiblical views of social justice, gay marriage, homosexual priests, women in the pulpits and far more.

Some may ask what about the remaining twenty percent of Christian denominations. Most of those are moderate in beliefs, which cast doubt on the trustworthiness of the Scriptures and give fodder to the liberal-progressive denominations. These are fence-riders, who have abandoned the truth and the Way of true, pure Christianity. Before delving into the so-called conservative parts of Christianity, let us look at the charismatics.

We have charismatic Christianity, the fastest growing segment, which emphasizes the work of the Holy Spirit, spiritual gifts, and modern-day miracles, speaking in tongues[30] and miraculous healing, even snake handling in some areas. All of this is **un**biblical and based on emotionalism.

Those who believe that charismatic Christianity is false Christianity, persons such as myself, are said to be overly critical. Supporters of Charismatic Christianity say we "should be focusing on the fact that while many in the church continue to abandon our Christian faith, the Pentecostal/Charismatic community continues to offer the church a legitimate growth mechanism."[31] I would respond that a denomination founded on, grounded in **un**biblical beliefs is not true Christianity, and are the false teachers and prophets that we were warned were coming by Jesus and the New Testament writers. Therefore, charismatic Christianity is no Christianity at all, and all who are being brought in, are being obscured from finding the path of true Christianity.

So-called conservative Christianity is so minuscule that it barely gets press. We should not confuse radical Christianity, such as the Westboro Baptist Church,[32] with truly conservative, fundamentalist Christianity. However, even here we find differences doctrinally, and yes, even in the so-called salvation doctrines. Are all of the 41,000 different varieties of Christianity just different roads leading to the same place? Are all of the various conservative churches the truth and the Way? The answer is no, as far as this writer is concerned. We need to return to the question that

---

[30] http://www.christianpublishers.org/speaking-in-tongues-truth

[31] http://tiny.cc/j5d7mx

[32] www.godhatesfags.com/

Jesus asked, "When the Son of Man comes, will he find faith on earth?" (Lu 18:8) Jesus would not find faith on earth, not at the level that one might expect, not at present. However, do not lose hope, because Jesus was able to

(1) found Christianity,

(2) lead the apostles to maintain its purity as one form of Christianity, and

(3) restrain the apostasy as it grew from 120 disciples to over a million within 70-80 years. It is not beyond his authority and power of merging and solidifying those who have a receptive heart into the faith, the truth and the Way of the 21st century.

The reader may be disappointed that I did not identify some of the Bible scholars of moderate and liberal Christianity, or the truly conservative denominations or churches, but that was done on purpose. It is up to each reader, to wade through these different forms of true Christianity, and find the path that best fits the first century Christianity example. How I best do that, one may ask. To personalize this, I will move to the second person pronoun, you because it is all about you.

- Be willing to buy out the time. If you do not have the time; then, all is for not. If you cannot invest a decent amount of time in our short life now, knowing that an eternity of time is on the horizon, you cannot see the forest for the trees.

- You need particular kinds of knowledge, which will enable you to make wise decisions.

- You need to have a good understanding of hermeneutics and exegesis, big words for biblical interpretation rules and their application. How can you identify a form of Christianity plagued with unbiblical doctrines, without the knowledge of how to interpret the Scriptures correctly? Yes, it is the same Bible scholars explaining these rules. Thus, we ask, 'how can we trust them to give us rules that do not lead us astray?' Generally, they do give the rules correctly, but violate them at times in their own commentaries. Below are the best books for such a venture.[33]

---

[33] **(1)** Basic Bible Interpretation by Roy B. Zuck; **(2)** A BASIC GUIDE TO BIBLICAL INTERPRETATION Understanding the Correct Methods of Interpretation by Edward D.

- You need to have a decent understanding of Bible translation differences and the translation process. Below are books that will help you in this venture.[34]

- You need to have a descent understanding of old and New Testament textual criticism. Below are books that will help you in this venture.[35]

- You need to have a descent understanding of the Bible as a whole. Below are books that will help you in this venture.[36]

- You should get a book on Bible difficulties as well. You should study it along with the commentary volumes, as you are doing your Bible reading.[37]

- Once you have invested a couple years in getting some foundational understanding, it is time to pay better attention.

- The apostle Paul went by his Jewish name "Saul" before he started using Paul. He was a Pharisee in Judaism. To him the truth was natural Israel, which was actually the truth and the way to Good for 1,500 years. Saul/Paul

---

Andrews **(3)** Protestant Biblical Interpretation: A Textbook of Hermeneutics By Bernard Ramm; **(4)** Evangelical Hermeneutics: The New Versus the Old by Robert L. Thomas; and **(5)** Biblical Hermeneutics: A Treatise on the Interpretation of the Old and New Testaments (Classic Reprint) By Milton Spenser Terry

[34] **(1)** The Word of God in English: Criteria for Excellence in Bible Translation By Leland Ryken; **(2)** Understanding English Bible Translation: The Case for an Essentially Literal Approach By Leland Ryken; **(3)** Do We Still Need a Literal Bible?: Discover the Truth about Literal Bibles Authored by Don Wilkins [Coming 2015]

[35] **(1)** Introduction to New Testament Textual Criticism By J. Harold Greenlee; **(2)** THE TEXT OF THE NEW TESTAMENT The Science and Art of Textual Criticism by Don Wilkins and Edward D. Andrews [coming 2015]; **(3)** Encountering the Manuscripts: An Introduction to New Testament Paleography & Textual Criticism By Philip Comfort

[36] **(1)** Holman Old Testament Commentary Series- 20 volume set [buy them one at a time, as you are doing your Bible reading]; **(2)** Holman New Testament Commentary (12 volume set). Note: Use your understanding of how to interpret Scripture, to see when the author gives a meaning that is not what the author meant. Holman is very good.

[37] **(1)** The Big Book of Bible Difficulties: Clear and Concise Answers from Genesis to Revelation By Norman L. Geisler, Thomas Howe; **(2)** New International Encyclopedia of Bible Difficulties By Gleason L. Archer Jr. **(3)** Bible Difficulties In the Book of Genesis: Answering the Bible Critics BIBLE BOOK NUMBER 1 Authored by Edward d Andrews; **(4)** Bible Difficulties In the Book of Exodus: Answering the Bible Critics BIBLE BOOK NUMBER 2 Authored by Edward D Andrews [more being developed]

saw Christianity as a sect of Judaism, a cultish-sect, and he persecuted them. Once he had a correct understanding of the Old Testament, he was better able to see that Christianity was now the truth and the Way. He had to **humble** himself and leave Judaism, who had lost favor with God. Then he had to join what he had formerly viewed as the enemy. **Humility!**

If ever we see that our variety of Christianity is not the truth, we need to be like Paul and find the truth, or the closest thing to it. Moreover, we need to keep our eyes open to Jesus' transitioning some of Christianity to be the faith that he will be looking for upon his return. If we fail to arm ourselves with knowledge, understanding, thinking ability and wisdom, we are subjecting ourselves **only** to other people's interpretations and our 21st-century opinions as to who has the truth.

EARLY CHRISTIANITY 1 The Holy Spirit in the First Century and Today

Acts 4:31 Updated American Standard Version (UASV)

31 And when they had prayed, the place in which they were gathered together was shaken, and **they were all filled with the Holy Spirit** and **began to speak the word of God with boldness.**

Just three days before Jesus was executed, Jesus told his disciples, "And this gospel of the kingdom will be proclaimed in all the inhabited earth[38] as a testimony to all the nations, and then the end will come." (Matt. 24:14) Jesus would speak on this again just before he ascended to heaven; Jesus said to his disciples, "Go therefore and make disciples of all the nations ... teaching them to observe all that I commanded you ..." (Matt 28:19-20) Of course, being curious, they were asking him, "Lord, is it at this time you are restoring the kingdom to Israel?" He said to them, "It is not for you to know times or seasons that the Father has fixed by his own authority. But you will receive power when the Holy Spirit has come upon you; and you will be my witnesses in both Jerusalem and in all Judea and Samaria, and to the extremity of the earth."–Acts 1:6-8

It has been and will be mentioned several times in this publication, Christianity has lost its way in the great commission of proclaiming the good news of the kingdom, teaching biblical truths, and making disciples, even in the face of centuries of intensified missionary work this is true. It is the mission of Christian Publishing House and this author that the first-century lifesaving work of evangelism is restored, so that, all Christians may play a role in making disciples. Therefore, it is tools like this publication and others by this author and other authors, which will enable any willing Christian to share biblical truths effectively within their family, their community, their workplace or their school, to make disciples. Within this chapter, we will cover how the Holy Spirit can enable us to be bold when we are sharing biblical truths with others.[39]

---

[38] Or *in the whole world*

[39] A recommend read THE HOLY SPIRIT AND THE CHRISTIAN How Are We to Understand the Work of and the Indwelling of the Holy Spirit? by Edward D. Andrews

http://www.christianpublishers.org/apps/webstore/products/show/5890475

The Need to Be Bold

One can only imagine the joy of making a disciple for Christ, who, in turn, goes out to make disciples himself. Congregation Evangelists, be it male or female should be very involved in evangelizing their communities and helping the church members play their role at the basic levels of evangelism. There is nothing to say that one church could not have many within, who have the calling of an evangelist, which would and should be cultivated. However, like in the first-century, we in the twenty-first-century have many challenges that get in our way. Generally speaking, few today are eager to hear from God's Word, mostly because the majority have preconceived ideas about it (just a man's book, full of errors and contradictions, and the like), many are of the same mindset as those who were living the days of Noah. "For as in those days before the flood they were eating and drinking, marrying and giving in marriage, until the day that Noah entered the ark." (Matt. 24:38-39, NASB) Then, the apostle Peter warned,

2 Peter 3:3-4 Updated American Standard Version (UASV)

[3] Know this first of all, that in the last days ridiculers will come with their ridicule, following after their own desires, [4] and saying: "Where is this promised coming of his? For ever since the fathers fell asleep, all continues just as it was from the beginning of creation."

On these verses, David Walls writes, **"In the last days"** refers to all the days between the first advent of the Messiah and the second advent. Characteristic of that time frame, however long it will be, is the fact that people will make fun of the doctrine of the Second Coming. **Ridiculing** toward Christians is to express derision or scorn about a Christian or Christianity, the Bible, or God. It describes the characteristic attitude of the day toward the Second Coming. False teachers argued that the promise of the Second Coming had been delayed so long that we may safely conclude that it would never happen. As far as they could see, the world was going on just as it always had—people lived and died, but nothing really changed." (Walls and Anders 1996, p. 141) Today, we have false teachers on both sides of the second coming fence: (1) ones that scoff at the idea of Jesus' second coming and (2) those that act as though they are prophets of God, knowing the very day and hour.[40] However, we also have those that from liberal and moderate "Christianity" that ridicule, mock and oppose conservative Christianity. All of this, and we

---

[40] A recommended read WHAT DOES THE BIBLE REALLY SAY ABOUT THE SECOND COMING OF CHRIST? by Edward D. Andrews

http://www.christianpublishers.org/apps/webstore/products/show/5383701

have not even gotten to those outside of Christianity, who also ridicule, mock and oppose the Almighty God and his Word, the Bible.

As true Christians, we may face ridicule, mocking and opposition from the governmental officials, the news and entertainment media, other religions, and the agnostics and atheists. However, even more, close to home, it may come from those that our children go to school with, their teachers or it may come from those we work with, even from close family members. All of these people need to be evangelized to if we are to carry out the Great Commission of proclaiming and teaching God's Word, to make disciples for Christ. We need to evangelize those in false forms of "Christianity," the unbelievers and those in either of these categories, who are closer to us.

However, we face yet more challenges that are in our way. One such challenge is our human imperfection, i.e., our human weaknesses, such as shyness and fear of being ridiculed, mocked and opposed. Lastly, our greatest obstacle is our church leaders, who are failing to train us to be effective evangelizers in our communities. James, Jesus' half-brother wrote, "One of you says to them [the poor], 'Go in peace, be warmed and filled," without giving them the things needed for the body, what good is that? So also faith by itself, if it does not have works, is dead." (Jam. 2:16-17, ESV) This principle can be carried over to pastors, elders, priests, ministers, who say to their congregation, "**You** need to share the gospel in **your** community so that **you** may help build up the church for Christ." All of this pointing the finger at them by using the second person pronoun, "**you**" repeatedly, and these leaders have not even given them the tools to be effective evangelists within their community. What good is that? Therefore, their supposed faith that the evangelism work will be done, but having no works of training such ones, means they have no genuine faith at all, it is dead. If we are to persist in sharing the Word of God, this will require that we have the tools to help us (i.e., this book and others like it), as well as boldness. In this chapter, we will focus on boldness.

Ephesians 6:19-20 Updated American Standard Version (UASV)

¹⁹ and for me, that a word may be given to me at the opening of my mouth **boldly**, to make known the mystery of the gospel, ²⁰ for which I am an ambassador in chains, that I may proclaim it **boldly**, as I ought to speak.

The Greek word, *parresia*, "boldness" in verse 19 has the sense of in boldness "in an evident or publicly known manner—'publicly, in an evident manner, well known.'"[41] The Greek word, *parresiazomai*, "boldly" in verse 19, is a "(derivative of *parresia* 'boldness,' 25.158) to speak openly about something and with complete confidence—'to speak boldly, to speak openly.'"[42] However, this boldness, confidence, courage, fearlessness does not give us a license to be blunt or rude to the ones we speak to, even if their demeanor is such. The apostle said to the Christians in Rome, "Never pay back evil for evil to anyone." (Rom. 12:17; See Col. 4:6, NASB) He went on to say, "If possible, so far as it depends on you, be at peace with all men." (Rom. 12:18, NASB) When we go about our evangelism work, sharing God's Word with others, we need to be bold in this hostile world, but it needs to be balanced with tact as well because our objective is not to offend the one we to whom we are witnessing.

To be sure, this sort of boldness calls for personal qualities that involve much effort that needs to be developed over time. We do not just wake up one morning and decide that we are going to be bold from here forward. In addition, we do not just read a couple of Bible verses about being bold, and then, we are all of a sudden able to be bold in our witness to others. "But after we [Paul and his companions] had already suffered and been mistreated in Philippi, as you know, **we had the boldness in our God** to speak to you the gospel of God amid much conflict." (1 Thess. 2:2) We today can acquire a similar boldness if we are hesitant, shy or nervous at the idea of speaking to others about the Word of God.

Paul and his traveling companions had boldness, which you can note he said in the above, "we had the boldness in our God." In other words, God removed Paul's fears and gave him boldness (courage). The rulers, elders, and scribes gathered in Jerusalem and commanded Peter and John to no longer witness about Jesus. These Jewish religious leaders had the power of life and death over them. Of course, they could only take their life, not their opportunity at eternal life. However, Peter and John answered them, "Whether it is right in the sight of God to listen to you rather than to God, you must judge, for we cannot but speak of what we have seen and heard." God was well aware of these threats, but he granted his servants to speak his word "*with all boldness*." Ac 4:5, 19-20, 29, ESV) The Father had provided them with Holy Spirit. What about us; Should we expect that the Holy Spirit under this direct and supernatural control will guide, lead, and direct us in the same bold way.

---

[41] Johannes P. Louw and Eugene Albert Nida, *Greek-English Lexicon of the New Testament: Based on Semantic Domains* (New York: United Bible Societies, 1996), 337.

[42] IBID., 398.

What Was the Reason for the Direct and Supernatural Work of the Holy Spirit in the First Century?

A significant change was in the offing. The Jews had followed the lead of their religious leaders in the last act of rebellion, resulting in their rejection as his people. The Mosaic Law was being replaced with the law of Christ. This does not mean that no Jew could be received into the newly founded Christian congregation. To the contrary, the next three and half years would be only the Jewish people, which would make up this new way to God. As was the case with Moses, there was to be a sign, miraculous events, which included the speaking in tongues, this as evidence to those, whose heart was receptive to the truth that the Son of God had come, had given his life for them, and ascended back to heaven. Exodus 19:16-19

However, there was much labor to be done. Beginning in 36 C.E., with the conversion of Cornelius, an uncircumcised Gentile, the gospel got underway in its spread to non-Jewish people of every nation. (Acts, chap. 10) In truth, so swiftly did it spread that by about 60 C.E., the apostle Paul could say that the gospel had been "proclaimed in all creation that is under heaven." (Col. 1:23) Consequently, by the time of the last apostle's death (John c. 100 C.E.), Jesus' faithful followers had made disciples all the way through the Roman Empire—in Asia, Europe, and Africa! By 125 C.E., there were over one million Christians.

If we objectively look at the history of first-century Christianity, the three and a half year ministry of Jesus, founding the Christian congregation, the apostles spreading the good news throughout the whole of the Roman Empire, and the Holy Spirit miraculously guiding, leading and showing the apostles the "things to come," reminding them of all that Jesus had said. The apostles and a select few of others, like Paul, Barnabas, Silas, Apollos, Timothy, Titus, Philip, were under direct and supernatural control as they established Christianity in the first century. While there may have been a few individuals, attempting to cause division in the first century, by 100 C.E. there was but one Christianity, the one Jesus founded and the apostle grew. The twenty-seven books of the New Testament were to be added to the Old Testament by 200 C.E. The particular work of the Holy Spirit that Jesus spoke of had run its course by the death of the apostle John in 100 C.E., as he was the last apostle. After John, no man has been miraculously guided or directed, in the same manner, and way, because that same specific work of the Holy Spirit was no longer needed. The work of the Holy Spirit from the second century forward has been the inspired, inerrant Word of God. There was no need for the Holy Spirit to operate the same as in the first century because the work of setting up Christianity and completing the Word of God was completed. The work of the Holy Spirit now takes place through the Spirit-inspired Word of God.

What Were the Gifts of the Holy Spirit in the First Century?

What miraculous, supernatural gifts were the apostles and a select few workers to receive, to establish first century Christianity? They would receive a helper, comforter, an instructor, a guide, a supporter, i.e., the Holy Spirit.

What did Jesus say about the Holy Spirit, being specifically applied to the apostles and a select few other fellow workers, to accomplish their work of establishing Christianity and completing the Bible? He had much to say on this, as we will discover from the texts below. Italics and underlines are mines.

John 14:15-17 Updated American Standard Version (UASV)

15 "If you love me, you will keep my commandments. 16 And I will ask the Father, and he will give you another Helper, that he may be with you forever; 17 the Spirit of truth, *whom the world cannot receive*, because it does not see him or know him, but you know him because *he dwells with <u>you</u>* and *will be in <u>you</u>*.

John 14:26 Updated American Standard Version (UASV)

26 But the Helper, the Holy Spirit, whom the Father will send in my name, *that one will <u>teach you</u> all things* and <u>bring to your remembrance</u> *all* that I have said to you.

John 15:26 Updated American Standard Version (UASV)

26 "But when the Helper comes, whom I will send to you from the Father, the Spirit of truth, who proceeds from the Father, *that one will bear <u>witness about me</u>*.

John 16:5-8 Updated American Standard Version (UASV)

5 But now I am going to him who sent me, and none of you asks me, 'Where are you going?' 6 But because I have said these things to you, sorrow has filled your heart. 7 Nevertheless, I tell you the truth: it is to your advantage that I go away; for if I do not go away, the Helper will not come to you; but if I go, I will send him to you. 8 And when that one

arrives, *he will convict the world concerning sin* and *righteousness* and *judgment*;

John 16:12-15 Updated American Standard Version (UASV)

12 "I still have many things to say to you, but you cannot bear them now. 13 But when that one, the Spirit of truth, comes, *he will guide you into all the truth*; for he will not speak from himself, but whatever he hears, he will speak; and *he will declare to you the things that are to come*. 14 That one will glorify me, for *he will take what is mine and declare it to you.* 15 All the things that the Father has are mine; therefore I said that he takes what is mine and will declare it to you.

In the above texts, we have a number of things that the Holy Spirit was to do for the apostles and a select few other fellow workers. While the apostle was not ignorant or illiterate as some commentators suppose, they did not possess training in the rabbinic study of Scripture, such as the apostle Paul had under Gamaliel. Luke tells us of an account of Peter and John before the Jewish religious leaders, where he writes,

Acts 4:13 Updated American Standard Version (UASV)

13 Now when they saw the boldness of Peter and John, and perceived that they were uneducated and untrained men, **they were astonished**, and they recognized that they had been with Jesus.

All of a sudden, Peter and John, literate fishermen were keeping pace with the Jewish religious leaders, who had training in the Rabbinic study of Scripture. This is the Holy Spirit teaching them, guiding them, instructing them, bringing back to their remembrance all that Jesus had said. Therefore, the apostles and a select few fellow workers needed the Holy Spirit if they were to establish Christianity on the grand scale that it was by the end of the first century and complete the New Testament. There was no way that the apostles alone could have educated themselves to the level of Paul, in such a short period, it was the Holy Spirit, who taught and instructed them miraculously. The Holy Spirit guided them as well. One way was in their writings, as no New Testament author contradicted another; they were all one because there was really one author, God. This is actually true of all forty plus authors of the entire Bible. From the second century forward, this has never repeated. In fact, today we have 41,000 different denominations, all teaching different things on the same doctrines.

Convicting the World Concerning Sin

Nisan 14, 33 C.E., the night of the Passover feast with Jesus, he told the apostles, "When he [the Holy Spirit] comes, he will convict the world concerning sin and righteousness and judgment." (John 16:8, ESV) How did the Holy Spirit do this on Pentecost? The first stage was to baptize the apostle in Holy Spirit, which means that they would have been miraculously endowed with guidance, instruction, teachings, and a remembrance of what Jesus had said. Again, looking at Jesus' words just before his ascension, he said, "for John baptized with water, but you will be baptized with the Holy Spirit not many days from now." (Acts 1:5, ESV) The second stage was the work that these ones would carry out in the first century, namely, putting the world on notice (convicting them concerning their sin and righteousness), which was very similar to what the Mosaic Law had done with the Israelites. Remember the words of the apostle Paul,

Romans 5:20-21 Updated American Standard Version (UASV)

20 The [Mosaic] Law came in so that the transgression would **increase**; but where sin increased, grace abounded all the more, 21 so that, as sin reigned in death, even so grace would reign through righteousness to eternal life through Jesus Christ our Lord.

How did the Mosaic Law make sin "increase"? From Adam's rebellion to the Mosaic Law, man was well aware of right and wrong because even in imperfection he had a sense of right and wrong. God had given Adam and Eve a conscience, an internal mechanism, to evidence the difference between right and wrong. In their perfection, they were able to sin still because even if a perfect person entertains bad thoughts, it will lead to sin and death. (Jam 1:14-15) Nevertheless, humankind in imperfection has a measure of that conscience that was given to Adam and Eve, meaning they have always had a sense of good and bad. However, the Mosaic Law laid our more explicitly what sin was and the different aspects of it. Therefore, the Mosaic Law caused sin to increase. On this Paul wrote,

Romans 7:7-8 Updated American Standard Version (UASV)

7 What shall we say then? Is the Law sin? May it never be! On the contrary, I would not have come to know sin except through the Law; for I would not have known about coveting if the Law had not said, "You shall not covet." 8 But sin, taking opportunity through the commandment, produced in me coveting of every kind; for apart from the Law sin *is* dead.

Like the apostle Paul, neither Jewish persons nor us today would know the full range of sin without the Mosaic Law. Paul gave us the example of coveting. The law exposed the coveting spirit that Paul would never have truly recognized in its fullest sense. This is how Paul could say, "apart from the Law sin *is* dead," specifically, it would not be as recognizable, as exposed, as highlighted. The Law made people more aware of the extent of their sinful nature. We should offer a word of caution, though, the Mosaic Law did not move them toward sin or make sin more appealing, but rather it exposed sin for what it was. Sin is missing the mark of perfection. Sin is being out of harmony with the Creator, his personality, standards, and ways, which he inculcated in his creation. The Law made it possible to convict more people concerning sin. Now, the apostles, baptized in Holy Spirit were going to take this a step further with the law of Christ. Again, Jesus said to his apostles, "When he [the Holy Spirit] comes, he will convict the world [by way of the apostle workers] concerning sin and righteousness and judgment." (John 16:8, ESV)

What do we mean by 'convicting the world concerning sin'? This is not a reference to sin in general, as though, the Holy Spirit would personally come upon a person who just watched a movie they should not have, or they just told a lie, or they committed any sin. When we feel this inner guilt, a groaning of our inner person, because we know we have just done wrong, this is not the Holy Spirit convicting us of that sin. It is the Holy Spirit working through the Word of God, which convicts us of sin. Sin will cause us to feel guilt, anxiety, insecurity, shame. We get a clearer understanding of this when we consider Paul's words that "the work of the law is written on their hearts, while their conscience also bears witness, and their conflicting thoughts accuse or even excuse them." (Rom 2:15, ESV) In other words, when we fall short of God's standards as they are laid out in Scripture or our God given conscience, we will feel an internal groaning within us, which is our conscience convicting us of wrongdoing.

We are born with the weaker version of the conscience that God had given Adam and Eve. It will prevent most humans from committing the obvious right and wrongs, even if they never read the Word of God their entire life. However, considering that almost all of the teachers and professors in the United States and Especially Europe and Canada are of a liberal progressive mindset, which is contrary to God's standards, the conscience is greatly weakened by Satan's world. If our conscience is ignored, it will become calloused and unfeeling, no longer warning us of our wrongdoing, because it will no longer notify us of wrongdoing in our heart and mind. On the other hand, if Scripture trains our conscience, it will not allow us to commit the wrongdoing in the first place. Returning to the being made bold by the Holy Spirit, we too can receive the Spirit in our evangelism work, but not in the same way and the same sense as the apostles and their fellow workers.

The Work of the Holy Spirit in the First Century

There was a different level of relationship between fist century Christianity and Christianity over the next 2,000 years. It must be remembered that Christ needed (1) **to train** those that would, (2) **establish Christianity**, and (3) **grow Christianity** to the point that it was **extensive** and **united**. This was needed to withstand the apostasy and false teachers that were to come over the next 2,000 years, who would split Christianity into so many factions, finding the truth and the way of the first century today is nigh impossible. All that Jesus and his apostles were to accomplish took place in a mere one hundred years while also publishing the twenty-seven books of the New Testament that later Christians would bring together as one book. There was a definite need for the Holy Spirit in first century Christianity. Let us look at the gifts of prophecy and speaking in tongues.

As for Tongues, They Will Cease

1 Corinthians 13:8-10 Updated American Standard Version (UASV)

[8] Love never fails. But if there are gifts of prophecy, they will be done away with; if there are tongues,[43] they will cease;[44] if there is knowledge, it will be done away with. [9] For we have partial knowledge and we prophesy partially, [10] but when what is complete comes, what is partial will be done away.

Some may argue that the evidence does not give one any idea of when the gift of tongues was to end. However, they would be mistaken in this case. There are three lines of evidence that present the fact that the gift of tongues would die out shortly after the death of the last apostle, which was the apostle John, who died about 98-100 C.E. **First**, the gift of tongues was always passed on to the person, only by an apostle: either by laying his hands on this one, or at least being present. (Acts 2:4, 14, 17; 10:44-46; 19:6; see also Acts 8:14-18.) **Second**, 1 Corinthians 13:8 informed the Corinthian reader specifically that this gift would "cease." In short, the Greek word for cease [*pausontai*], means to 'peter out,' or 'to die out,' not to be brought to a halt. We will deal with *pausontai* more extensively in a moment. **Third**, both one and two are exactly what happened when we look at the history of this gift of tongues. M'Clintock

---

[43] Namely, miraculous speaking in other languages.

[44] MIRACLES - DO THEY STILL HAPPEN TODAY? God Miraculously Saving People's Lives, Apparitions, Speaking In Tongues, Faith Healing by Edward D. Andrews

http://www.christianpublishers.org/apps/webstore/products/show/5823391

and Strong's *Cyclopaedia* (Vol. VI, p. 320) says that it is "an uncontested statement that during the first hundred years after the death of the apostles we hear little or nothing of the working of miracles by the early Christians." Therefore, following their passing off the scene and after those who in that way had obtained the gift of tongues breathed their last breath; the gift of tongues should have died out with these ones. (Elwell, 2001, 1207-8) This analysis concurs with the intention of those gifts as acknowledged at Hebrews 2:2-4. In other words, The gifts of the Spirit in the first century, which includes speaking in tongues, was evidence that God had abandoned the 1,600 years of the nation of Israel being the way to God to the Christian congregation.

Daniel B. Wallace in his *Greek Grammar Beyond the Basics* helps us to comprehend better how we are to understand *pausontai* of 1 Corinthians 13:8:

> If the voice of the verb here is significant, then Paul is saying either that tongues will cut themselves off (direct middle) or, more likely, cease of their own accord, i.e., 'die out' without an intervening agent (indirect middle). It may be significant with reference to prophecy and knowledge, Paul used a different verb ([*katargeo*]) and out it in the passive voice. In vv 9-10, the argument continues: 'for we *know* in part and we *prophecy* in part; but when the perfect comes, the partial shall be done away with [*katargethesontai*].' Here again, Paul uses the same passive verb he had used with prophecy and knowledge and he speaks of the verbal counterpart to the nominal 'prophecy' and 'knowledge.' Yet he does not speak about *tongues* being done away 'when the perfect comes.' The implication *may* be that tongues were to have 'died out' on their own *before* the perfect comes. (Wallace 1996, 422)

These abilities were only established by the presence or lying on of hands by the apostles. This coincides with 1 Corinthians 13:8 and the history of these phenomena. Our Greek word for "cease" means that the gift of tongues was to 'die out' over time as the last of those who had received this gift passed off the scene of this earth. This is established by the historical fact that the second century saw just that being evidenced. Today, the Christian is moved by Spirit to speak with his heart and mind, defending and establishing the gospel, and destroying false doctrines, snatching some back from the fire. It is these things, which will give credence to the words of the modern-day Christian congregation: "God is really among you."—1 Corinthians 14:24-25.

The special, supernatural gifts, such as speaking in tongues gave impetus to the evangelism work that needed to be done in the first century, into many different lands throughout the Roman Empire. (Matt 28:19-20; Ac 1:8; 2:1-11) In the first century, the ones who spoke in tongues did so in languages that others could understand. (Ac 2:4, 8) If we look at those who claim to do so today, it is some ecstatic explosion of incomprehensible sounds, which only draws attention to them.

1 Corinthians 12:7-11 Updated American Standard Version (UASV)

7 But the manifestation of the Spirit is given to each one for a beneficial purpose. **8** For to one is given speech of wisdom through the Spirit, to another speech of knowledge according to the same Spirit, **9** to another faith by the same Spirit, to another gifts of healing by that one Spirit, **10** to yet another operations of miraculous powers, to another prophesying, to another the distinguishing of spirits, to another different tongues, and to another interpretation of tongues. **11** But all these operations are performed by the very same Spirit, distributing to each one respectively just as it wills.

What we see here mentioned by Paul, apparently does not take place today in any Christian congregation. He is indicating various direct and supernatural manifestations of the Spirit, which was a direct gift from the Holy Spirit. There was a reason for these miraculous gifts, which Paul mentions in his letter to the Ephesians,

Ephesians 4:11-13 Updated American Standard Version (UASV)

11 And he gave some as apostles, and some as prophets, and some as evangelists, and some as shepherds and teachers, **12** for the equipping of the holy ones or the work of ministry, to the building up of the body of Christ; **13** until we all attain to the unity of the faith, and of the knowledge of the Son of God, to a mature man, to the measure of the stature which belongs to the fullness of Christ.

If we look at the above mention history of the Christian congregation of the first century and what was accomplished, it perfectly fits Paul's reasons here. The reason for the direct gifts of the Holy Spirit was (1) **to train** those that would, (2) **establish Christianity**, and (3) **grow Christianity** to the point that it was **extensive** and **united**. This gift of the Spirit accompanied the baptism of the Spirit on the day of Pentecost. As has been mentioned, the 120 disciples in that upper room grew to become a united, one denomination of Christianity, which numbered over one million all throughout the Roman Empire, after a mere century. Therefore, when Peter promised the gift of the Holy Spirit on the day of Pentecost, it **was not** to be universally given across the whole of Christianity until the return of Jesus Christ, applying to all who obeyed the Word of God. Rather, it was limited to those of the first century. Even so, it was the apostles and a select few fellow workers, who manifested the Holy Spirit in a supernatural way, by being miraculously taught, instructed, guided, and bringing to their remembrance exactly what Jesus taught for three and a half years, and what Jesus meant by the words that he used. Yes, there were a number, in the first century, who were used as apostles [those caring for many congregations], and some as prophets [those proclaiming God's Word], and some as evangelists [a proclaimer of the gospel or good news],[45] and some as shepherds [elders or overseers in the congregation] and teachers [those who teach within the congregation].

Philip the Evangelist

Philip preached the Word of God to the Samaritans in the city of Samaria after the great persecution arose following the death of Stephen.

Acts 8:12-17 Updated American Standard Version (UASV)

[12] But when they believed Philip as he preached good news about the kingdom of God and the name of Jesus Christ, they were baptized, both men and women. [13] Simon himself also believed, and after being baptized, he continued with Philip; and he was amazed at seeing the signs and great powerful works taking place.

[14] Now when the apostles in Jerusalem heard that Samaria had received the word of God, they sent them Peter and John, [15] who came down and prayed for them that they might receive the Holy Spirit. [16] for he had not yet fallen on any of them, but they had only been baptized in the name of the Lord Jesus. [17] Then they laid their hands on them and they received the Holy Spirit.

What do we notice here? We have Philip, a very important and prominent evangelist, who took the good news to Samaria. He preached and baptized the Samaritans. Philip was endowed with Holy Spirit with six other men, who were selected for a special service. "These [seven men] set before the apostles, and they prayed and **laid their hands on them**." (Ac 6:6) We see that Philip was able to perform signs and great miracles. If the gift of the Holy Spirit was to be for all who accepted Jesus

---

[45] Basic Evangelism is planting seeds of truth and watering any seeds that have been planted. [In the basic sense of this word (*euaggelistes*), this would involve all Christians.] In some cases, it may be that one Christian planted the seeds, which were initially rejected, so he was left in a good way because the planter did not try to force the truth down his throat. However, sometime later he faces something in life that moves him to reconsider those seeds, and some other Christian waters what had already been planted. This evangelism can be carried out in all of the methods that are available: informal, house-to-house, street, and the like. What amount of time is invested in the evangelism work is up to each Christian to decide for themselves.

and was baptized, why did the Samaritans not receive the Spirit? Philip was not an apostle, meaning he could not confer the gift of the Spirit by laying hands on them, even though he had had hands laid on him, and he could perform signs and great miracles. Therefore, Peter and John were dispatched to Samaria, to lay hands on the Samaritans, so that "they might receive the Holy Spirit." It should be noted that the gifts of the Holy Spirit were **always** conveyed to others by the apostles of Jesus Christ (1) laying on of hands (2) or in their presence.

The Holy Spirit Falls on the Gentile

Cornelius was a Gentile an army officer (centurion, KJV), who commanded 100 soldiers. He was "a devout man" who "feared God with all his household, gave alms generously to the people, and prayed continually to God," "an upright and God-fearing man, who is well spoken of by the whole Jewish nation." About the ninth hour of the day, he saw clearly in a vision an angel of God come in and say to him, "Cornelius." And he stared at him in terror and said, "What is it, Lord?" And he said to him, "Your prayers and your alms have ascended as a memorial before God." The angel also told Cornelius, "send men to Joppa and bring one Simon who is called Peter." (Acts 10:1-22) Again, the gifts of the Holy Spirit were always conveyed to others by the apostles of Jesus Christ (1) laying on of hands (2) or in their presence.

Acts 10:44-48 Updated American Standard Version (UASV)

44 While Peter was still speaking these words, the Holy Spirit fell upon all who heard the word. **45** All the circumcised believers[46] who came with Peter were amazed, because the gift of the Holy Spirit had been poured out on the Gentiles also. **46** For they were hearing them speaking with tongues and magnifying God. Then Peter answered, **47** "Can anyone withhold water for baptizing these people, who have received the Holy Spirit just as we have?" **48** And he commanded them to be baptized in the name of Jesus Christ. Then they asked him to remain for some days.

Disciples at Ephesus

In Acts chapter 19, we find Paul meeting up with certain disciples that had been baptized by the John the Baptist. Paul explained that John was not aware of the full Gospel before his death. Below you will notice that these disciples of John had not even heard of the Holy Spirit, even though John pointed his disciples toward Jesus. Yet again, the gifts of the Holy

---

[46] I.e., faithful ones

Spirit were always conveyed to others by the apostles of Jesus Christ (1) laying on of hands (2) or in their presence.

Acts 19:1-7 Updated American Standard Version (UASV)

[1] And it happened that while Apollos was in Corinth, Paul traveled through the inland regions and came to Ephesus and found some disciples. [2] And he said to them, "Did you receive the Holy Spirit when you believed?" And they said to him, "But we have not even heard that there is a Holy Spirit!" [3] And he said, "Into what then were you baptized?" And they said, "Into the baptism of John." [4] And Paul said, "John baptized with a baptism of repentance, telling the people that they should believe in the one who was to come after him, that is, in Jesus." [5] On hearing this, they were baptized in the name of the Lord Jesus. [6] And when Paul had laid his hands on them, the Holy Spirit came on them, and they began speaking in tongues and prophesying. [7] There were in all about twelve men.

Young Timothy

Here is yet another experience where someone has received the Holy Spirit by an apostle laying hands on him or her. Once more, the gifts of the Holy Spirit were always conveyed to others by the apostles of Jesus Christ (1) laying on of hands (2) or in their presence.

2 Timothy 1:4-7 Updated American Standard Version (UASV)

[4] longing to see you, even as I recall your tears, so that I may be filled with joy. [5] For I am reminded of the sincere faith within you, which first dwelt in your grandmother Lois and your mother Eunice, and I am sure that it is in you as well. [6] For this reason I remind you to kindle afresh the gift of God which is in you through the laying on of my hands. [7] For God did not give us a spirit of cowardice, but one of power and of love and of soundness of mind.

Christians In Rome

That the gifts of the Holy Spirit were always conveyed to others by the apostles of Jesus Christ (1) laying on of hands (2) or in their presence was clear. Listen to the praise of Paul to these ones in Rome. He writes, "To all those in Rome who are loved by God and called to be holy ones: 'Grace to you and peace from God our Father and the Lord Jesus Christ. First, I thank my God through Jesus Christ for all of you, because your faith is proclaimed in all the world. For God is my witness, whom I serve with my spirit in the gospel of his Son, that without ceasing I mention you always in my prayers, asking that somehow by God's will I may now at last succeed in coming to you.'" Paul goes on to tell these Christians.

Romans 1:11 Updated American Standard Version (UASV)

¹¹ For I am longing to see you, that I may impart some spiritual gift to you for you to be strengthened;

Notice that Paul could encourage and counsel them from a distance in the longest letter he had penned. However, it was necessary that he be present to convey gifts of the Spirit by his presence or the laying on of hands.

What have we learned thus far? First, the gift of the Spirit was a miraculous, supernatural gift for helping the first-century believers to be bold, to perform signs and miracles, to speak in foreign languages, to be Jesus' "witnesses in Jerusalem and in all Judea and Samaria, and to the end of the earth." (Ac 1:8) We also notice that the gifts of the Holy Spirit were **always** conveyed to others by the apostles of Jesus Christ (1) laying on of hands (2) or in their presence. Moreover, once the last apostle died, John, in 100 C.E., there was no longer one available to convey the gifts of the Spirit.

Therefore, the Greek word at 1 Corinthians 13:8 for "cease" [pausontai], became a reality in that the gifts that had been given 'petered out,' or 'died out,' namely, they were not brought to a halt, as some were, like prophecy. In other words, they died out as the last ones who were given them died at the beginning of the second century. Second, we can see from the letters of the New Testament authors that in the first century, many of the congregations were filled with members that had the supernatural power of the Spirit. Moreover, when we interpret those letters, this must be a part of the historical setting. Below are a few examples from these letters,

Romans 8:9, 23 Updated American Standard Version (UASV)

⁹ However, you are not in the flesh but in the Spirit, if indeed **the Spirit of God dwells in you**. But if anyone does not have the Spirit of Christ, he does not belong to him. ²³ And not only this, but also we ourselves, having the **first fruits of the Spirit**, even we ourselves groan within ourselves, waiting eagerly for our adoption as sons, the redemption of our body.

Romans 15:30 Updated American Standard Version (UASV)

³⁰ Now I urge you, brothers, through our Lord Jesus Christ and through **the love of the Spirit**, that you exert yourselves with me in prayers to God for me,

2 Corinthians 5:5 Updated American Standard Version (UASV)

5 Now the one who prepared us for this very thing is God, who gave us **the Spirit as a down payment** of what is to come.

Ephesians 1:13-14 Updated American Standard Version (UASV)

13 In whom also, you having heard the word of truth, the gospel of your salvation, in whom also having trusted, were **sealed with the Holy Spirit** of promise, **14** who is a down payment of our inheritance for the redemption of the possession, to the praise of his glory.

Ephesians 2:18 Updated American Standard Version (UASV)

18 for through him we both have our **access in one Spirit** to the Father.

Ephesians 5:18 Updated American Standard Version (UASV)

18 And do not get drunk with wine, for that is[47] dissipation,[48] but be **filled with the Spirit,**

1 Thessalonians 4:8 Updated American Standard Version (UASV)

8 Therefore the one who rejects this is not rejecting man, but God, who also **gives his Holy Spirit to you**.

Titus 3:5 Updated American Standard Version (UASV)

5 he saved us, not by deeds of righteousness that we have done, but because of his mercy, through the **washing** of **regeneration** and **renewal by the Holy Spirit,**

Hebrews 2:4 Updated American Standard Version (UASV)

4 God also testifying with them, both by **signs** and **wonders** and by various **miracles** and by **gifts of the Holy Spirit** <u>according to His own will</u>.

James 4:5 Updated American Standard Version (UASV)

5 Or do you think that the Scripture speaks to no purpose, "The **spirit that dwells in us** strongly desires to envy"?

1 John 2:20, 27 Updated American Standard Version (UASV)

20 But you have been **anointed by the Holy One**, and you all have knowledge. **27** As for you, the **anointing which you received from him**

---

[47] Lit *in which is*

[48] behavior which shows lack of concern or thought for the consequences of an action—'senseless deeds, reckless deeds, recklessness.'—GELNTBSD

remains in you, and you have no need for anyone to teach you; but as his anointing teaches you about all things, and is true and is not a lie, and just as it has taught you, you remain in him.

1 John 4:13 Updated American Standard Version (UASV)

[13] By this we know that we are remaining in him and he in us, because he has given **his Spirit to us**.

The Holy Spirit and Today's Christians

Can The Holy Spirit do the same for us? No, the Holy Spirit cannot, at least not in the same way and the same sense. How, then, can we receive the Holy Spirit, to be instructed, guided, taught, reminded and to be directed in our witnessing to others in our evangelism work? As an aside, the answer will apply to every other facet of our Christian life as well, we just happen to be focusing on the evangelism aspect. Let us look at the thought of the Holy Spirit instructing and teaching Christians. Today we have over 41,000 different denominations, all teaching different doctrinal positions on the same subject matter. If we choose just one denomination, we find that each of the tens of thousands of pastors in the churches does not have to teach the same thing about the same doctrine. Then, let us take and one church within that denominations, and we will find that the church members do not all believe the same thing as their pastor.

Thus, we have all sorts of men teaching different views on every doctrine. Let us look at a few examples, so we can better understand. In dealing with the inspiration of God's Word, most church leaders teach The Infallibilist View, meaning that they believe the Bible is infallible only in matters of faith, but that it contains many mistakes, errors, and contradictions in matters when it touches on science, history, and geography. On the other hand, few conservative church leaders still teach The Inerrantist View, meaning that they believe the Bible is without error of any kind. On the doctrine of the atonement, some leaders have The Penal Substitution View, meaning that they believe that Christ died in our place. Others have the Christus Victor View, meaning that they believe Christ destroyed Satan and his works. While others have The Moral Government View, meaning that they believe Christ displayed God's wrath against sin. Concerning the doctrine of Sanctification, there are four main views. We have the Lutheran View, meaning sanctification as a declaration by God. We have the Calvinist view, meaning sanctification as holiness in Christ and personal conduct. Then, we have the Keswick View, meaning sanctification as resting-faith in the sufficiency of Christ. In addition, we have the Wesleyan, View, meaning entire sanctification as perfect love. Even these four beliefs on sanctification are not completely accepted because each church leader can tweak it to fit his understanding of things. These doctrines are just the beginning. We could cover The Providence Debate, i.e., the sovereignty of God. We could talk about different foreknowledge beliefs, the divine image differences the different salvation beliefs, the different beliefs about the human constitution, eternal security, the destiny of the evangelized, baptism, charismatic gifts, hellfire, and numerous others.

These differences in the Christian leader's beliefs are often contradictory. Are we to believe that the Holy Spirit one church leader to teach that sinners are destined to enteral torment in hellfire while other leaders teach eternal destruction for the sinners? Are we to believe that the Holy Spirit teaches different church leaders four different views on sanctification? The belief that the Holy Spirit is still carrying out the same work today as what the Father and the Son assigned in the first century, place the Holy Spirit in a very unenviable position, i.e., teaching different views on the same doctrine, some of which are even contradictory. Can we accept that the Holy Spirit teaches different views on all doctrinal positions, even being contradictory? Remember, it was the Holy Spirit, who taught and instructed the apostles miraculously. The Holy Spirit guided them as well. One way was in their writings, as no New Testament author contradicted another, they were all one because there was really one author, God. This is actually true of all forty plus authors of the entire Bible. Thus, we are to believe that the Holy Spirit moved over forty Bible authors miraculously, over a 1,600 year period, to pen sixty-six Bible books, in all of which there is not one contraction, error or mistake, but now the Holy Spirit is teaching different views and contradictory information? We would not say in the church of and leader, who taught contradictory information, so why would we accept that the Holy Spirit would do such a thing. Supposing that churches evangelized their own communities, which they do not, but let us suppose they did. How should an atheist feel if different churches came to his home to witness to him and they told him contradictory views about the same doctrine?

The problem is the belief that the Holy Spirit is carrying out the same work after that work was completed in the first century. Only the apostles and a select few fellow workers received the Holy Spirit in a direct and supernatural way, teaching them, guiding them, instructing them, bringing back to their remembrance all that Jesus had said. The apostle Paul told Timothy, "The things which you have heard from me in the presence of many witnesses, entrust these to faithful men who will be able to teach others also." (2 Tim. 2:2) We all know that Timothy traveled with Paul for 15 years, being taught by Paul (Paul already being extremely educated by Gamaliel), but more importantly, miraculously taught and instructed by the Holy Spirit. This clearly was not the case with Timothy (his being taught and instructed by the Holy Spirit in the same way and to the same extent), as Timothy was taught by Paul and his study of the Old Testament Scriptures. This text evidences that we are to be taught and instructed by Holy Spirit by way of our study the Holy, Spirit-inspired Scriptures.

If the Holy Spirit were miraculously teaching and instructing Christians today, as took place with the apostles and a select few fellow workers, there would be no need for any sort of Bible study tools, such as Bible dictionaries, encyclopedias, word study dictionaries, commentaries, and the like. Even so, while there are no direct Scriptures to evidence Timothy receiving Holy Spirit in the same way as Paul and the twelve apostles, we know that Holy Spirit led Paul to Timothy on his second missionary tour. We know that Paul saw something in Timothy that brought about a 15-year friendship and bond between the two like no other. Timothy became an extremely valuable co-worker of the apostle Paul, in a time, when the Holy Spirit was building the first-century Christian congregation. Therefore, we cannot discount the possibility that Timothy was guided by the Holy Spirit as Paul had been, maybe not to the same degree, and that he was not taught and instructed in the same way and sense but used more directly by the Holy Spirit than those after the first century, including us today. Let us get back to the apostles for a moment. Let us look at the apostles in the very beginning of Acts, as Jesus tells them,

Acts 1:8 Updated American Standard Version (UASV)

8 But you will receive power when **the Holy Spirit has come upon you**; and you will be my witnesses in both Jerusalem and in all Judea and Samaria, and to the extremity of the earth."

Earlier, Jesus had told them that he was going away and that he was sending them a helper, the Holy Spirit. Now, he specifically tells them, "You [namely, the apostles] will receive power when the Holy Spirit has come upon you, and you will be my witnesses in Jerusalem and in all Judea and Samaria, and to the end of the earth." Just after Jesus said these things, as they were watching, he ascended back to heaven to be with the Father. Some days later on Sivan 6, 33 C.E., they would receive the power of the Holy Spirit, where there was an outpouring of Holy Spirit. (Acts 2:1-17, 38) If they had already received the Holy Spirit, they would not have needed to call the brothers together to determine who was going to replace Judas as the twelfth apostle. Moreover, "they cast lots for them [Joseph called Barsabbas, who was also called Justus, and

Matthias], and the lot fell on Matthias, and he was numbered with the eleven apostles."–Acts 1:15-26

Obtain Boldness

Jesus told his listeners,

Luke 11:13 Updated American Standard Version (UASV)

¹³ If you then, being evil, know how to give good gifts to your children, how much more will your heavenly Father give the Holy Spirit to those who ask Him?"

If we want to receive the Holy Spirit, we just go to the Father in prayer and ask him. If want to be bolder in our sharing of the good news, we can pray to God for the Holy Spirit. However, we must not misunderstand the Scriptures, so as to expect the miraculous, supernatural gifts of the Holy Spirit in the same sense and the same way as the apostle, their fellow workers, and the Christians of the first century. If want to become a better teacher in the Bible class at our churches, we will have to be a better Bible student, take in many Scriptures that deal with the principles of being a more effective teacher, put these into practice, and maybe pick up some good Christian books on being a better teacher. In this way, we would be working in harmony with our prayer, because the Word of God is Spirit inspired, and thus the more we delve into it and apply it in a correct and balanced manner; in essence, we are getting more Holy Spirit. If we want to teach the Bible to the Spanish-speaking people in our community, we may want to learn the Spanish language.

Some might believe that I am suggesting that the Holy Spirit is not active today. This is not the case. It is not the question of whether the Spirit is active, but how the Spirit is active. We can all agree that the Holy Spirit is pleading with the unsaved world, to help them find the path of salvation that leads to accepting Jesus Christ. This is not accomplished in some miraculous, supernatural way, but rather through our work as ambassadors for Christ. New Testament Bible scholar Richard L. Pratt Jr., made the following comment on 2 Corinthians 5:20a,

> Paul's role in the divine plan of reconciliation led him to a remarkable claim. He and his company were **Christ's ambassadors**. "Ambassadors" was a technical political term used in Paul's day that closely parallels our English word "ambassadors." An ambassador represented a nation or kingdom in communication with other nations. Paul had in mind his apostolic call to represent the kingdom of Christ to the nations of the earth. Ambassadors held positions of great honor

in the ancient world because they represented the authority of the kings on whose behalf they spoke.

This was also true for Paul as the ambassador of Christ. When he spoke the message of reconciliation, it was **as though God were making his appeal through** him. Rather than speaking directly to the nations of earth, God ordained that human spokespersons would speak for him. As an apostle, Paul had authority to lead and guide the church (2 Cor. 13:3, 10). Yet, this description applies to all who bear the gospel of Christ to others—even to those who do not bear apostolic authority (1 Pet. 4:11). Though we may not present the gospel as perfectly as Paul did, we do speak on God's behalf when we bring the message of grace to others. But Paul and his company were to be received as mouthpieces of God in the most authoritative sense. (Pratt Jr 2000, p. 359)

2 Corinthians 5:16-20 Updated American Standard Version (UASV)

[16] From now on, therefore, we regard no one according to the flesh. Even though we once regarded Christ according to the flesh, we regard him thus no longer. [17] Therefore if anyone is in Christ, he is a new creation; the old things have passed away; behold, new things have come. [18] And all these things are from God, who has reconciled us to himself through Christ, and who has given us the ministry of reconciliation, [19] namely, that God was in Christ reconciling the world to himself, not counting their trespasses against them, and entrusting to us the message of reconciliation. [20] Therefore, we are ambassadors for Christ, as though God were making an appeal through us; we beg you on behalf of Christ, be reconciled to God.

As ambassadors for Christ, we are not seeking to offer superficial feel-good solutions to the problems of their imperfection, nor the wicked world in which we live. We are not telling them that, if they accept Christ, God will take care of their problems, and they will feel better about life. Sadly, many who first come to a Christian meeting are looking for just that; they want God to help them cope with the imperfection that surrounds their every waking moment. We certainly can counsel them biblically, which will enable them to improve their lot in life, will help them be stronger in dealing with this imperfection we all face, and, generally speaking, if they live a Christlike life, there will be fewer problems that a worldly life. However, our serving as ambassadors for Christ, this is not the goal of our service to the unbelieving world. We are offering them the same gospel that Paul did. In other words, the Father loved the world of humankind so much, he offered the only begotten

Son, and the Father is willing to forgive any of their Adamic, inherited sin, by means of Christ Jesus. Paul wrote,

Romans 5:10-12, 8:32 Updated American Standard Version (UASV)

[10] For if while we were enemies we were reconciled to God through the death of his Son, much more, having been reconciled, we shall be saved by his life. [11] Not only that, but we are also exulting in God through our Lord Jesus Christ, through whom we have now received the reconciliation.

[12] Therefore, just as through one man sin entered into the world, and death through sin, and so death spread to all men, because all sinned,

[32] He who did not spare his own Son, but delivered him over for us all, how will he not also with him freely give us all things?

EARLY CHRISTIANITY 2 Clement of Rome - Apostolic Father

[A.D. 30–100.] Clement was probably a Gentile and a Roman. He seems to have been at Philippi with St. Paul (A.D. 57) when that first-born of the Western churches was passing through great trials of faith. There, with holy women and others, he ministered to the apostle and to the saints. As this city was a Roman colony, we need not inquire how a Roman happened to be there. He was possibly in some public service, and it is not improbable that he had visited Corinth in those days. From the apostle, and his companion, St. Luke, he had no doubt learned the use of the Septuagint, in which his knowledge of the Greek tongue soon rendered him an adept. His copy of that version, however, does not always agree with the Received Text, as the reader will perceive.

A co-presbyter with Linus and Cletus, he succeeded them in the government of the Roman Church. I have reluctantly adopted the opinion that his Epistle was written near the close of his life, and not just after the persecution of Nero. It is not improbable that Linus and Cletus both perished in that fiery trial, and that Clement's immediate succession to their work and place occasions the chronological difficulties of the period. After the death of the apostles, for the Roman imprisonment and martyrdom of St. Peter seem historical, Clement was the natural representative of St. Paul, and even of his companion, the "apostle of the circumcision;" and naturally he wrote the Epistle in the name of the local church, when brethren looked to them for advice. St. John, no doubt, was still surviving at Patmos or in Ephesus; but the Philippians, whose intercourse with Rome is attested by the visit of Epaphroditus, looked naturally to the surviving friends of their great founder; nor was the aged apostle in the East equally accessible. All roads pointed towards the Imperial City and started from its *Milliarium Aureum*. However, though Clement doubtless wrote the letter, he conceals his own name and puts forth the brethren, who seem to have met in council, and sent a brotherly delegation (Chap. lix.). The entire absence of the spirit of Diotrephes (St. John, Ep. 3. 9), and the close accordance of the Epistle, in humility and meekness, with that of St. Peter (Ep. 1, 5:1–5), are noteworthy features. The whole will be found animated with the loving and faithful spirit of St. Paul's dear Philippians, among whom the writer had learned the Gospel.

Clement fell asleep, probably soon after he despatched his letter. It is the legacy of one who reflects the apostolic age in all the beauty and evangelical truth which were the first-fruits of the Spirit's presence with the Church. He shares with others the aureole of glory attributed by St. Paul (Phil. 4:3), "His name is in the Book of Life."

The plan of this publication does not permit the restoration, in this volume, of the recently discovered portions of his work. It is the purpose of the editor to present this, however, with other recently discovered relics of primitive antiquity, in a supplementary volume, should the undertaking meet with sufficient encouragement. The so-called second Epistle of Clement is now known to be the work of another and has been relegated to another place in this series.

The following is the Introductory Notice of the original editors and translators, Drs. Roberts and Donaldson:—

The first Epistle, bearing the name of Clement, has been preserved to us in a single manuscript only. Though very frequently referred to by ancient Christian writers, it remained unknown to the scholars of Western Europe until happily discovered in the Alexandrian manuscript. This ms. of the Sacred Scriptures (known and generally referred to as Codex A) was presented in 1628 by Cyril, Patriarch of Constantinople, to Charles I., and is now preserved in the British Museum. Subjoined to the books of the New Testament contained in it, there are two writings described as the Epistles of one Clement. Of these, that now before us is the first. It is tolerably perfect, but there are many slight *lacunæ*, or gaps, in the ms., and one whole leaf is supposed to have been lost towards the close. These *lacunæ*, however, so numerous in some chapters, do not generally extend beyond a word or syllable, and can, for the most part, be easily supplied.

Who the Clement was to whom these writings are ascribed, cannot with absolute certainty be determined. The general opinion is, that he is the same as the person of that name referred to by St. Paul (Phil. 4:3). The writings themselves contain no statement as to their author. The first, and by far the longer of them, simply purports to have been written in the name of the Church at Rome to the Church at Corinth. But in the catalog of contents prefixed to the MS, they are both plainly attributed to one Clement; and the judgment of most scholars is, that, in regard to the first Epistle at least, this statement is correct, and that it is to be regarded as an authentic production of the friend and fellow-worker of St. Paul. This belief may be traced to an early period in the history of the Church. It is found in the writings of Eusebius (*Hist. Eccl.*, iii. 15), of Origen (*Comm. in Joan.*, i. 29), and others. The internal evidence also tends to support this opinion. The doctrine, style, and manner of thought are all in accordance with it; so that, although, as has been said, positive certainty cannot be reached on the subject, we may with great probability conclude that we have in this Epistle a composition of that Clement who is known to us from Scripture as having been an associate of the great apostle.

The date of this Epistle has been the subject of considerable controversy. It is clear from the writing itself that it was composed soon after some persecution (chap. i.) which the Roman Church had endured; and the only question is, whether we are to fix upon the persecution under Nero or Domitian. If the former, the date will be about the year 68; if the latter, we must place it towards the close of the first century or the beginning of the second. We possess no external aid to the settlement of this question. The lists of early Roman bishops are in hopeless confusion, some making Clement the immediate successor of St. Peter, others placing Linus, and others still Linus and Anacletus, between him and the apostle. The internal evidence, again, leaves the matter doubtful, though it has been strongly pressed on both sides. The probability seems, on the whole, to be in favor of the Domitian period, so that the Epistle may be dated about A.D. 97.

The early Church held this Epistle in very great esteem. The account given of it by Eusebius (Hist. Eccl., iii. 16) is as follows: "There is one acknowledged Epistle of this Clement (whom he has just identified with the friend of St. Paul), great and admirable, which he wrote in the name of the Church of Rome to the Church at Corinth, sedition having then arisen in the latter Church. We are aware that this Epistle has been publicly read in very many churches both in old times, and also in our own day." The Epistle before us thus appears to have been read in numerous churches, as being almost on a level with the canonical writings. And its place in the Alexandrian MS, immediately after the inspired books, is in harmony with the position thus assigned it in the primitive Church. There does indeed appear a great difference between it and the inspired writings in many respects, such as the fanciful use sometimes made of Old-Testament statements, the fabulous stories which are accepted by its author, and the general diffuseness and feebleness of style by which it is distinguished. But the high tone of evangelical truth which pervades it, the simple and earnest appeals which it makes to the heart and conscience, and the anxiety which its writer so constantly shows to promote the best interests of the Church of Christ, still impart an undying charm to this precious relic of later apostolic times.[49]

---

[49] Alexander Roberts, James Donaldson, and A. Cleveland Coxe, eds., "Introductory Note to the First Epistle of Clement to the Corinthians," in The Apostolic Fathers with Justin Martyr and Irenaeus, vol. 1, The Ante-Nicene Fathers (Buffalo, NY: Christian Literature Company, 1885), 1–3.

EARLY CHRISTIANITY 3 Ignatius of Antioch - Early Christian Writings

[A.D. 30–107.] The seductive myth which represents this Father as the little child whom the Lord placed in the midst of his apostles (St. Matt. 18:2) indicates at least the period when he may be supposed to have been born. That he and Polycarp were fellow-disciples under St. John, is a tradition by no means inconsistent with anything in the Epistles of either. His subsequent history is sufficiently indicated in the Epistles which follow.

Had not the plan of this series been so exclusively that of a mere revised reprint, the writings of Ignatius themselves would have made me diffident as to the undertaking. It seems impossible for anyone to write upon the subject of these precious remains, without provoking controversy. This publication is designed as an *Eirenicon*, and hence "few words are best," from one who might be supposed incapable of an unbiassed opinion on most of the points which have been raised in connection with these Epistles. I must content myself therefore, by referring the studious reader to the originals as edited by Bishop Jacobson, with a Latin version and copious annotations. That revered and learned divine honored me with his friendship; and his precious edition has been my frequent study, with theological students, almost ever since it appeared in 1840. It is by no means superannuated by the vigorous Ignatian literature which has since sprung up, and to which reference will he made elsewhere. But I am content to leave the whole matter, without comment, to the minds of Christians of whatever school and to their independent conclusions. It is a great thing to present them in a single volume with the shorter and longer Epistles duly compared, and with the Curetonian version besides. One luxury only I may claim, to relieve the drudging task-work of a mere reviser. Surely I may point out some of the proverbial wisdom of this great disciple, which has often stirred my soul, as with the trumpet heard by St. John in Patmos. In him, indeed, the lions encountered a lion, one truly begotten of "the Lion of the tribe of Judah." Take, then, as a specimen, these thrilling injunctions from his letter to Polycarp, to whom he bequeathed his own spirit, and in whom he well knew the Church would recognize a sort of survival of St. John himself. If the reader has any true perception of the rhythm and force of the Greek language, let him learn by heart the originals of the following aphorisms:—

1.   Find time to pray without ceasing.

2.   Every wound is not healed with the same remedy.

3.   The times demand thee, as pilots the haven.

4.   The crown is immortality.

5.   Stand like a beaten anvil.

6.   It is the part of a good athlete to be bruised and to prevail.

7.   Consider the times: look for Him who is above time.

8.   Slight not the menservants and the handmaids.

9.   Let your stewardship define your work.

10.   A Christian is not his own master, but waits upon God.

Ignatius so delighted in his name Theophorus (sufficiently expounded in his own words to Trajan or his official representative), that it is worth noting how deeply the early Christians felt and believed in (2 Cor. 6:16) the indwelling Spirit.

Ignatius has been censured for his language to the Romans, in which he seems to crave martyrdom. But he was already condemned, in law a dead man, and felt himself at liberty to glory in his tribulations. Is it more than modern Christians often too lightly sing?—

"Let cares like a wild deluge come,

And storms of sorrow fall," etc.

So the holy martyr adds, "Only let me attain unto Jesus Christ."

The Epistle to the Romans is utterly inconsistent with any conception on his part, that Rome was the see and residence of a bishop holding any other than fraternal relations with himself. It is very noteworthy that it is devoid of expressions, elsewhere made emphatic, which would have been much insisted upon had they been found herein. Think what use would have been made of it, had the words which he addresses to the Smyrnæans (cap. viii.) to strengthen their fidelity to Polycarp, been found in this letter to the Romans, especially as in this letter we first find the use of the phrase "Catholic Church" in patristic writings. He defines it as to be found "where Jesus Christ is," words which certainly do not limit it to communion with a professed successor of St. Peter.

The following is the original Introductory Notice:—

The epistles ascribed to Ignatius have given rise to more controversy than any other documents connected with the primitive Church. As is evident to every reader on the very first glance at these writings, they contain numerous statements which bear on points of ecclesiastical order that have long divided the Christian world; and a strong temptation has thus been felt to allow some amount of prepossession to enter into the discussion of their authenticity or spuriousness. At the same time, this question has furnished a noble field for the display of learning and acuteness, and has, in the various forms under which it has been debated, given rise to not a few works of the very highest ability and scholarship. We shall present such an outline of the controversy as may enable the reader to understand its position at the present day.

There are, in all, fifteen Epistles which bear the name of Ignatius. These are the following: One to the Virgin Mary, two to the Apostle John, one to Mary of Cassobelæ, one to the Tarsians, one to the Antiochians, one to Hero, a deacon of Antioch, one to the Philippians; one to the Ephesians, one to the Magnesians, one to the Trallians, one to the Romans, one to the Philadelphians, one to the Smyrnæans, and one to Polycarp. The first three exist only in Latin: all the rest are extant also in Greek.

It is now the universal opinion of critics, that the first eight of these professedly Ignatian letters are spurious. They bear in themselves indubitable proofs of being the production of a later age than that in which Ignatius lived. Neither Eusebius nor Jerome makes the least reference to them; and they are now by common consent set aside as forgeries, which were at various dates, and to serve special purposes, put forth under the name of the celebrated Bishop of Antioch.

But after the question has been thus simplified, it still remains sufficiently complex. Of the seven Epistles which are acknowledged by Eusebius (*Hist. Eccl.*, iii. 36), we possess two Greek recensions, a shorter and a longer. It is plain that one or other of these exhibits a corrupt text, and scholars have for the most part agreed to accept the shorter form as representing the genuine letters of Ignatius. This was the opinion generally acquiesced in, from the time when critical editions of these Epistles began to be issued, down to our own day. Criticism, indeed, fluctuated a good deal as to which Epistles should be accepted and which rejected. Archp. Usher (1644), Isaac Vossius (1646), J. B. Cotelerius (1672), Dr. T. Smith (1709), and others, edited the writings ascribed to Ignatius in forms differing very considerably as to the order in which they were arranged, and the degree of authority assigned them, until at length, from about the beginning of the eighteenth century, the seven Greek Epistles, of which a translation is here given, came to be generally accepted in their *shorter* form as the genuine writings of Ignatius.

Before this date, however, there had not been wanting some who refused to acknowledge the authenticity of these Epistles in either of the recensions in which they were then known to exist. By far the most learned and elaborate work maintaining this position was that of Daillé (or Dallæus), published in 1666. This drew forth in reply the celebrated *Vindiciæ* of Bishop Pearson, which appeared in 1672. It was generally supposed that this latter work had established on an immoveable foundation the genuineness of the shorter form of the Ignatian Epistles; and, as we have stated above, this was the conclusion almost universally accepted down to our own day. The only considerable exception to this concurrence was presented by Whiston, who laboured to maintain in his *Primitive Christianity Revived* (1711) the superior claims of the longer recension of the Epistles, apparently influenced in doing so by the support which he thought they furnished to the kind of Arianism which he had adopted.

However, although the shorter form of the Ignatian letters had been generally accepted in preference to the longer, there was still a pretty prevalent opinion among scholars, that even it could not be regarded as absolutely free from interpolations, or as of undoubted authenticity. Thus said Lardner, in his *Credibility of the Gospel History* (1743): "I have carefully compared the two editions, and am very well satisfied, upon that comparison, that the larger are an interpolation of the smaller, and not the smaller an epitome or abridgment of the larger.... But whether the smaller themselves are the genuine writings of Ignatius, Bishop of Antioch, is a question that has been much disputed, and has employed the pens of the ablest critics. And whatever positiveness some may have shown on either side, I must own I have found it a very difficult question."

This expression of uncertainty was repeated in substance by Jortin (1751), Mosheim (1755), Griesbach (1768), Rosenmüller (1795), Neander (1826), and many others; some going so far as to deny that we have any authentic remains of Ignatius at all, while others, though admitting the seven shorter letters as being probably his, yet strongly suspected that they were not free from interpolation. Upon the whole, however, the shorter recension was, until recently, accepted without much opposition, and chiefly in dependence on the work of Bishop Pearson above mentioned, as exhibiting the genuine form of the Epistles of Ignatius.

But a totally different aspect was given to the question by the discovery of a Syriac version of three of these Epistles among the mss. procured from the monastery of St. Mary Deipara, in the desert of Nitria, in Egypt. In the years 1838, 1839, and again in 1842, Archdeacon Tattam visited that monastery, and succeeded in obtaining for the English Government a vast number of ancient Syriac manuscripts. On these being deposited in the British Museum, the late Dr. Cureton, who then had charge of the Syriac department, discovered among them, first, the Epistle to Polycarp, and then again, the same Epistle, with those to the Ephesians and to the Romans, in two other volumes of manuscripts.

As the result of this discovery, Cureton published in 1845 a work, entitled, *The Ancient Syriac Version of the Epistles of St. Ignatius to St. Polycarp, the Ephesians, and the Romans*, etc., in which he argued that these Epistles represented more accurately than any formerly published what Ignatius had actually written. This, of course, opened up the controversy afresh. While some accepted the views of Cureton, others very strenuously opposed them. Among the former was the late Chev. Bunsen; among the latter, an anonymous writer in the *English Review*, and Dr. Hefele, in his third edition of the *Apostolic Fathers*. In reply to those who had controverted his arguments, Cureton published his *Vindiciæ Ignatianæ* in 1846, and his *Corpus Ignatianum* in 1849. He begins his introduction to the last-named work with the following sentences: "Exactly three centuries and a half intervened between the time when three Epistles in Latin, attributed to St. Ignatius, first issued from the press, and the publication in 1845 of three letters in Syriac bearing the name of the same apostolic writer. Very few years passed before the former were almost universally regarded as false and spurious; and it seems not improbable that scarcely a longer period will elapse before the latter be almost as generally acknowledged and received as the only true and genuine letters of the venerable Bishop of Antioch that have either come down to our times, or were ever known in the earliest ages of the Christian Church."

Had the somewhat sanguine hope thus expressed been realized, it would have been unnecessary for us to present to the English reader more than a translation of these three Syriac Epistles. But the Ignatian controversy is not yet settled. There are still those who hold that the balance of argument is in favour of the shorter Greek, as against these Syriac Epistles. They regard the latter as an epitome of the former, and think the harshness which, according to them, exists in the sequence of thoughts and sentences, clearly shows that this is the case. We have therefore given all the forms of the Ignatian letters which have the least claim on our attention. The reader may judge, by comparison for himself, which of these is to be accepted as genuine, supposing him disposed to admit the claims of any one of them. We content ourselves with laying the materials for judgment before him, and with referring to the above-named works in which we find the whole subject discussed.

As to the personal history of Ignatius, almost nothing is known. The principal source of information regarding him is found in the account of his martyrdom, to which the reader is referred. Polycarp alludes to him in his Epistle to the Philippians (chap. ix.), and also to his letters (chap. xiii.).

Irenæus quotes a passage from his Epistle to the Romans (*Adv. Hær.*, v. 28; *Epist. ad Rom.*, chap. iv.), without, however, naming him. Origen twice refers to him, first in the preface to his Comm. on the Song of Solomon, where he quotes a passage from the Epistle of Ignatius to the Romans, and again in his sixth homily on St. Luke, where he quotes from the Epistle to the Ephesians, both times naming the author. It is unnecessary to give later references.

Supposing the letters of Ignatius and the account of his martyrdom to be authentic, we learn from them that he voluntarily presented himself before Trajan at Antioch, the seat of his bishopric, when that prince was on his *first* expedition against the Parthians and Armenians (a.d. 107); and on professing himself a Christian, was condemned to the wild beasts. After a long and dangerous voyage he came to Smyrna, of which Polycarp was bishop, and thence wrote his four Epistles to the Ephesians, the Magnesians, the Trallians, and the Romans. From Smyrna he came to Troas, and tarrying there a few days, he wrote to the Philadelphians, the Smyrnæans, and Polycarp. He then came on to Neapolis, and passed through the whole of Macedonia. Finding a ship at Dyrrachium in Epirus about to sail into Italy, he embarked, and crossing the Adriatic, was brought to Rome, where he perished on the 20th of December 107, or, as some think, who deny a twofold expedition of Trajan against the Parthians, on the same day of the year A.D. 116.[50]

---

[50] Alexander Roberts, James Donaldson, and A. Cleveland Coxe, eds., "Introductory Note to the Epistle of Ignatius to the Ephesians," in *The Apostolic Fathers with Justin Martyr and Irenaeus*, vol. 1, The Ante-Nicene Fathers (Buffalo, NY: Christian Literature Company, 1885), 45–48.

EARLY CHRISTIANITY 4 Polycarp of Smyrna - A Disciple of John

[A.D. 69-155.] The thousands, who surrounded him in the arena, viewed him as a godless man, who was causing their countrymen to abandon their worship, believing that this man worked toward the destruction of their gods. The crowd's stares were of malicious hatred, as they despised his very presence. The governor called him forward; this dignified man of 86 years of age stepped into the open and acknowledged his identity. His name was Polycarp.

However, as Polycarp entered the stadium, there came a voice from heaven: "Be strong, Polycarp, and act like a man." And no one saw the speaker, but those of our people who were present heard the voice. And then, as he was brought forward, there was a great tumult when they heard that Polycarp had been arrested. (2) Therefore, when he was brought before him, the proconsul asked if he were Polycarp.[51] And when he confessed that he was, the proconsul tried to persuade him to recant, saying, "Have respect for your age," and other such things as they are accustomed to say: "Swear by the Genius[52] of Caesar; repent; say, 'Away with the atheists!' " So Polycarp solemnly looked at the whole crowd of lawless heathen who were in the stadium, motioned toward them with

---

[51] *Polycarp*: so gE; m (followed by Lightfoot) omits.

[52] Genius: i.e., the guardian spirit.

his hand, and then (groaning as he looked up to heaven) said, "Away with the atheists!" (3) But when the magistrate persisted and said, "Swear the oath, and I will release you; revile Christ," Polycarp replied, "For eighty-six years I have been his servant,[53] and he has done me no wrong. How can I blaspheme my King who saved me?"[54]

You are the reader are likely asking why is the 86 year old man on trial? Who exactly was Polycarp? And what was it that brought him to this point in his life?

Early Life and Ministry

Polycarp was born to Christian parents about 69 C.E. in Asia Minor, at Smyrna. As he grew into a man, he was known for his kindness, self-discipline, compassionate treatment of others, and thorough study of God's Word. Soon enough he became an elder in the Christian congregation at Smyrna.

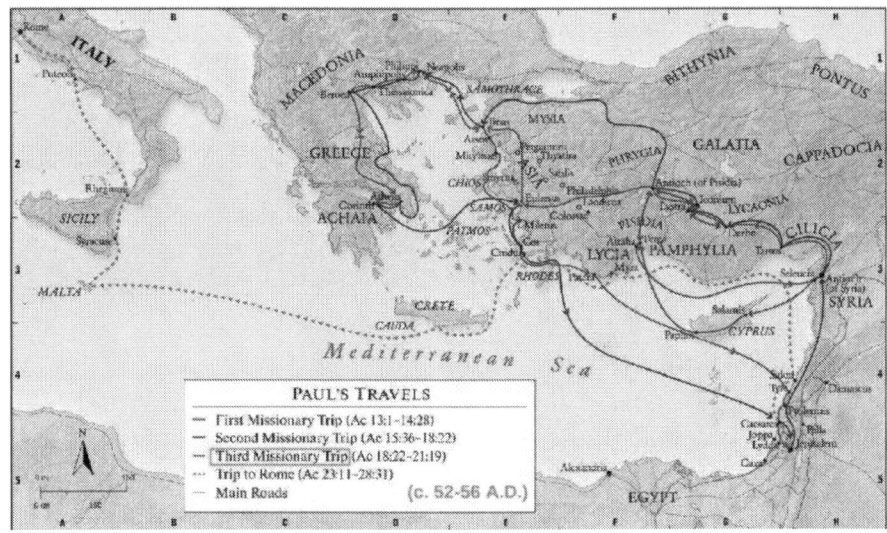

Third Missionary Journey of Paul

Polycarp was very fortunate to live in a time, where he was able to learn from the apostles themselves. In fact, the apostle John was one of his teachers. Listen to Irenaeus'[55] own words about Polycarp:

---

[53] have ... servant: so g; mE read have served him.

[54] Michael William Holmes, The Apostolic Fathers: Greek Texts and English Translations, Third ed. (Grand Rapids, Mich.: Baker Books, 2007), 315, 317.

[55] Irenaeus was born between 120 C.E. and 140 C.E. in or near the city of Smyrna, who died about 200 C.E. He served as an elder in Gaul. He was an early apologist, who

Polycarp was not only instructed by apostles and conversant with many who had seen the Lord, but was appointed by apostles to serve in Asia as Bishop of Smyrna. I myself saw him in my early years, for he lived a long time and was very old indeed when he laid down his life by a glorious and most splendid martyrdom. At all times he taught the things which he had learnt from the apostles, which the Church transmits, which alone are true. These facts are attested by all the churches of Asia and the successors of Polycarp to this day—and he was a much more trustworthy and dependable witness to the truth than Valentinus and Marcion and all other wrong–headed persons. In the time of Anicetus he stayed for a while in Rome, where he won over many from the camp of these heretics in the Church of God, proclaiming that the one and only truth he had received from the apostles was the truth transmitted by the Church. And there are people who heard him describe how John, the Lord's disciple, when at Ephesus went to take a bath, but seeing Cerinthus inside rushed out of the building without taking a bath, crying: "Let us get out of here, for fear the place falls in, now that Cerinthus, the enemy of the truth, is inside!" Polycarp himself on one occasion came face to face with Marcion, and when Marcion said "Don't you recognize me?" he replied: "I do indeed: I recognize the firstborn of Satan!" So careful were the apostles and their disciples to avoid even exchanging words with any falsifier of the truth, in obedience to the Pauline injunction: "If a man remains heretical after more than one warning, have no more to do with him, recognizing that a person of that type is a perverted sinner, self–condemned.[56]

A Witness to the Truth

It is very fortunate that Polycarp received the training that he did, from the apostles, especially John. He was entering the beginning of the time period of the foretold apostasy [rebellion, falling away]:

2 Thessalonians 2:1-3 New American Standard Bible (NASB)

[1] Now we request you, brethren, with regard to the coming of our Lord Jesus Christ and our gathering together to Him, [2] that you not be quickly shaken from your composure or be disturbed either by a spirit or a message or a letter as if from us, to the effect that the day of the Lord

---

wrote in defense of the Christian truth as he knew it. His principal writing was *The Refutation and Overthrow of the Knowledge Falsely So Called*," which was commonly referred to as "*Against Heresies*."

[56] Irenaeus Against Heresies 3.3.4; Eusebius, Ecclesiastical History 4.14.3–8. This translation from edition cited above.

has come. **3** Let no one in any way deceive you, for **it will not come unless the apostasy [rebellion, falling away] comes first**, and the man of lawlessness is revealed, the son of destruction.

Polycarp was often moved to go out of his way to be there for others. For example, when Ignatius of Antioch, Syria, on the way to his martyrdom in Rome, asked the Philippians to send a letter to his congregation, Polycarp of Smyrna made sure it was delivered.

In Polycarp's letter to the Philippians, we can appreciate the truths he shares with his readers.

I greatly rejoice with you in our Lord Jesus Christ, because you welcomed the representations of the true love[57] and, as was proper for you, helped on their way those men confined by chains suitable for saints, which are the diadems of those who are truly chosen by God and our Lord; (2) and because your firmly rooted faith, renowned from the earliest times, still perseveres and bears fruit to our Lord Jesus Christ, who endured for our sins, facing even death, "whom God raised up, having loosed the pangs of Hades." (3) "Though you have not seen him, you believe in him with an inexpressible and glorious joy" (which many desire to experience), knowing that "by grace you have been saved, not because of works," but by the will of God through Jesus Christ.

"Therefore prepare for action and serve God in fear" and truth, leaving behind the empty and meaningless talk and the error of the crowd, and "believing in him who raised" our Lord Jesus Christ "from the dead and gave him glory" and a throne at his right hand; to whom all things in heaven and on earth were subjected, whom every breathing creature serves, who is coming as "Judge of the living and the dead," for whose blood God will hold responsible those who disobey him. (2) But "he who raised him from the dead will raise us also," if we do his will and follow his commandments and love the things he loved, while avoiding every kind of unrighteousness, greed, love of money, slander and false testimony; "not repaying evil for evil or insult for insult" or blow for blow or curse for curse, (3) but instead remembering what the Lord said as he taught: "Do not judge, that you may not be judged; forgive, and you will be forgiven; show mercy, that you may be shown mercy; with the measure you use, it will be measured back to you"; and "blessed are the poor and those who are persecuted for righteousness' sake, for theirs is the kingdom of God."[58]—Luke 6:20 and Matt. 5:10; cf. Matt. 5:3.

---

[57] I.e., Ignatius and his companions.

[58] Michael William Holmes, The Apostolic Fathers: Greek Texts and English Translations, Updated ed. (Grand Rapids, Mich.: Baker Books, 2007), 281, 283.

As you can see from the footnotes Polycarp quoted abundantly from the Scriptures. In his letter to the Philippians, he referred to Matthew, Acts, Romans, 1 Corinthians, 2 Corinthians, Galatians, Ephesians, 2 Thessalonians, 1 Timothy, 1 Peter, to mention just a few. This sets a good example for us to follow, and should help us to appreciate that the apologist, who lived right after the death of the last apostle, John; used the Scriptures to defend the truth as they understood it.

Polycarp in Smyrna

Smyrna was an ancient coastal city of Asia Minor, on the Aegean shore of what is now Asiatic Turkey. It was full of activity and a flourishing trading center. It had a temple of Tiberius Caesar and so sponsored emperor worship. In addition, Roman emperors were presented importantly as deities on coins and in inscriptions. Pagan religious philosophies were endorsed by royal authority.

Regardless of the wealth that was flowing into Smyrna, many of those within the Christian congregation were materially poor. However, in the time of the apostle John (c. 96 C.E.), they were commended for being spiritually rich.

Revelation 2:8-10 English Standard Version (ESV)

[8] "And to the angel of the church in Smyrna write: 'The words of the first and the last, who died and came to life.

[9] "'I know your tribulation and your poverty (but you are rich) and the slander of those who say that they are Jews and are not, but are a synagogue of Satan. [10] Do not fear what you are about to suffer. Behold, the devil is about to throw some of you into prison, that you may be

tested, and for ten days you will have tribulation. Be faithful unto death, and I will give you the crown of life.

We can attribute this spiritual maturity among the Christians in Smyrna, to the hard work of the elders, like Polycarp. Throughout the time of Polycarp's serving as oversight in the congregation, these ones lived through one difficult religious struggle after another. There was the pressure from the Roman government, the fleshly non-Christian Jews, as well as conflicting creeds and cults. The community that they had to go into, to spread the gospel, was widespread with demonic practices, such as sorcery and astrology, and thus the atmosphere was one of godlessness. The martyrdom of Polycarp took place on February 23, 155 C.E., where extremist Jews apparently helped with the gathering of firewood. They did this even though the execution took place on a great Sabbath day!

The Godless

After withdrawing from the city, Polycarp is hunted by a police captain named Herod and betrayed by young slaves who belong to his own house (6:2). He is arrested late in the evening in an "upper room" by police armed as if advancing against a robber (7:1; cf. Mt. 26:55). He refuses to flee, but like Jesus in Gethsemane says "the will of God be done." After a long prayer (7:3) he is taken back to the city riding on an ass on a "great Sabbath day" (8:1).[59]

Back in the arena, Polycarp was standing before the governor and an enormous crowd, looking for blood. The governor continued to push him to profess worshipful honor to Caesar:

But as he continued to insist, saying, "Swear by the Genius of Caesar," he answered: "If you vainly suppose that I will swear by the Genius of Caesar, as you request, and pretend not to know who I am, listen carefully: I am a Christian. Now if you want to learn the doctrine of Christianity, name a day and give me a hearing." (2) The proconsul said: "Persuade the people." But Polycarp said: "You I might have considered worthy of a reply, for we have been taught to pay proper respect to rulers and authorities appointed by God, as long as it does us no harm; but as for these, I do not think they are worthy, that I should have to defend myself before them."[60]

Just moments later Polycarp was burned to death because he would not forsake Jesus Christ.

[A.D. 65–100–155.] The Epistle of Polycarp is usually made a sort of preface to those of Ignatius, for reasons which will be obvious to the reader. Yet he was born later, and lived to a much later period. They seem to have been friends from the days of their common pupilage under St. John; and there is nothing improbable in the conjecture of Usher, that he was the "angel of the church in Smyrna," to whom the Master says, "Be thou faithful unto death, and I will give thee a crown of life." His pupil Irenæus gives us one of the very few portraits of an apostolic man which are to be found in antiquity, in a few sentences which are a picture: "I could describe the very place in which the blessed Polycarp sat and taught; his going out and coming in; the whole tenor of his life; his personal appearance; how he would speak of the conversations he had held with John and with others who had seen the Lord. How did he make mention of their words and of whatever he had heard from them respecting the Lord." Thus he unconsciously tantalizes our reverent curiosity. Alas! that such conversations were not written for our learning. But there is a wise Providence in what is withheld, as well as in the inestimable treasures we have received.

Irenæus will tell us more concerning him, his visit to Rome, his

---

[59] Geoffrey W. Bromiley, vol. 1, *The International Standard Bible Encyclopedia, Revised* (Wm. B. Eerdmans, 1988; 2002), 211.

[60] Michael William Holmes, *The Apostolic Fathers: Greek Texts and English Translations*, Third ed. (Grand Rapids, Mich.: Baker Books, 2007), 315, 317.

rebuke of Marcion, and incidental anecdotes, all which are instructive. The expression which he applied to Marcion is found in this Epistle. Other facts of interest are found in the Martyrdom, which follows in these pages. His death, in extreme old age under the first of the Antonines, has been variously dated; but we may accept the date we have given, as rendered probable by that of the Paschal question, which he so lovingly settled with Anicetus, Bishop of Rome.

The Epistle to the Philippians is the more interesting as denoting the state of that beloved church, the firstborn of European churches, and so greatly endeared to St. Paul. It abounds in practical wisdom, and is rich in Scripture and Scriptural allusions. It reflects the spirit of St. John, alike in its lamb-like and its aquiline features: he is as loving as the beloved disciple himself when he speaks of Christ and his church, but "the son of thunder" is echoed in his rebukes of threatened corruptions in faith and morals. Nothing can be more clear than his view of the doctrines of grace; but he writes like the disciple of St. John, though in perfect harmony with St. Paul's hymn-like eulogy of Christian love.

The following is the original Introductory Notice:—

The authenticity of the following Epistle can on no fair grounds be questioned. It is abundantly established by external testimony, and is also supported by the internal evidence. Irenæus says (*Adv. Hær.*, iii. 3): "There is extant an Epistle of Polycarp written to the Philippians, most satisfactory, from which those that have a mind to do so may learn the character of his faith," etc. This passage is embodied by Eusebius in his *Ecclesiastical History* (iv. 14); and in another place the same writer refers to the Epistle before us as an undoubted production of Polycarp (*Hist. Eccl.*, iii. 36). Other ancient testimonies might easily be added, but are superfluous, inasmuch as there is a general consent among scholars at the present day that we have in this letter an authentic production of the renowned Bishop of Smyrna.

Of Polycarp's life little is known, but that little is highly interesting. Irenæus was his disciple, and tells us that "Polycarp was instructed by the apostles, and was brought into contact with many who had seen Christ" (*Adv. Hær.*, iii. 3; Euseb. *Hist. Eccl.*, iv. 14). There is also a very graphic account given of Polycarp by Irenæus in his Epistle to Florinus, to which the reader is referred. It has been preserved by Eusebius (*Hist. Eccl.*, v. 20).

The Epistle before us is not perfect in any of the Greek mss. which contain it. But the chapters wanting in Greek are contained in an ancient Latin version. While there is no ground for supposing, as some have done, that the whole Epistle is spurious, there seems considerable force in the arguments by which many others have sought to prove chap. xiii. to be an interpolation.

The date of the Epistle cannot be satisfactorily determined. It depends on the conclusion we reach as to some points, very difficult and obscure, connected with that account of the martyrdom of Polycarp which has come down to us. We shall not, however, probably be far wrong if we fix it about the middle of the second century.[61]

---

[61] Alexander Roberts, James Donaldson, and A. Cleveland Coxe, eds., "Introductory Note to the Epistle of Polycarp to the Philippians," in *The Apostolic Fathers with Justin Martyr and Irenaeus*, vol. 1, The Ante-Nicene Fathers (Buffalo, NY: Christian Literature Company, 1885), 31–32.

EARLY CHRISTIANITY 5 Barnabas - The Anonymous Teacher

[A.D. 100.] The writer of this Epistle is supposed to have been an Alexandrian Jew of the times of Trajan and Hadrian. He was a layman; but possibly he bore the name of "Barnabas," and so has been confounded with his holy and apostolic name-sire. It is more probable that the Epistle, being anonymous, was attributed to St. Barnabas, by those who supposed that apostle to be the author of the Epistle to the Hebrews, and who discovered similarities in the plan and purpose of the two works. It is with great reluctance that I yield to modern scholars, in dismissing the ingenious and temperate argument of Archbishop Wake for the apostolic origin of this treatise. The learned Lardner[2] shares his convictions; and the very interesting and ingenious views of Jones never appeared to me satisfactory, weighed with preponderating arguments, on the other side.[4]

The Maccabæan spirit of the Jews never burned more furiously than after the destruction of Jerusalem, and while it was kindling the conflagration that broke out under Barchochebas, and blazed so terribly in the insurrection against Hadrian. It is not credible that the Jewish Christians at Alexandria and elsewhere were able to emancipate themselves from their national spirit; and accordingly the old Judaizing, which St. Paul had anathematized and confuted, would assert itself again. If such was the occasion of this Epistle, as I venture to suppose, a higher character must be ascribed to it than could otherwise be claimed. This accounts, also, for the degree of favour with which it was accepted by the primitive faithful.

It is interesting as a specimen of their conflicts with a persistent Judaism which St. Paul had defeated and anathematized, but which was ever cropping out among believers originally of the Hebrews. Their own habits of allegorizing, and their Oriental tastes, must be borne in mind, if we are readily disgusted with our author's fancies and refinements. St. Paul himself pays a practical tribute to their modes of thought, in his Epistle to the Galatians 4:24. This is the *ad hominem* form of rhetoric, familiar to all speakers, which laid even the apostle open to the slander of enemies (2 Cor. 12:16),—that he was "crafty," and caught men with guile. It is interesting to note the more Occidental spirit of Cyprian, as compared with our author, when he also contends with Judaism. Doubtless we have in the pseudo-Barnabas something of that *œconomy* which is always capable of abuse, and which was destined too soon to overleap the bounds of its moral limitations.

It is to be observed that this writer sometimes speaks as a Gentile, a fact which some have found it difficult to account for, on the supposition that he was a Hebrew, if not a Levite as well. But so, also, St. Paul sometimes speaks as a Roman, and sometimes as a Jew; and, owing to the mixed character of the early Church, he writes to the Romans (4:1) as if they were all Israelites, and again to the same Church (Rom. 11:13) as if they were all Gentiles. So this writer sometimes identifies himself with Jewish thought as a son of Abraham, and again speaks from the Christian position as if he were a Gentile, thus identifying himself with the catholicity of the Church.

But the subject thus opened is vast; and "the Epistle of Barnabas," so called, still awaits a critical editor, who at the same time shall be a competent expositor. Nobody can answer these requisitions, who is unable, for this purpose, to be a Christian of the days of Trajan.

But it will be observed that this version has great advantages over any of its predecessor, and is a valuable acquisition to the student. The learned translators have had before them the entire Greek text of the fourth century, disfigured is true by corruptions, but still very precious, the rather as they have been able to compare it with the text of Hilgenfeld. Their editorial notes are sufficient for our own plan; and little has been left for me to do, according to the scheme of this publication, save to revise the "copy" for printing. I am glad to presume no further into such a labyrinth, concerning which the learned and careful Wake modestly professes, "I have endeavoured to attain to the sense of my author, and to make him as plain and easy as I was able. If in anything I have chanced to mistake him, I have only this to say for myself: that he must be better acquainted with the road than I pretend to be, who will undertake to travel so long a journey in the dark and never to miss his way."

The following is the original Introductory Notice:—

Nothing certain is known as to the author of the following Epistle. The writer's name is Barnabas, but scarcely any scholars now ascribe it to the illustrious friend and companion of St. Paul. External and internal evidence here come into direct collision. The ancient writers who refer to this Epistle unanimously attribute it to Barnabas the Levite, of Cyprus, who held such an honourable place in the infant Church. Clement of Alexandria does so again and again (*Strom.*, ii. 6, ii. 7, etc.). Origen describes it as "a Catholic Epistle" (*Cont. Cels.*, i. 63), and seems to rank it among the Sacred Scriptures (*Comm. in Rom.*, i. 24). Other statements have been quoted from the fathers, to show that they held this to be an authentic production of the apostolic Barnabas; and certainly no other name is ever hinted at in Christian antiquity as that of the writer. But notwithstanding this, the internal evidence is now generally regarded as conclusive against this opinion. On perusing the Epistle, the reader will be in circumstances to judge of this matter for himself. He will be led to consider whether the spirit and tone of the writing, as so decidedly opposed to all respect for Judaism—the numerous inaccuracies which it contains with respect to Mosaic enactments and observances—the absurd and trifling interpretations of Scripture which it suggests—and the many silly vaunts of superior knowledge in which its writer indulges—can possibly comport with its ascription to the fellow-labourer of St. Paul. When it is remembered that no one ascribes the Epistle to the apostolic Barnabas till the times of Clement of Alexandria, and that it is ranked by Eusebius among the "spurious" writings, which, however much known and read in the Church, were never regarded as authoritative, little doubt can remain that the external evidence is of itself weak, and should not make us hesitate for a moment in refusing to ascribe this writing to Barnabas the Apostle.

The date, object, and intended reader of the Epistle can only be doubtfully inferred from some statements which it contains. It was clearly written after the destruction of Jerusalem, since reference is made to that event (chap. xvi.), but how long after is matter of much dispute. The general opinion is, that its date is not later than the middle of the second century, and that it cannot be placed earlier than some twenty or thirty years before. In point of style, both as respects thought and expression, a very low place must be assigned it. We know nothing certain of the region in which the author lived, or where the first readers were to be found. The intention of the writer, as he himself states (chap. i.), was "to perfect the knowledge" of those to whom he wrote. Hilgenfeld, who has devoted much attention to this Epistle, holds that "it was written at the close of the first century by a Gentile Christian of the school of Alexandria, with the view of winning back, or guarding from a Judaic form of Christianity, those Christians belonging to the same class as himself."

Until the recent discovery of the Codex Sinaiticus by Tischendorf, the first four and a half chapters were known only in an ancient Latin version. The whole Greek text is now happily recovered, though it is in many places very corrupt. We have compared its readings throughout, and noted the principal variations from the text represented in our version. We have also made frequent reference to the text adopted by Hilgenfeld in his recent edition of the Epistle (Lipsiæ, T. O. Weigel, 1886).[62]

---

[62] Alexander Roberts, James Donaldson, and A. Cleveland Coxe, eds., "Introductory Note to the Epistle of Barnabas," in The Apostolic Fathers with Justin Martyr and Irenaeus, vol. 1, The Ante-Nicene Fathers (Buffalo, NY: Christian Literature Company, 1885), 133–135.

EARLY CHRISTIANITY 6 Hermas - Early Christian Writer

Barry Hofstetter

Introduction

The Shepherd of Hermas is part of that collection of writings that since the 19th century has been termed "The Apostolic Fathers," the first generation of Christian leaders writing after the end of the apostolic age and the completion of the New Testament (NT) canonical documents. These writings are a vital part of our understanding regarding the development of Christianity. How did the ancient Christians understand the Gospel and apply it to their own context? We find in them a witness to the fact that certain documents of the NT were known to the ancient Christians. We see development regarding doctrine and practical issues which contribute significantly to the later history of the church. The Shepherd of Hermas is arguably somewhat later than some of the other documents in the collection (see below), but still provides a fascinating witness to the way in which one ancient author saw the *paradosis* (tradition) in application to his own context.[63] As we shall see, however, the author's conception of that tradition is quite different from the NT and even the other writings contemporaneous with him.

Summary, Structure and Genre

The Shepherd of Hermas begins with a Christian slave named Hermas who is sold by his master to a woman in Rome named Rhoda. He is apparently set free by her, and as a freedman goes on to live a moderately successful life engaging in the types of business to which freedmen were accustomed to pursue.[64] Many years later he sees her bathing in the Tiber river and is sorely tempted by her beauty. This moral lapse results in a great deal of soul searching on his behalf, and provides the segue into the rest of the work and its primary concern with the issues

---

[63] I am using the Lightfoot edition of the Apostolic Fathers, both Greek (mostly) and English translation. The English translation is readily available on the Web, and though usually attributed to Lightfoot, was actually produced by his colleague J.R. Harmer, as the introductory note to the text indicates. Citations in this article are actually from the Logos collection, derived from the 1891 edition published by Macmillan and Co., London.

[64] Freedmen, *liberti*, were a very important part of the economic context of ancient Rome, providing the backbone of what today we would call the business and mercantile classes.

of what it means to live a moral Christian life, and particularly the issue of repentance. Hermas is the central character of the work with regard to whom these issues are explored. He successively meets, as he seeks to improve his life as a Christian, the Woman (the church) and the Shepherd (who may or may not stand in a position similar to that of the Lord). The work therefore take the shape of a novella or a morality play with a definite plot. It is divided historically into three sections, the Visions, the Mandates (precepts or instructions) and Similitudes (parables). Unlike a modern writing in which the author might endeavor to give each section more or less equal weight, these sections are not equal in either length or content. The Visions are actually introductory and provide what we might call now the "backstory" for the work. The great weight of the moral and theological instruction are contained in the second and third parts. The genre is partly in the form of an apocalypse, showing the triumph of the church over and against the secular forces arrayed against her, and partly in the form of parables.

Authorship, Date and Provenance

There is more than one theory concerning the authorship of the work. One is that the Hermas of the story is the individual known to the apostle Paul (cf. Rom 16:14). This is by far the least likely theory, but demonstrates the tendency of both ancients and some moderns to make connections based on very tenuous facts, in this case the same name. Another theory is that Hermas was a contemporary of yet another of the apostolic fathers, Clement of Rome, and this connection is made from Vision 2.4.3:

Thou shalt therefore write two little books, and shalt send one to Clement, and one to Grapte. So Clement shall send to the foreign cities, for this is his duty; while Grapte shall instruct the widows and the orphans. But thou shalt read (the book) to this city along with the elders that preside over the Church.[65]

This theory, based on actual textual evidence from the document, has much greater weight, but is still unlikely. The Clement mentioned is not referred to as presiding over the church at Rome, but seems to have the duty of passing correspondence on to "foreign" cities (Grk, "outside" cities), a duty which may or may not have belonged to someone of the rank of bishop, but one might expect a little more description if it was the bishop of Rome.

---

[65] Lightfoot, J. B., & Harmer, J. R. (1891). *The Apostolic Fathers* (409). London: Macmillan and Co.

The third and most likely theory is that Hermas was the brother of "Pope"[66] Pius the first of Rome (c. 140-155). The authority for this is the famous Muratorian Canon, a list of writings considered canonical or non-canonical by the compiler. This provides an external referent that in the absence of any competing facts to the contrary is likely to be accurate.

However, Hermas composed The Shepherd quite recently in our times in the city of Rome, while his brother, Pius, the bishop, occupied the [episcopal] seat of the city of Rome. [45] And therefore, it should indeed be read, but it cannot be published for the people in the Church, [46] neither among the Prophets, since their number is complete, [47] nor among the Apostles for it is after their time...[67]

Most scholars are agreed that the Muratorian Canon was originally composed in the second century, although some think it may have been as late as the fourth. It is on interesting grounds that the compiler rejects the canonicity of the text. We shall see below that that there are even more compelling reasons for not including it in the canon of Scripture.

If this is accurate, it also gives us the approximate date of the composition, which would be mid- to later second century A.D. This assumes single authorship of the text, something which several scholars dispute (for what I think are insufficient reasons, discussed below).

The provenance is the place where the text was written. The simplest explanation would be city of Rome. The author in several places shows familiarity with the city and its environs, and clearly represents the action as taking place in that locale. Whether this is actually the case is less important than the fact that the church of Rome even in ancient times had a certain priority, both due to the legends of the apostles who had resided there and due its location in the capital of the empire. By placing the action there the writer lends a certain gravitas to the work which would help his readers take it more seriously.

Manuscripts and Language

An incomplete Greek copy of the Shepherd is included in codes Sinaiticus, perhaps the most important ancient manuscript left to us from ancient times. The other Greek manuscript (also incomplete) is the Athos manuscript, dating from the fourth century. There are also a number of Latin manuscripts in two distinct textual traditions (the Old Latin Version

---

[66] The term "pope" of so early a figure is almost certainly anachronistic, but he is so called even by Protestant scholars.

[67] Found online at http://www.earlychristianwritings.com/text/muratorian-latin.html

and the Palatine). These are complete. In the Lightfoot edition, the two Greek manuscripts are combined to produce the text, but the reader may be surprised that the final part of the text finishes in Latin. There is also an Aethiopic version, and occasional citations by ancient authorities, and especially Clement of Alexandria and Origen.[68]

The character of the Greek is quite interesting. The syntax (the actual grammar and order of the words) is quite simple. We have reasonably short sentences which tend to use a paratactic arrangement, similar to the style found in the Johannine writings in the NT. This means that the author favors coordinating conjunctions rather than subordinate clauses or the equivalent, and avoids long sentences with several clauses. The style is very consistent throughout. This indicates to me that there is one author for the text, though arguably you could have an editor who simply made sure that the combined parts are consistent in style, but that seems less likely. Usually in a redacted text, one can find sufficient inconsistencies in style to at least make the case. If the reference to Clement is to the bishop of Rome, then this might indicate that the text was written in several parts over a long period of time, concluding in the mid-second century.

The author also seems to have a fairly limited vocabulary, which might indicate familiarity in Greek only with early Christian writings. Most of his vocabulary will be familiar to students of NT Greek. He tends to communicate the same ideas in the same words over and over again. This is often a feature of people who are writing in a second language that they do not know that well. A native or bi-lingual speaker of a language will often vary his vocabulary and expressions intuitively according to the context, but one who is not fluent but at a lesser level of mastery will tend to stay in the confines of what he has learned. If he is familiar with a particular body of literature or a particular linguaculture his speech and writing will reflect that. If in fact the provenance of the text is Rome, it may be that Hermas' first language was Latin, and that his Greek was limited to the Christian writings available to him and the Greek that may still have been spoken in the church of Rome at that time.

At the same time, like the NT authors, although his language would not be the polished and educated Greek of the literati, he still uses quite sophisticated literary devices and figures to communicate his content. This suggests to me that the style may actually be to some extent affected. In other words, he may be deliberately imitating the simpler style of the NT and other early Christians authors, for the simple reason that this might have sounded to his readers more authentic, much as Joseph Smith wrote

---

[68] Lightfoot, p. 294-297.

the Book of Mormon in 17ᵗʰ century English, even though writing in the 19ᵗʰ century 200 hundred years after that dialect had gone out of style.

The Latin manuscripts faithfully represent the style of the Greek original.[69]

Comparison with the NT

Many years ago, I once had a dream, as a teenager and very young Christian, that I was visiting hell (along with several of my friends!). A demon came and gave us what looked like a NT. As I opened it up and read it, with a sinking feeling I realized it was nothing like the Bible that I had already come to cherish. This is precisely how many Christians feel when they read the Shepherd of Hermas. It clearly borrows imagery and ideas from canonical materials and the early Christian tradition, yet in content it is significantly different from the majority of the NT.

Specifically it maintains what many would call salvation by works and a very strict code of moralism as the rule for the Christian life. This can be seen by a simple vocabulary study (in addition to reading the actual content). The word grace (Grk., *charis*) appears four times in the Shepherd, and in the more general sense of "gift" or "favor," and not the semi-technical sense of "divine forgiveness" that it often has in the NT. In contrast, in the NT, the same word appears 155 times, the majority of these in the Pauline epistles. Grace is clearly not an important concept for the author of the Shepherd. By contrast, repentance (Grk., *metanoia*) appears 13 times in the Shepherd and the verb repent (Grk., *metanoeo*) appears 93 times. The verb appears 34 times in the NT and the noun 22 times. While word studies are not the whole story (the context and usage of the words is very important) here it reveals a clear difference in the emphasis, indeed, a difference in conceptualization, between the Shepherd and the NT. For Hermas, the focus is on the deeds of the individual, and particularly repentance, and not on the work of grace from God that produces that repentance, as in in the NT.

This becomes even clearer when we read the actual content of the Shepherd. One of the major problems of the early church was repentance after baptism. Baptism covered sin up until the time of the baptism, but what if one sinned after baptism? Related to his was the problem of lapsing during persecution. If one recanted the faith in order to save his life and property, could he then repent and return to the fold after the persecution was over? You can imagine the very human reaction of many who remained faithful and suffered great loss. Their answer was often a

---

[69] I can't comment on the Aethiopic, since I know nothing about that language.

resounding "no!" and this led directly to the "second repentence" controversy. Because of The Shepherd's handling of this, some have dated the text later, but it was an issue of continuing concern for the ancient church, and was applicable to all sins, not just lapsing under persecution. The Shepherd's answer to this issue is that one repentance for sin after baptism is acceptable, but no more.

After that thou hast made known unto them all these words, which the Master commanded me that they should be revealed unto thee, then all their sins which they sinned aforetime are forgiven to them; yea, and to all the saints that have sinned unto this day, if they repent with their whole heart, and remove double-mindedness from their heart. 5For the Master sware by His own glory, as concerning His elect; that if, now that this day has been set as a limit, sin shall hereafter be committed, they shall not find salvation; for repentance for the righteous hath an end; the days of repentance are accomplished for all the saints; whereas for the Gentiles there is repentance until the last day.[70]

Sir,' say I, 'to ask a further question.' 'Speak on,' saith he. 'I have heard, Sir,' say I, 'from certain teachers, that there is no other repentance, save that which took place when we went down into the water and obtained remission of our former sins.'...But I say unto you,' saith he, 'if after this great and holy calling any one, being tempted of the devil, shall commit sin, he hath only one (opportunity of) repentance.[71]

Now, what would the NT perspective on this be? Is there a limit on forgiveness for sins? For one thing, baptism is seen as a sign and symbol for the forgiveness of sins, not that which actually produces that forgiveness. In the NT, it is particularly faith which obtains forgiveness. Of the many verses that could be cited:

21 But now the righteousness of God has been manifested apart from the law, although the Law and the Prophets bear witness to it— 22 the righteousness of God through faith in Jesus Christ for all who believe. For there is no distinction: 23 for all have sinned and fall short of the glory of God, 24 and are justified by his grace as a gift, through the redemption that is in Christ Jesus, 25 whom God put forward as a propitiation by his blood, to be received by faith. This was to show God's righteousness, because in his divine forbearance he had passed over former sins. 26 It was

---

[70] Lightfoot, J. B., & Harmer, J. R. (1891). *The Apostolic Fathers* (408). London: Macmillan and Co.

[71] Lightfoot, J. B., & Harmer, J. R. (1891). *The Apostolic Fathers* (425). London: Macmillan and Co.

to show his righteousness at the present time, so that he might be just and the justifier of the one who has faith in Jesus. [72]

We also have:

If we confess our sins, he is faithful and just to forgive us our sins and to cleanse us from all unrighteousness. [73]

My little children, I am writing these things to you so that you may not sin. But if anyone does sin, we have an advocate with the Father, Jesus Christ the righteous.[74]

From these and other NT passages, a case could be made that there is no limit at all to forgiveness of sins. One issue that the Shepherd is clearly concerned with is antinomianism, the idea that one can, after having received forgiveness, sin with impunity. The answer the Shepherd invents is that this simply means one loses his salvation. Even if one repentance is valid after baptism, that is still essentially salvation by works. The answer of the NT is that forgiveness is radical, total and eternal, but if that forgiveness is truly obtained, then it results in a completely different lifestyle for the individual. The Christian will become concerned with living in gratitude to God for the immense gift he has received. When he does sin, he will grieve, and immediately seek to restore his relationship with God. It is the love of God which is the motivation for living a moral life in the NT. It is the fear of God, not in the biblical sense of awe or reverence, but in the sense of true fear, of losing eternal life and eternal punishment, that is presented as the motivation in the Shepherd.

Conclusion

The Shepherd is an important document from early church history, a witness to the different ways in which the early Christian tradition could be interpreted. From a literary perspective it is a fascinating use of allegory and parable used to communicate its message. From a biblical and evangelical perspective however, the doctrine of the work is completely contrary to the Gospel. For this reason the ancient church did well not to include it in the canon, and not simply because it was a later work not to be included with the apostles. It reminds us that heresy can

---

[72] *The Holy Bible: English Standard Version*. 2001 (Ro 3:21–26). Wheaton: Standard Bible Society.

[73] *The Holy Bible: English Standard Version*. 2001 (1 Jn 1:9). Wheaton: Standard Bible Society.

[74] *The Holy Bible: English Standard Version*. 2001 (1 Jn 2:1). Wheaton: Standard Bible Society.

be produced at any time, and even become popular in certain circles, and that we must be ever vigilant to guard the truth as expressed in the canonical Scriptures. Reading the Shepherd and other writings produced after the completion of the NT also highlights the superiority of the NT with its high view of soteriology (salvation) and Christology (doctrine of Christ), both of which are severely lacking in the Shepherd.

EARLY CHRISTIANITY 7 Papias - Enjoyed the Lord's Sayings

[A.D. 70–155.] It seems unjust to the holy man of whose comparatively large contributions to early Christian literature such mere relics have been preserved, to set them forth in these versions, unaccompanied by the copious annotations of Dr. Routh. If even such crumbs from his table are not by any means without a practical value, with reference to the Canon and other matters, we may well credit the testimony (though disputed) of Eusebius, that he was a learned man, and well versed in the Holy Scripture. All who name poor Papias are sure to do so with the apologetic qualification of that historian, that he was of slender capacity. Nobody who attributes to him the millenarian fancies, of which he was but a narrator, as if these were the characteristics rather than the blemishes of his works, can fail to accept this estimate of our author. But more may be said when we come to the great name of Irenæus, who seems to make himself responsible for them.[2]

Papias has the credit of association with Polycarp, in the friendship of St. John himself, and of "others who had seen the Lord." He is said to have been bishop of Hierapolis, in Phrygia, and to have died about the same time that Polycarp suffered; but even this is questioned. So little do we know of one whose lost books, could they be recovered, might reverse the received judgment, and establish his claim to the disputed tribute which makes him, like Apollos, "an eloquent man, and mighty in the Scriptures."

The following is the original Introductory Notice:—

The principal information in regard to Papias is given in the extracts made among the fragments from the works of Irenæus and Eusebius. He was bishop of the Church in Hierapolis, a city of Phrygia, in the first half of the second century. Later writers affirm that he suffered martyrdom about a.d. 163; some saying that Rome, others that Pergamus, was the scene of his death.

He was a hearer of the Apostle John, and was on terms of intimate intercourse with many who had known the Lord and His apostles. From these he gathered the floating traditions in regard to the sayings of our Lord, and wove them into a production divided into five books. This work does not seem to have been confined to an exposition of the sayings of Christ, but to have contained much historical information.

Eusebius speaks of Papias as a man most learned in all things, and well acquainted with the Scriptures. In another passage[2] he describes him as of small capacity. The fragments of Papias are translated from the text given in Routh's *Reliquiæ Sacræ*, vol. i.[75]

Papias of Hierapolis: Papias (70 – 163 C.E.) was a bishop of the early Church. Eusebius of Caesarea calls him "Bishop of Hierapolis," a city in the region of Asia, which is 6.2 miles (10 km) north of Laodicea and near Colossae (Col. 4:12-13), in the northern edge of the Lycus Valley of Asia Minor, but should not be confused with the Hierapolis of Syria. Christianity came to Hierapolis through the 'efforts' of Epaphras. Papias wrote a five-volume work titled *An Exposition of the Oracles of the Lord*.

Papias describes his way of gathering information,

I will not hesitate to set down for you, along with my interpretations, everything I carefully learned then from the elders and carefully remembered, guaranteeing their truth. For unlike most people I did not enjoy those who have a great deal to say, but those who teach the truth. Nor did I enjoy those who recall someone else's commandments, but those who remember the commandments given by the Lord to the faith and proceeding from the truth itself. And if by chance someone who had been a follower of the elders should come my way, I inquired about the words of the elders–what Andrew and Peter said, or Philip or Thomas or James or John or Matthew or any other of the Lord's disciples, were saying. For I did not think that information from books would profit me as much as information from a living and abiding voice.[76]

John 14:26 New American Standard Bible (NASB)

[26] But the Helper, the Holy Spirit, whom the Father will send in My name, He will teach you all things, and bring to your remembrance all that I said to you.

Papias would have been about 28 years old when John penned First, Second and Third John in 98 C.E. from Ephesus. We know that Papias was a friend and associate of Polycarp (69 – 155 C.E.), who was one year younger than he. As we learned from the above, Polycarp was a student of the apostle John. When we consider the years, in which Papias lived, whom he likely studied under, his associates, his positions as an overseer in the congregation of Hierapolis, his way of taking in knowledge; it is likely that he was very knowledgeable about the Christianity of his era.

---

[75] Alexander Roberts, James Donaldson, and A. Cleveland Coxe, eds., "Introductory Note to the Fragments of Papias," in *The Apostolic Fathers with Justin Martyr and Irenaeus*, vol. 1, The Ante-Nicene Fathers (Buffalo, NY: Christian Literature Company, 1885), 151–152.

[76] Michael William Holmes, *The Apostolic Fathers: Greek Texts and English Translations*, Third ed. (Grand Rapids, Mich.: Baker Books, 2007), 735.

According to Irenaeus (130 – 202 C.E.), Papias was an exceptionally learned man, who was held in high esteem and respected as a reliable source for the apostolic teachings. Eusebius (260/265–339/340 C.E.), an early church historian, on the other hand, offers us contradictory information regarding Papias. "Eusebius ('Hist. Eccl.,' iii. 36) says, 'While Polycarp was in Asia, and was Bishop of Smyrna, Papias was well known as Bishop of the Church in Hierapolis, **a man well skilled in all manner of learning**, and well acquainted with 'the Scriptures.' In 3.39 Eusebius again speaks of him as σφόδρα σμικρὸς ὢν τὸν νοῦν, as being intellectually small or weak. These apparently contradictory passages are not difficult to reconcile."[77] The reason Eusebius took issue with Papias was apparently because Papias believed in a literal millennium, a thousand-year reign of Christ upon the earth. However, this was actually the prevalent view of Christians in the second century, while Eusebius was a determined anti-millenarian.[78]

Papias was writing at a time when Gnosticism was widespread. Gnosticism an early apostate Christian movement teaching that salvation comes by learning esoteric spiritual truths that free humanity from the material world, intertwining philosophy, speculation, as well as pagan mysticism. It would seem that Papias' writings of Jesus sayings were an attempt to slow the rampant growth of Gnosticism. After that came Irenaeus, an apologist specifically fighting the Gnostics' false and exaggerated spirituality. The Gnostic literature may have sparked Papias' sarcastic reference to "**those who have so very much to say**, but in those who teach the truth; nor in those who relate foreign commandments, but in those (who record) such as were given from the Lord to the Faith, and are derived from the Truth itself."[79] It would seem that Papias' objective was to shine a light on the false teachings with the truth. – 1 Timothy 6:4; Philippians 4:5.

About 150 C.E., Papias says of Mark's Gospel, "'Mark, having become the interpreter of Peter, wrote down accurately everything that he remembered.'[80] Irenaeus writing about A.D. 185 stated: 'Now after their decease (Peter and Paul) Mark, the disciple, and interpreter of Peter,

---

[77] H. D. M. Spence-Jones, ed., *St. John*, vol. 1, The Pulpit Commentary (London; New York: Funk & Wagnalls Company, 1909), xxxii.

[78] Philip Schaff and David Schley Schaff, *History of the Christian Church*, vol. 2 (New York: Charles Scribner's Sons, 1910), 696.

[79] Joseph Barber Lightfoot and J. R. Harmer, *The Apostolic Fathers* (London: Macmillan and Co., 1891), 528.

[80] "The Fragments of Papias," p. 265.

also handed down to us in writing what Peter had preached.'"[81] (Irenaeus, "Against Heresies," 370) Further confirming this Gospel's accuracy, Papias continues, "So then Mark made no mistake when he wrote down thus some things as he remembered them; for he concentrated on this alone— not to omit anything that he had heard, nor to include any false statement among them."[82] Papias also provides external evidence that Matthew initially penned his Gospel in Hebrew. Papias says, "Matthew put together the oracles [of the Lord] in the Hebrew language, and each one interpreted them as best he could."[83] It is likely that Papias referred to the Gospel of Luke and John, as well as to other writings of the Christian Greek New Testament books. If true, he would undoubtedly be one of the earliest witnesses establishing their authority, authenticity and divine inspiration. Sadly, though, only scanty fragments of the writings of Papias have survived. Papias seemingly suffered martyrdom at Pergamum in 161 or 165 C.E.

Richard Heard offers the following balanced observation, "Papias is primarily of interest to us as the last link in a chain of oral tradition going back to the Apostles, and for the information—difficult as it sometimes is to interpret—which he preserved about Peter and Mark, Matthew, Philip, and the Elder John. We are profoundly thankful for his curiosity and for his belief 'that things out of the books did not profit me so much as the utterances of a voice which liveth and abideth', even if some of the oral traditions which he wrote down appear to us legendary, e.g. the report attributed to John, the disciple of the Lord, of the Lord's teaching on the material delights of Paradise, and the account which Papias gives of the death of Judas."[84]

Agnostic Bible scholar, Bart D. Ehrman, makes the following observation about Papias, "There's an even bigger problem with taking Papias at his word when he indicates that Marks Gospel is based on an eyewitness report of Peter: virtually everything else that Papias says is widely, and rightly, discounted by scholars as pious imagination rather

---

[81] Paul P. Enns, *The Moody Handbook of Theology* (Chicago, IL: Moody Press, 1989), 84.

[82] R. A. Cole, "Mark, Gospel Of," ed. D. R. W. Wood et al., *New Bible Dictionary* (Leicester, England; Downers Grove, IL: InterVarsity Press, 1996), 727–728.

[83] Papias, "Fragments of Papias," in *The Apostolic Fathers with Justin Martyr and Irenaeus*, ed. Alexander Roberts, James Donaldson, and A. Cleveland Coxe, vol. 1, The Ante-Nicene Fathers (Buffalo, NY: Christian Literature Company, 1885), 155.

[84] Richard Heard (1954). (B) Papias' Quotations from the New Testament. New Testament Studies, 1, pp 130-134. doi:10.1017/S0028688500003647.

than historical fact."[85] An Apologetic Bible scholar, Timothy Paul Jones makes the following response,

"In fairness to Ehrman's position, some early Christian theologians did engage in pious-as well as, in the descriptions of the heretical Carpocratians in the writings of Clement of Alexandria and Epiphanius of Salamis, quite impious–imaginings.

Still, Ehrman's own declaration at this point is, I think, a bit of an overstatement. The fragments of Papias's writings include stories about a man named Justus Barsabas who was poisoned but didn't die and about a dead man who was raised to life. Papias also described traditions, allegedly from John the author of Revelation, about a future epoch of earthly bliss and material blessings following the return of Jesus to earth ("the millennium"). Such ideas may strike some per sans as odd, but they do not differ significantly from notions that were already present in the New Testament.

Papias did record at least one tradition that could qualify as 'pious imagination.' Recounting the death of Judas Iscariot, Papias recorded a story in which the betrayer-apparently having survived the suicide attempt described in Matthew 27:5–swelled until his eyes could not be seen and his genitals oozed putrid pus. In the end, Judas died on his own land in such a way that the entire property stank; this account seems to expand on the tradition found in Acts 1:18. Although scholars in previous generations were hesitant to ascribe this story to Papias, it appears-based on the report recorded in the writings of Apollinarius of Laodicea-that Papias may actually have preserved this tale about Judas. Responding to the tale of Judas's death, Ehrman comments that 'Papias was obviously given to flights of fancy.'

So what effect do these stories have on the tradition that Papias preserved regarding the Gospels According to Matthew and Mark? Very little, really.

The importance of Papias's testimony is that it verifies that the type of authorial traditions cited by Irenaeus of Lyons–traditions that connected the four New Testament Gospels to Matthew, Mark, Luke and John–existed long before the mid to late second century. Through what remains of Papias's writings, it is clear that these traditions were at least as ancient as the late first or early second century.

Papias faithfully recorded stories that he heard, and it is possible that

---

[85] Bart D. Ehrman, *Peter, Paul and Mary Magdalene: The Followers of Jesus in History and Legend* (Oxford, NY: Oxford University Press, 2006), 95.

some of these stories were exaggerated. But the fact that Papias may have recorded some exaggerated stories does not negate the crucial fact that he recorded oral traditions about the Gospels that were in circulation fewer than twenty years after the last of the four New Testament Gospels was written. This fact is already suggested by the consistency with which the various manuscripts connect the four Gospels to the same authors; the testimony of Papias simply confirms this suggestion. (Jones 2007, 148-7)

EARLY CHRISTIANITY 8 Justin Martyr - Early Apologist

[A.D. 110–165.] Justin was a Gentile, but born in Samaria, near Jacob's well. He must have been well educated: he had traveled extensively, and he seems to have been a person enjoying at least a competence. After trying all other systems, his elevated tastes and refined perceptions made him a disciple of Socrates and Plato. So he climbed towards Christ. As he himself narrates the story of his conversion, it need not be anticipated here. What Plato was feeling after, he found in Jesus of Nazareth. The conversion of such a man marks a new era in the gospel history. The sub-apostolic age begins with the first Christian author,—the founder of theological literature. It introduced to mankind, as the mother of true philosophy, the despised teaching of those Galileans to whom their Master had said, "Ye are the light of the world."

And this is the epoch which forced this great truth upon the attention of contemplative minds. It was more than a hundred years since the angels had sung "Good-will to men;" and that song had now been heard for successive generations, breaking forth from the lips of sufferers on the cross, among lions, and amid blazing faggots. Here was a nobler Stoicism that needed interpretation. Not only choice spirits, despising the herd and boasting of a loftier intellectual sphere, were its professors; but thousands of men, women, and children, withdrawing themselves not at all from the ordinary and humble lot of the people, were inspired by it to live and die heroically and sublimely,—exhibiting a superiority to revenge and hate entirely unaccountable, praying for their enemies, and seeking to glorify their God by love to their fellow-men.

And in spite of Gallios and Neros alike, the gospel was dispelling the gross darkness. Of this, Pliny's letter to Trajan is decisive evidence. Even in Seneca we detect reflections of the daybreak. Plutarch writes as never a Gentile could have written until now. Plato is practically surpassed by him in his thoughts upon the "delays of the Divine Justice." Hadrian's address to his soul, in his dying moments, is a tribute to the new ideas which had been sown in the popular mind. And now the Antonines, impelled by something in the age, came forward to reign as "philosophers." At this moment, Justin Martyr confronts them like a Daniel. The "little stone" smites the imperial image in the face, not yet "in the toes." He tells the professional philosophers on a throne how false and hollow is all wisdom that is not meant for all humanity, and that is not capable of leavening the masses. He exposes the impotency of even Socratic philosophy: he shows, in contrast, the force that works in the words of Jesus; he points out their regenerating power. It is the mission of Justin to be a star in the West, leading its Wise Men to the cradle of Bethlehem.

The writings of Justin are deficient in charms of style; and, for us, there is something the reverse of attractive in the forms of thought which he had learned from the philosophers. If Plato had left us nothing but the Timæus, a Renan would doubtless have reproached him as of feeble intellectual power. So a dancing-master might criticize the movements of an athlete, or the writhings of St. Sebastian shot with arrows. The practical wisdom of Justin using the rhetoric of his times, and discomfiting false philosophy with its own weapons, is not appreciated by the fastidious Parisian. But the manly and heroic pleadings of the man, for a despised people with whom he had boldly identified himself; the intrepidity with which he defends them before despots, whose mere caprice might punish him with death; above all, the undaunted spirit with which he exposes the shame and absurdity of their inveterate superstition and reproaches the memory of Hadrian whom Antoninus had deified, as he had deified Antinous of loathsome history,—these are characteristics which every instinct of the unvitiated soul delights to honour. Justin cannot be refuted by a sneer.

He wore his philosopher's gown after his conversion, as a token that he had attained the only true philosophy. And seeing, that, after the conflicts and tests of ages, it is the only philosophy that lasts and lives and triumphs, its discoverer deserves the homage of mankind. Of the philosophic gown we shall hear again when we come to Tertullian.

The residue of Justin's history may be found in "The Martyrdom" and other pages soon to follow, as well as in the following Introductory Note of the able translators, Messrs. Dods and Reith:—

Justin Martyr was born in Flavia Neapolis, a city of Samaria, the modern Nablous. The date of his birth is uncertain, but may be fixed about a.d. 114. His father and grandfather were probably of Roman origin. Before his conversion to Christianity he studied in the schools of the philosophers, searching after some knowledge which should satisfy the cravings of his soul. At last he became acquainted with Christianity, being at once impressed with the extraordinary fearlessness which the Christians displayed in the presence of death, and with the grandeur, stability, and truth of the teachings of the Old Testament. From this time he acted as an evangelist, taking every opportunity to proclaim the gospel as the only safe and certain philosophy, the only way to salvation. It is probable that he travelled much. We know that he was some time in Ephesus, and he must have lived for a considerable period in Rome. Probably he settled in Rome as a Christian teacher. While he was there, the philosophers, especially the Cynics, plotted against him, and he sealed his testimony to the truth by martyrdom.

The principal facts of Justin's life are gathered from his own writings. There is little clue to dates. It is agreed on all hands that he lived in the reign of Antoninus Pius, and the testimony of Eusebius and most credible historians renders it nearly certain that he suffered martyrdom in the reign of Marcus Aurelius. The *Chronicon Paschale* gives as the date 165 a.d.

The writings of Justin Martyr are among the most important that have come down to us from the second century. He was not the first that wrote an Apology in behalf of the Christians, but his Apologies are the earliest extant. They are characterized by intense Christian fervour, and they give us an insight into the relations existing between heathens and Christians in those days. His other principal writing, the Dialogue with Trypho, is the first elaborate exposition of the reasons for regarding Christ as the Messiah of the Old Testament, and the first systematic attempt to exhibit the false position of the Jews in regard to Christianity.

Many of Justin's writings have perished. Those works which have come to us bearing his name have been divided into three classes.

The first class embraces those which are unquestionably genuine, viz. the two Apologies, and the Dialogue with Trypho. Some critics have urged objections against Justin's authorship of the Dialogue; but the objections are regarded now as possessing no weight.

The second class consists of those works which are regarded by some critics as Justin's, and by others as not his. They are: 1. An Address to the Greeks; 2. A Hortatory Address to the Greeks; 3. On the Sole Government of God; 4. An Epistle to Diognetus; 5. Fragments from a work on the Resurrection; 6. And other Fragments. Whatever difficulty there may be in settling the authorship of these treatises, there is but one opinion as to their earliness. The latest of them, in all probability, was not written later than the third century.

The third class consists of those that are unquestionably not the works of Justin. These are: 1. An Exposition of the True Faith; 2. Replies to the Orthodox; 3. Christian Questions to Gentiles; 4. Gentile Questions to Christians; 5. Epistle to Zenas and Serenus; and 6. A Refutation of certain Doctrines of Aristotle. There is no clue to the date of the two last. There can be no doubt that the others were written after the Council of Nicæa, though, immediately after the Reformation, Calvin and others appealed to the first as a genuine writing of Justin's.

There is a curious question connected with the Apologies of Justin which have come down to us. Eusebius mentions two Apologies,—one written in the reign of Antoninus Pius, the other in the reign of Marcus Aurelius. Critics have disputed much whether we have these two Apologies in those now extant. Some have maintained, that what is now called the Second Apology was the preface of the first, and that the second is lost. Others have tried to show, that the so-called Second Apology is the continuation of the first, and that the second is lost. Others have supposed that the two Apologies which we have are Justin's two Apologies, but that Eusebius was wrong in affirming that the second was addressed to Marcus Aurelius; and others maintain, that we have in our two Apologies the two Apologies mentioned by Eusebius, and that our first is his first, and our second his second.[86]

---

[86] Alexander Roberts, James Donaldson, and A. Cleveland Coxe, eds., "Introductory Note to the First Apology of Justin Martyr," in *The Apostolic Fathers with Justin Martyr and Irenaeus*, vol. 1, The Ante-Nicene Fathers (Buffalo, NY: Christian Literature Company, 1885), 159–161.

EARLY CHRISTIANITY 9 Irenaeus of Lyons - Against Heresies

[A.D. 120–202.] This history introduces us to the Church in her western outposts. We reach the banks of the Rhone, where for nearly a century Christian missions have flourished. Between Marseilles and Smyrna there seems to have been a brisk trade, and Polycarp had sent Pothinus into Celtic Gaul at an early date as its evangelist. He had fixed his see at Lyons, when Irenæus joined him as a presbyter, having been his fellow-pupil under Polycarp. There, under the "good Aurelius," as he is miscalled (A.D. 177), arose the terrible persecution which made "the martyrs of Lyons and Vienne" so memorable. It was during this persecution that Irenæus was sent to Rome with letters of remonstrance against the rising pestilence of heresy; and he was probably the author of the account of the sufferings of the martyrs which is appended to their testimony. But he had the mortification of finding the Montanist heresy patronized by Eleutherus the Bishop of Rome; and there he met an old friend from the school of Polycarp, who had embraced the Valentinian heresy. We cannot doubt that to this visit we owe the lifelong struggle of Irenæus against the heresies that now came in, like locusts, to devour the harvests of the Gospel. But let it be noted here, that, so far from being "the mother and mistress" of even the Western Churches, Rome herself is a mission of the Greeks;[2] Southern Gaul is evangelized from Asia Minor, and Lyons checks the heretical tendencies of the Bishop at Rome. Ante-Nicene Christianity, and indeed the Church herself, appears in Greek costume which lasts through the synodical period; and Latin Christianity, when it begins to appear, is African, and not Roman. It is strange that those who have recorded this great historical fact have so little perceived its bearings upon Roman pretensions in the Middle Ages and modern times.

Returning to Lyons, our author found that the venerable Pothinus had closed his holy career by a martyr's death; and naturally Irenæus became his successor. When the emissaries of heresy followed him, and began to disseminate their licentious practices and foolish doctrines by the aid of "silly women," the great work of his life began. He condescended to study these diseases of the human mind like a wise physician; and, sickening as was the process of classifying and describing them, he made this also his laborious task, that he might enable others to withstand and to overcome them. The works he has left us are monuments of his fidelity to Christ, and to the charges of St. Paul, St. Peter, and St. Jude, whose solemn warnings now proved to be prophecies. No marvel that the great apostle, "night and day with tears," had forewarned the churches of "the grievous wolves" which were to make havoc of the fold.

If it shocks the young student of the virgin years of Christianity to find such a state of things, let him reflect that it was all foretold by Christ himself, and demonstrates the malice and power of the adversary. "An enemy hath done this," said the Master. The spirit that was then working "in the children of disobedience," now manifested itself. The awful visions of the Apocalypse began to be realized. It was now evident in what sense "the Prince of peace" had pronounced His mission, "not peace, but a sword." In short, it became a conspicuous fact, that the Church here on earth is "militant;" while, at the same time, there was seen to be a profound philosophy in the apostolic comment, "There must be also heresies among you, that they which are approved may be made manifest." In the divine economy of Providence it was permitted that every form of heresy which was ever to infest the Church should now exhibit its essential principle, and attract the censures of the faithful. Thus testimony to primitive truth was secured and recorded: the language of catholic orthodoxy was developed and defined, and landmarks of faith were set up for perpetual memorial to all generations. It is a striking example of this divine economy, that the see of Rome was allowed to exhibit its fallibility very conspicuously at this time, and not only to receive the rebukes of Irenæus, but to accept them as wholesome and necessary; so that the heresy of Eleutherus, and the spirit of Diotrephes in Victor, have enabled reformers ever since, and even in the darkest days of pontifical despotism, to testify against the manifold errors patronized by Rome. Hilary and other Gallicans have been strengthened by the example of Irenæus, and by his faithful words of reproof and exhortation, to resist Rome, even down to our own times.

That the intolerable absurdities of Gnosticism should have gained so many disciples, and proved itself an adversary to be grappled with and not despised, throws light on the condition of the human mind under heathenism, even when it professed "knowledge" and "philosophy." The task of Irenæus was twofold: (1) to render it impossible for any one to confound Gnosticism with Christianity, and (2) to make it impossible for such a monstrous system to survive, or ever to rise again. His task was a nauseous one; but never was the spirit enjoined by Scripture more patiently exhibited, nor with more entire success. If Julian had found Gnosticism just made to his hand, and powerful enough to suit his purposes, the whole history of his attempt to revive Paganism would have been widely different. Irenæus demonstrated its essential unity with the old mythology, and with heathen systems of philosophy. If the fog and malaria that rose with the Day-star, and obscured it, were speedily dispersed, our author is largely to be identified with the radiance which flowed from the Sun of righteousness, and with the breath of the Spirit that banished them forever.

The Episcopate of Irenæus was distinguished by labours, "in season and out of season," for the evangelization of Southern Gaul; and he seems to have sent missionaries into other regions of what we now call France. In spite of Paganism and heresy, he rendered Lyons a Christian city; and Marcus seems to have retreated before his terrible castigation, taking himself off to regions beyond the Pyrenees. But the pacific name he bears, was rendered yet more illustrious by his interposition to compose the Easter Controversy, then threatening to impair, if not to destroy, the unity of the Church. The beautiful *concordat* between East and West, in which Polycarp and Anicetus had left the question, was now disturbed by Victor, Bishop of Rome, whose turbulent spirit would not accept the compromise of his predecessor. Irenæus remonstrates with him in a catholic spirit, and overrules his impetuous temper. At the Council of Nice, the rule for the observance of Easter was finally settled by the whole Church; and the forbearing example of Irenæus, no doubt contributed greatly to this happy result. The blessed peacemaker survived this great triumph, for a short time only, closing his life, like a true shepherd, with thousands of his flock, in the massacre (a.d. 202) stimulated by the wolfish Emperor Severus.

The Introductory Notice of the learned translators is as follows:—

The work of Irenæus *Against Heresies* is one of the most precious remains of early Christian antiquity. It is devoted, on the one hand, to an account and refutation of those multiform Gnostic heresies which prevailed in the latter half of the second century; and, on the other hand, to an exposition and defence of the Catholic faith.

In the prosecution of this plan, the author divides his work into five books. The first of these contains a minute description of the tenets of the various heretical sects, with occasional brief remarks in illustration of their absurdity, and in confirmation of the truth to which they were opposed. In his second book, Irenæus proceeds to a more complete demolition of those heresies which he has already explained, and argues at great length against them, on grounds principally of reason. The three remaining books set forth more directly the true doctrines of revelation, as being in utter antagonism to the views held by the Gnostic teachers. In the course of this argument, many passages of Scripture are quoted and commented on; many interesting statements are made, bearing on the rule of faith; and much important light is shed on the doctrines, held, as well as the practices observed, by the Church of the second century.

It may be made matter of regret, that so large a portion of the work of Irenæus is given to an exposition of the manifold Gnostic speculations. Nothing more absurd than these has probably ever been imagined by rational beings. Some ingenious and learned men have indeed endeavoured to reconcile the wild theories of these heretics with the principles of reason; but, as Bishop Kaye remarks (*Eccl. Hist. of the Second and Third Centuries*, p. 524), "a more arduous or unpromising undertaking cannot well be conceived." The fundamental object of the Gnostic speculations was doubtless to solve the two grand problems of all religious philosophy, viz., How to account for the existence of evil; and, How to reconcile the finite with the infinite. But these ancient theorists were not more successful in grappling with such questions than have been their successors in modern times. And by giving loose reins to their imagination, they built up the most incongruous and ridiculous systems; while, by deserting the guidance of Scripture they were betrayed into the most pernicious and extravagant errors.

Accordingly, the patience of the reader is sorely tried, in following our author through those mazes of absurdity which he treads, in explaining and refuting these Gnostic speculations. This is especially felt in the perusal of the first two books, which, as has been said, are principally devoted to an exposition and subversion of the various heretical systems. But the vagaries of the human mind, however melancholy in themselves, are never altogether destitute of instruction. And in dealing with those set before us in this work, we have not only the satisfaction of becoming acquainted with the currents of thought prevalent in these early times, but we obtain much valuable information regarding the primitive Church, which, had it not been for these heretical schemes, might never have reached our day.

Not a little of what is contained in the following pages will seem almost unintelligible to the English reader. And it is scarcely more comprehensible to those who have pondered long on the original. We have inserted brief notes of explanation where these seemed specially necessary. But we have not thought it worthwhile to devote a great deal of space to the elucidation of those obscure Gnostic views which, in so many varying forms, are set forth in this work. For the same reason, we give here no account of the origin, history, and successive phases of Gnosticism. Those who wish to know the views of the learned on these points, may consult the writings of Neander, Baur, and others, among the Germans, or the lectures of Dr. Burton in English; while a succinct description of the whole matter will be found in the "Preliminary Observations on the Gnostic System," prefixed to Harvey's edition of Irenæus.

The great work of Irenæus, now for the first time translated into English, is unfortunately no longer extant in the original. It has come down to us only in an ancient Latin version, with the exception of the greater part of the first book, which has been preserved in the original Greek, through means of copious quotations made by Hippolytus and Epiphanius. The text, both Latin and Greek, is often most uncertain. Only three mss. of the work *Against Heresies* are at present known to exist. Others, however, were used in the earliest printed editions put forth by Erasmus. And as these codices were more ancient than any now available, it is greatly to be regretted that they have disappeared or perished. One of our difficulties throughout, has been to fix the readings we should adopt, especially in the first book. Varieties of reading, actual or conjectural, have been noted only when some point of special importance seemed to be involved.

After the text has been settled, according to the best judgment which can be formed, the work of translation remains; and that is, in this case, a matter of no small difficulty. Irenæus, even in the original Greek, is often a very obscure writer. At times he expresses himself with remarkable clearness and terseness; but, upon the whole, his style is very involved and prolix. And the Latin version adds to these difficulties of the original, by being itself of the most barbarous character. In fact, it is often necessary to make a conjectural re-translation of it into Greek, in order to obtain some inkling of what the author wrote. Dodwell supposes this Latin version to have been made about the end of the fourth century; but as Tertullian seems to have used it, we must rather place it in the beginning of the third. Its author is unknown, but he was certainly little qualified for his task. We have endeavoured to give as close and accurate a translation of the work as possible, but there are not a few passages in which a guess can only be made as to the probable meaning.

Irenæus had manifestly taken great pains to make himself acquainted with the various heretical systems which he describes. His mode of exposing and refuting these is generally very effective. It is plain that he possessed a good share of learning, and that he had a firm grasp of the doctrines of Scripture. Not unfrequently he indulges in a kind of sarcastic humour, while inveighing against the folly and impiety of the heretics. But at times he gives expression to very strange opinions. He is, for example, quite peculiar in imagining that our Lord lived to be an *old* man, and that His public ministry embraced at least *ten* years. But though, on these and some other points, the judgment of Irenæus is clearly at fault, his work contains a vast deal of sound and valuable exposition of Scripture, in opposition to the fanciful systems of interpretation which prevailed in his day.

We possess only very scanty accounts of the personal history of Irenæus. It has been generally supposed that he was a native of Smyrna, or some neighbouring city, in Asia Minor. Harvey, however, thinks that he was probably born in Syria, and removed in boyhood to Smyrna. He himself tells us (iii. 3, 4) that he was in early youth acquainted with Polycarp, the illustrious bishop of that city. A sort of clue is thus furnished as to the date of his birth. Dodwell supposes that he was born so early as a.d. 97, but this is clearly a mistake; and the general date assigned to his birth is somewhere between a.d. 120 and a.d. 140.

It is certain that Irenæus was bishop of Lyons, in France, during the latter quarter of the second century. The exact period or circumstances of his ordination cannot be determined. Eusebius states (*Hist. Eccl.*, v. 4) that he was, while yet a presbyter, sent with a letter, from certain members of the Church of Lyons awaiting martyrdom, to Eleutherus, bishop of Rome; and that (v. 5) he succeeded Pothinus as bishop of Lyons, probably about a.d. 177. His great work *Against Heresies* was, we learn, written during the episcopate of Eleutherus, that is, between a.d. 182 and a.d. 188, for Victor succeeded to the bishopric of Rome in a.d. 189. This new bishop of Rome took very harsh measures for enforcing uniformity throughout the Church as to the observance of the paschal solemnities. On account of the severity thus evinced, Irenæus addressed to him a letter (only a fragment of which remains), warning him that if he persisted in the course on which he had entered, the effect would be to rend the Catholic Church in pieces. This letter had the desired result; and the question was more temperately debated, until finally settled by the Council of Nice.

The full title of the principal work of Irenæus, as given by Eusebius (*Hist. Eccl.*, v. 7), and indicated frequently by the author himself, was *A Refutation and Subversion of Knowledge falsely so called*, but it is generally referred to under the shorter title, *Against Heresies*. Several other smaller treatises are ascribed to Irenæus; viz., *An Epistle to Florinus*, of which a small fragment has been preserved by Eusebius; a treatise *On the Valentinian Ogdoad*; a work called forth by the paschal controversy, entitled *On Schism*, and another *On Science*; all of which that remain will be found in our next volume of his writings. Irenæus is supposed to have died about A.D. 202; but there is probably no real ground for the statement of Jerome, repeated by subsequent writers, that he suffered martyrdom, since neither Tertullian nor Eusebius, nor other early authorities, make any mention of such a fact.[87]

---

[87] Alexander Roberts, James Donaldson, and A. Cleveland Coxe, eds., "Introductory Note to Irenæus Against Heresies," in *The Apostolic Fathers with Justin Martyr and Irenaeus*, vol. 1, The Ante-Nicene Fathers (Buffalo, NY: Christian Literature Company, 1885), 309–313.

EARLY CHRISTIANITY 10 Tatian the Assyrian

[A.D. 110–172.] Tatian stands in an equivocal position, as half Father and half heretic. His good seems to have been largely due to Justin's teaching and influence. One may trust that his falling away, in the decline of life, is attributable to infirmity of mind and body; his severe asceticism countenancing this charitable thought. Many instances of human frailty, which the experience of ages has taught Christians to view with compassion rather than censure, are doubtless to be ascribed to mental aberration and decay. Early Christians had not yet been taught this lesson; for, socially, neither Judaism nor Paganism had wholly surrendered their unloving influences upon their minds. Moreover, their high valuation of discipline, as an essential condition of self-preservation amid the fires of surrounding scorn and hatred, led them to practise, perhaps too sternly, upon offenders, what they often heroically performed upon themselves,—the amputation of the scandalous hand, or the plucking out of the evil eye.

In Tatian, another Assyrian follows the Star of Bethlehem, from Euphrates and the Tigris. The scanty facts of his personal history are sufficiently detailed by the translator, in his Introductory Note. We owe to himself the pleasing story of his conversion from heathenism. But I think it important to qualify the impressions the translation may otherwise leave upon the student's mind, by a little more sympathy with the better side of his character, and a more just statement of his great services to the infant Church.

His works, which were very numerous, have perished, in consequence of his lapse from orthodoxy. Give him due credit for his *Diatessaron*, of which the very name is a valuable testimony to the Four Gospels as recognized by the primitive churches. It is lost, with the "infinite number" of other books, which St. Jerome attributes to him. All honour to this earliest harmonist for such a work; and let us believe, with Mill and other learned authorities, that, if Eusebius had seen the work he censures, he might have expressed himself more charitably concerning it.

We know something of Tatian, already, from the melancholy pages of Irenæus. Theodoret finds no other fault with his *Diatessaron* than its omission of the genealogies, which he, probably, could not harmonize on any theory of his own. The errors into which he fell in his old age were so absurd, and so contrary to the Church's doctrine and discipline, that he could not be tolerated as one of the faithful, without giving to the heathen new grounds for the malignant slanders with which they were ever assailing the Christians. At the same time, let us reflect, that his fall is to be attributed to extravagant ideas of that encraty which is a precept of the Gospel, and which a pure abhorrence of pagan abominations led many of the orthodox to practice with extreme rigidity. And this is the place to say, once for all, that the figures of Elijah upon Mt. Carmel and of John Baptist in the wilderness, approved by our Lord's teachings, but moderated, as a lesson to others, by his own holy but less austere example, justify the early Church in making room for the two classes of Christians which must always be found in earnest religion, and which seem to have their warrant in the fundamental constitution of human nature. There must be men like St. Paul, living in the world, though not of it; and there must be men like the Baptist, of whom the world will say, "he hath a devil." Marvelously the early Catholics were piloted between the rocks and the whirlpools, in the narrow drift of the Gospel; and always the Holy Spirit of counsel and might was their guardian, amid their terrible trials and temptations. This must suggest, to every reflecting mind, a gratitude the most profound. To preserve evangelical encraty, and to restrain fanatical asceticism, was the spirit of early Christianity, as one sees in the ethics of Hermas. But the awful malaria of Montanism was even now rising like a fog of the marshes, and was destined to leave its lasting impress upon Western Christianity; "forbidding to marry, and commanding to abstain from meats." Our author, alas, laid the egg which Tertullian hatched, and invented terms which that great author raised to their highest power; for he was rather the disciple of Tatian than of the Phrygians, though they kindled his strange fire. After Tertullian, the whole subject of marriage became entangled with sophistries, which have ever since adhered to the Latin churches, and introduced the most corrosive results into the vitals of individuals and of nations. Southey suggests, that, in the Roman Communion, John Wesley would have been accommodated with full scope for his genius, and canonized as a saint, while his Anglican mother had no place for him. But, on the other hand, let us reflect that while Rome had no place for Wiclif and Hus, or Jerome of Prague, she has used and glorified and canonized many fanatics whose errors were far more disgraceful than those of Tatian and Tertullian. In fact, she would have utilized and beatified these very enthusiasts, had they risen in the Middle Ages, to combine their follies with equal extravagance in persecuting the Albigenses, while aggrandizing the papal ascendency.

I have enlarged upon the equivocal character of Tatian with melancholy interest, because I shall make sparing use of notes, in editing his sole surviving work, pronounced by Eusebius his masterpiece. I read it with sympathy, admiration, and instruction. I enjoy his biting satire of heathenism, his Pauline contempt for all philosophy save that of the Gospel, his touching reference to his own experiences, and his brilliant delineation of Christian innocence and of his own emancipation from the seductions of a deceitful and transient world. In short, I feel that Tatian deserves critical editing, in the original, at the hand and heart of some expert who can thoroughly appreciate his merits, and his relations to primitive Christianity.

The following is the original Introductory Notice:—

We learn from several sources that Tatian was an Assyrian, but know nothing very definite either as to the time or place of his birth. Epiphanius (*Hær.*, xlvi.) declares that he was a native of Mesopotamia; and we infer from other ascertained facts regarding him, that he flourished about the middle of the second century. He was at first an eager student of heathen literature, and seems to have been especially devoted to researches in philosophy. But he found no satisfaction in the bewildering mazes of Greek speculation, while he became utterly disgusted with what heathenism presented to him under the name of religion. In these circumstances, he happily met with the sacred books of the Christians, and was powerfully attracted by the purity of morals which these inculcated, and by the means of deliverance from the bondage of sin which they revealed. He seems to have embraced Christianity at Rome, where he became acquainted with Justin Martyr, and enjoyed the instructions of that eminent teacher of the Gospel. After the death of Justin, Tatian unfortunately fell under the influence of the Gnostic heresy, and founded an ascetic sect, which, from the rigid principles it professed, was called that of the Encratites, that is, "*The self-controlled*," or, "*The masters of themselves.*" Tatian latterly established himself at Antioch, and acquired a considerable number of disciples, who continued after his death to be distinguished by the practice of those austerities which he had enjoined. The sect of the Encratites is supposed to have been established about a.d. 166, and Tatian appears to have died some few years afterwards.

The only extant work of Tatian is his "Address to the Greeks." It is a most unsparing and direct exposure of the enormities of heathenism. Several other works are said to have been composed by Tatian; and of these, a *Diatessaron*, or *Harmony of the Four Gospels*, is specially mentioned. His Gnostic views led him to exclude from the continuous narrative of our Lord's life, given in this work, all those passages which bear upon the incarnation and true humanity of Christ. Notwithstanding this defect, we cannot but regret the loss of this earliest Gospel harmony; but the very title it bore is important, as showing that the Four Gospels, and these only, were deemed authoritative about the middle of the second century.[88]

---

[88] Alexander Roberts, James Donaldson, and A. Cleveland Coxe, eds., "Introductory Note to Tatian the Assyrian," in *Fathers of the Second*

EARLY CHRISTIANITY 11 Athenagoras of Athens

[A.D. 177.] To some extent we must recognize, in collocation, the principles of affinity and historic growth. Closing up the bright succession of the earlier Apologists, this favorite author affords also a fitting introduction to the great founder of the Alexandrian School, who comes next into view. His work opens the way for Clement's elaboration of Justin's claim, that the whole of philosophy is embraced in Christianity. It is charming to find the primal fountains of Christian thought uniting here, to flow on forever in the widening and deepening channel of Catholic orthodoxy, as it gathers into itself all human culture, and enriches the world with products of regenerated mind, harvested from its overflow into the fields of philosophy and poetry and art and science. More of this when we come to Clement, that man of genius who introduced Christianity to itself, as reflected in the burnished mirror of his intellect. Shackles are falling from the persecuted and imprisoned faculties of the faithful, and soon the Faith is to speak out, no more in tones of apology, but as mistress of the human mind, and its pilot to new worlds of discovery and broad domains of conquest. All hail the freedom with which, henceforth, Christians are to assume the overthrow of heathenism as a foregone conclusion. The distasteful exposure of heresies was the inevitable task after the first victory. It was the chase and following-up of the adversary in his limping and cowardly retreat, "the scattering of the rear of darkness." With Athenagoras, we touch upon tokens of things to come; we see philosophy yoked to the chariot of Messiah; we begin to realize that sibylline surrender of outworn Paganism, and its forecast of an era of light:—

"Magnus ab integro sæclorum nascitur ordo,

....................quo ferrea primum

Desinet, ac toto surget gens aurea mundo."

In Athenagoras, whose very name is a retrospect, we discover a remote result of St. Paul's speech on Mars Hill. The apostle had cast his bread upon the waters of Ilissus and Cephisus to find it after many days. "When they heard of the resurrection of the dead, some mocked; "but here comes a philosopher, from the Athenian *agora*, a convert to St.

Century: Hermas, Tatian, Athenagoras, Theophilus, and Clement of Alexandria (Entire), vol. 2, The Ante-Nicene Fathers (Buffalo, NY: Christian Literature Company, 1885), 61–63.

Paul's argument in his Epistle to the Corinthians, confessing "the unknown God," demolishing the marble mob of deities that so "stirred the apostle's spirit within him," and teaching alike the Platonist and the Stoic to sit at the feet of Jesus. "Dionysius the Areopagite, and the woman named Damaris," are no longer to be despised as the scanty first-fruits of Attica. They too have found a voice in this splendid trophy of the Gospel; and, "being dead, they yet speak" through him.

To the meagre facts of his biography, which appear below, there is nothing to be added; and I shall restrain my disposition to be a commentator, within the limits of scanty an notations. In the notes to Tatian and Theophilus, I have made the student acquainted with that useful addition to his treatise on *Justin Martyr*, in which the able and judicious Bishop Kaye harmonizes those authors with Justin. The same harmony enfolds the works of Athenagoras, and thus affords a synopsis of Christian teaching under the Antonines; in which precision of theological language is yet unattained, but identity of faith is clearly exhibited. While the Germans are furnishing the scholar with critical editions of the ancients, invaluable for their patient accumulations of fact and illustration, they are so daring in theory and conjecture when they come to exposition, that one enjoys the earnest and wholesome tone of sober comment that distinguishes the English theologian. It has the great merit of being inspired by profound sympathy with primitive writers, and unadulterated faith in the Scriptures. Too often a German critic treats one of these venerable witnesses, who yet live and yet speak, as if they were dead subjects on the dissecting-table. They cut and carve with anatomical display, and use the microscope with scientific skill; but, oh! how frequently they surrender the saints of God as mere corpses, into the hands of those who count them victims of a blind faith in a dead Christ.

It will not be necessary, after my quotations from Kaye in the foregoing sheets, to do more than indicate similar illustrations of Athenagoras to be found in his pages. The dry version often requires lubrications of devoutly fragrant exegesis; and providentially they are at hand in that elaborate but modest work, of which even this generation should not be allowed to lose sight.

The annotations of Conrad Gesner and Henry Stephans would have greatly enriched this edition, had I been permitted to enlarge the work by adding a version of them. They are often curious, and are supplemented by the interesting letter of Stephans to Peter Nannius, "the eminent pillar of Louvain," on the earliest copies of Athenagoras, from which modern editions have proceeded. The Paris edition of Justin Martyr (1615) contains these notes, as well as the Greek of Tatian, Theophilus, and Athenagoras, with a Latin rendering. As Bishop Kaye constantly refers to this edition. I have considered myself fortunate in possessing it; using it largely in comparing his learned comments with the Edinburgh Version.

A few words as to the noble treatise of our author, on the Resurrection. As a firm and loving voice to this keynote of Christian faith, it rings like an anthem through all the variations of his thought and argument. Comparing his own blessed hope with the delusions of a world lying in wickedness, and looking stedfastly to the life of the world to come, what a sublime contrast we find in this figure of Christ's witness to the sensual life of the heathen, and even to the groping wisdom of the Attic sages. I think this treatise a sort of growth from the mind of one who had studied in the Academe, pitying yet loving poor Socrates and his disciples. Yet more, it is the outcome of meditation on that sad history in the Acts, which expounds St. Paul's bitter reminiscences, when he says that his gospel was, "to the Greeks, foolishness." They never "heard him again on this matter." He left them under the confused impressions they had expressed in the *agora*, when they said, "he seemeth to be a setter-forth of new gods." St. Luke allows himself a smile only half suppressed when he adds, "because he preached unto them *Jesus and Anastasis*," which in their ears was only a barbarian echo to their own *Phœbus and Artemis*; and what did Athenians want of any more wares of that sort, especially under the introduction of a poor Jew from parts unknown? Did the apostle's prophetic soul foresee Athenagoras, as he "departed from among them"? However that may be, his blessed Master "knew what he would do." He could let none of Paul's words fall to the ground, without taking care that some seeds should bring forth fruit a thousand-fold. Here come the sheaves at last. Athenagoras proves, also, what our Saviour meant, when he said to the Galileans, "Ye are the light of the world."

The following is the original Introductory Notice:—

It is one of the most singular facts in early ecclesiastical history, that the name of Athenagoras is scarcely ever mentioned. Only two references to him and his writings have been discovered. One of these occurs in the work of Methodius, *On the Resurrection of the Body*, as preserved by Epiphanius (*Hœr.*, lxiv.) and Photius (*Biblioth.*, ccxxxiv.). The other notice of him is found in the writings of Philip of Side, in Pamphylia, who flourished in the early part of the fifth century. It is very remarkable that Eusebius should have been altogether silent regarding him; and that writings, so elegant and powerful as are those which still exist under his name, should have been allowed in early times to sink into almost entire oblivion.

We know with certainty regarding Athenagoras, that he was an Athenian philosopher who had embraced Christianity, and that his *Apology*, or, as he styles it, "Embassy" (πρεσβεία), was presented to the

Emperors Aurelius and Commodus about A.D. 177. He is supposed to have written a considerable number of works, but the only other production of his extant is his treatise on the Resurrection. It is probable that this work was composed somewhat later than the *Apology* (see chap. xxxvi.), though its exact date cannot be determined. Philip of Side also states that he preceded Pantænus as head of the catechetical school at Alexandria; but this is probably incorrect, and is contradicted by Eusebius. A more interesting and perhaps well-founded statement is made by the same writer respecting Athenagoras, to the effect that he was won over to Christianity while reading the Scriptures in order to controvert them. Both his *Apology* and his treatise on the Resurrection display a practiced pen and a richly cultured mind. He is by far the most elegant, and certainly at the same time one of the ablest, of the early Christian Apologists.[89]

---

[89] Alexander Roberts, James Donaldson, and A. Cleveland Coxe, eds., "Introductory Note to the Writings of Athenagoras," in *Fathers of the Second Century: Hermas, Tatian, Athenagoras, Theophilus, and Clement of Alexandria (Entire)*, vol. 2, The Ante-Nicene Fathers (Buffalo, NY: Christian Literature Company, 1885), 125–127.

EARLY CHRISTIANITY 12 Clement of Alexandria - Christian Theologian

[A.D. 153–193–217.] The second century of illumination is drawing to a close, as the great name of this Father comes into view, and introduces us to a new stage of the Church's progress. From Britain to the Ganges it had already made its mark. In all its Oriental identity, we have found it vigorous in Gaul and penetrating to other regions of the West. From its primitive base on the Orontes, it has extended itself to the deltas of the Nile; and the Alexandria of Apollos and of St. Mark has become the earliest seat of Christian learning. There, already, have the catechetical schools gathered the finest intellectual trophies of the Cross; and under the aliment of its library springs up something like a Christian university. Pantænus, "the Sicilian bee" from the flowery fields of Enna, comes to frame it by his industry, and store it with the sweets of his eloquence and wisdom. Clement, who had followed Tatian to the East, tracks Pantænus to Egypt, and comes with his Attic scholarship to be his pupil in the school of Christ. After Justin and Irenæus, he is to be reckoned the founder of Christian literature; and it is noteworthy how sublimely he begins to treat Paganism as a creed outworn, to be dismissed with contempt, rather than seriously wrestled with any longer.

His merciless exposure of the entire system of "lords many and gods many," seems to us, indeed, unnecessarily offensive. Why not spare us such details? But let us reflect, that, if such are our Christian instincts of delicacy, we owe it to this great reformer in no small proportion. For not content to show the Pagans that the very atmosphere was polluted by their mythologies, so that Christians, turn which way they would, must encounter pestilence, he becomes the ethical philosopher of Christians; and while he proceeds to dictate, even in minute details, the transformations to which the faithful must subject themselves in order "to escape the pollutions of the world," he sketches in outline the reformations which the Gospel imposes on society, and which nothing but the Gospel has ever enabled mankind to realize. "For with a celerity unsurpassable, and a benevolence to which we have ready access," says Clement, "the Divine Power hath filled the universe with the seed of salvation." Socrates and Plato had talked sublimely four hundred years before; but Lust and Murder were yet the gods of Greece, and men and women were like what they worshipped. Clement had been their disciple; but now, as the disciple of Christ, he was to exert a power over men and manners, of which they never dreamed.

Alexandria becomes the brain of Christendom: its heart was yet beating at Antioch, but the West was still receptive only, its hands and arms stretched forth towards the sunrise for further enlightenment. From the East it had obtained the Scriptures and their authentication, and from the same source was deriving the canons, the liturgies, and the creed of Christendom. The universal language of Christians is Greek. To a pagan emperor who had outgrown the ideas of Nero's time, it was no longer Judaism; but it was not less an Oriental superstition, essentially Greek in its features and its dress. "All the churches of the West," says the historian of Latin Christianity, "were Greek religious colonies. Their language was Greek, their organization Greek, their writers Greek, their Scriptures and their ritual were Greek. Through Greek, the communications of the churches of the West were constantly kept up with the East.... Thus the Church at Rome was but one of a confederation of Greek religious republics founded by Christianity." Now this confederation was the Holy Catholic Church.

Every Christian must recognize the career of Alexander, and the history of his empire, as an immediate precursor of the Gospel. The patronage of letters by the Ptolemies at Alexandria, the translation of the Hebrew Scriptures into the dialect of the Hellenes, the creation of a new terminology in the language of the Greeks, by which ideas of faith and of truth might find access to the mind of a heathen world,—these were preliminaries to the preaching of the Gospel to mankind, and to the composition of the New Testament of our Lord and Savior. He Himself had prophetically visited Egypt, and the idols were now to be removed before his presence. There a powerful Christian school was to make itself felt for ever in the definitions of orthodoxy; and in a new sense was that prophecy to be understood, "Out of Egypt have I called my Son."

The genius of Apollos was revived in his native city. A succession of doctors was there to arise, like him, "eloquent men, and mighty in the Scriptures." Clement tells us of his masters in Christ, and how, coming to Pantænus, his soul was filled with a deathless element of divine knowledge. He speaks of the apostolic tradition as received through his teachers hardly at second-hand. He met in that school, no doubt, some, at least, who recalled Ignatius and Polycarp; some, perhaps, who as children had heard St. John when he could only exhort his congregations to "love one another." He could afterwards speak of himself as in the next succession after the apostles.

He became the successor of Pantænus in the catechetical school, and had Origen for his pupil, with other eminent men. He was also ordained a presbyter. He seems to have compiled his *Stromata* in the reigns of Commodus and Severus. If, at this time, he was about forty years of age, as seems likely, we must conceive of his birth at Athens, while Antoninus Pius was emperor, while Polycarp was yet living, and while Justin and Irenæus were in their prime.

Alexander, bishop of Jerusalem, speaks of Clement, in turn, as his master: "for we acknowledge as fathers those blessed saints who are gone before us, and *to whom we shall go after a little time*; the truly blest Pantænus, I mean, and the holy Clemens, my teacher, who was to me so greatly useful and helpful." St. Cyril of Alexandria calls him "a man admirably learned and skilful, and one that searched to the depths all the learning of the Greeks, with an exactness rarely attained before." So Theodoret says, "He surpassed all others, and *was a holy man*." St. Jerome pronounces him the most learned of all the ancients; while Eusebius testifies to his theological attainments, and applauds him as an "incomparable master of Christian philosophy." But the rest shall be narrated by our translator, Mr. Wilson.

The following is the original Introductory Notice:—

Titus Flavius Clemens, the illustrious head of the Catechetical School at Alexandria at the close of the second century, was originally a pagan philosopher. The date of his birth is unknown. It is also uncertain whether Alexandria or Athens was his birthplace.

On embracing Christianity, he eagerly sought the instructions of its most eminent teachers; for this purpose travelling extensively over Greece, Italy, Egypt, Palestine, and other regions of the East.

Only one of these teachers (who, from a reference in the *Stromata*, all appear to have been alive when he wrote) can be with certainty identified, viz., Pantænus, of whom he speaks in terms of profound reverence, and whom he describes as the greatest of them all. Returning to Alexandria, he succeeded his master Pantænus in the catechetical school, probably on the latter departing on his missionary tour to the East, somewhere about A.D. 189. He was also made a presbyter of the Church, either then or somewhat later.[3] He continued to teach with great distinction till A.D. 202, when the persecution under Severus compelled him to retire from Alexandria. In the beginning of the reign of Caracalla we find him at Jerusalem, even then a great resort of Christian, and especially clerical, pilgrims. We also hear of him travelling to Antioch, furnished with a letter of recommendation by Alexander, bishop of Jerusalem. The close of his career is covered with obscurity. He is supposed to have died about a.d. 220.

Among his pupils were his distinguished successor in the Alexandrian school, Origen, Alexander bishop of Jerusalem, and, according to Baronius, Combefisius, and Bull, also Hippolytus.

The above is positively the sum of what we know of Clement's history.

His three great works, *The Exhortation to the Heathen* (λόγος ὁ προτρεπτικὸς πρὸς Ἕλληνας), *The Instructor*, or *Pædagogus* (παιδαγωγός), *The Miscellanies*, or *Stromata* (Στρωματεῖς), are among the most valuable remains of Christian antiquity, and the largest that belong to that early period.

The Exhortation, the object of which is to win pagans to the Christian faith, contains a complete and withering exposure of the abominable licentiousness, the gross imposture and sordidness of paganism. With clearness and cogency of argument, great earnestness and eloquence, Clement sets forth in contrast the truth as taught in the inspired Scriptures, the true God, and especially the personal Christ, the living Word of God, the Saviour of men. It is an elaborate and masterly work, rich in felicitous classical allusion and quotation, breathing throughout the spirit of philosophy and of the Gospel, and abounding in passages of power and beauty.

The *Pædagogus*, or *Instructor*, is addressed to those who have been rescued from the darkness and pollutions of heathenism, and is an exhibition of Christian morals and manners,—a guide for the formation and development of Christian character, and for living a Christian life. It consists of three books. It is the grand aim of the whole work to set before the converts Christ as the only Instructor, and to expound and enforce His precepts. In the first book Clement exhibits the person, the function, the means, methods, and ends of the Instructor, who is the Word and Son of God; and lovingly dwells on His benignity and philanthropy, His wisdom, faithfulness, and righteousness.

The second and third books lay down rules for the regulation of the Christian, in all the relations, circumstances, and actions of life, entering most minutely into the details of dress, eating, drinking, bathing, sleeping, etc. The delineation of a life in all respects agreeable to the Word, a truly Christian life, attempted here, may, now that the Gospel has transformed social and private life to the extent it has, appear unnecessary, or a proof of the influence of ascetic tendencies. But a code of Christian morals and manners (a sort of "whole duty of man" and manual of good breeding combined) was eminently needed by those whose habits and characters had been moulded under the debasing and polluting influences of heathenism; and who were bound, and were aiming, to shape their lives according to the principles of the Gospel, in the midst of the all but incredible licentiousness and luxury by which society around was incurably tainted. The disclosures which Clement, with solemn sternness, and often with caustic wit, makes of the prevalent voluptuousness and vice, form a very valuable contribution to our knowledge of that period.

The full title of the *Stromata*, according to Eusebius and Photius, was Τίτου Φλαυίου Κλήμεντος τῶν κατὰ τὴν ἀληθῆ φιλοσοφίαν γνωστικῶν ὑτ ομνημάτων στρωματεῖς—"Titus Flavius Clement's miscellaneous collections of speculative (gnostic) notes bearing upon the true philosophy." The aim of the work, in accordance with this title, is, in opposition to Gnosticism, to furnish the materials for the construction of a true gnosis, a Christian philosophy, on the basis of faith, and to lead on to this higher knowledge those who, by the discipline of the Pædagogus, had been trained for it. The work consisted originally of eight books. The eighth book is lost; that which appears under this name has plainly no connection with the rest of the *Stromata*. Various accounts have been given of the meaning of the distinctive word in the title (Στρωματεύς); but all agree in regarding it as indicating the miscellaneous character of its contents. And they are very miscellaneous. They consist of the speculations of Greek philosophers, of heretics, and of those who cultivated the true Christian gnosis, and of quotations from sacred Scripture. The latter he affirms to be the source from which the higher Christian knowledge is to be drawn; as it was that from which the germs of truth in Plato and the Hellenic philosophy were derived. He describes philosophy as a divinely ordered preparation of the Greeks for faith in Christ, as the law was for the Hebrews; and shows the necessity and value of literature and philosophic culture for the attainment of true Christian knowledge, in opposition to the numerous body among Christians who regarded learning as useless and dangerous. He proclaims himself an eclectic, believing in the existence of fragments of truth in all systems, which may be separated from error; but declaring that the truth can be found in unity and completeness only in Christ, as it was from Him that all its scattered germs originally proceeded. The *Stromata* are written carelessly, and even confusedly; but the work is one of prodigious learning, and supplies materials of the greatest value for understanding the various conflicting systems which Christianity had to combat.

It was regarded so much as the author's great work, that, on the testimony of Theodoret, Cassiodorus, and others, we learn that Clement received the appellation of Στρωματεύς (the Stromatist). In all probability, the first part of it was given to the world about a.d. 194. The latest date to which he brings down his chronology in the first book is the death of Commodus, which happened in A.D. 192; from which Eusebius concludes that he wrote this work during the reign of Severus, who ascended the imperial throne in A.D. 193, and reigned until A.D. 211. It is likely that the whole was composed ere Clement quitted Alexandria in A.D. 202. The publication of the *Pædagogus* preceded by a short time that of the *Stromata*; and the *Cohortatio* was written a short time before the *Pædagogus*, as is clear from statements made by Clement himself.

So multifarious is the erudition, so multitudinous are the quotations and the references to authors in all departments, and of all countries, the most of whose works have perished, that the works in question could only have been composed near an extensive library—hardly anywhere but in the vicinity of the famous library of Alexandria. They are a storehouse of curious ancient lore,—a museum of the fossil remains of the beauties and monstrosities of the world of pagan antiquity, during all the epochs and phases of its history. The three compositions are really parts of one whole. The central connecting idea is that of the Logos—the Word—the Son of God; whom in the first work he exhibits drawing men from the superstitions and corruptions of heathenism to faith; in the second, as training them by precepts and discipline; and in the last, as conducting them to that higher knowledge of the things of God, to which those only who devote themselves assiduously to spiritual, moral, and intellectual culture can attain. Ever before his eye is the grand form of the living personal Christ,—the Word, who "was with God, and who was God, but who became man, and dwelt among us."

Of course there is throughout plenty Of false science, and frivolous and fanciful speculation.

Who is the rich man that shall be saved? (τίς ὁ σωζόμενος πλούσιος;) is the title of a practical treatise, in which Clement shows, in opposition to those who interpreted our Lord's words to the young ruler as requiring the renunciation of worldly goods, that the disposition of the soul is the great essential. Of other numerous works of Clement, of which only a few stray fragments have been preserved, the chief are the eight books of *The Hypotyposes*, which consisted of expositions of all the books of Scripture. Of these we have a few undoubted fragments. *The Adumbrations*, or *Commentaries on some of the Catholic Epistles*, and *The Selections from the Prophetic Scriptures*, are compositions of the same character, as far as we can judge, as *The Hypotyposes*, and are supposed by some to have formed part of that work.

Other lost works of Clement are:—

The Treatise of Clement, the Stromatist, on the Prophet Amos.

On Providence.

Treatise on Easter.

On Evil-speaking.

Discussion on Fasting.

Exhortation to Patience; or, To the newly baptized.

Ecclesiastical Canon; or, Against the Judaizers.

Different Terms.

The following are the names of treatises which Clement refers to as written or about to be written by him, but of which otherwise we have no trace or mention:—*On First Principles; On Prophecy; On the Allegorical Interpretation of Members and Affections when ascribed to God; On Angels; On the Devil; On the Origin of the Universe; On the Unity and Excellence of the Church; On the Offices of Bishops, Presbyters, Deacons, and Widows; On the Soul; On the Resurrection; On Marriage; On Continence; Against Heresies.*

Preserved among Clement's works is a fragment called *Epitomes of the Writings of Theodotus, and of the Eastern Doctrine,* most likely abridged extracts made by Clement for his own use, and giving considerable insight into Gnosticism.

Clement's quotations from Scripture are made from the Septuagint version, often inaccurately from memory, sometimes from a different text from what we possess, often with verbal adaptations; and not rarely different texts are blended together.

The works of Clement present considerable difficulties to the translator; and one of the chief is the state of the text, which greatly needs to be expurgated and amended. For this there are abundant materials, in the copious annotations and disquisitions, by various hands, collected together in Migne's edition; where, however, corruptions the most obvious have been allowed to remain in the text.[90]

---

[90] Alexander Roberts, James Donaldson, and A. Cleveland Coxe, eds., "Introductory Note to Clement of Alexandria," in *Fathers of the Second Century: Hermas, Tatian, Athenagoras, Theophilus, and Clement of Alexandria (Entire),* vol. 2, The Ante-Nicene Fathers (Buffalo, NY: Christian Literature Company, 1885), 165–169.

EARLY CHRISTIANITY 13 Cyprian of Carthage

[A.D. 200–258.] If Hippolytus reflects the spirit of Irenæus in all his writings, it is not remarkable. He was the spiritual son of the great Bishop of Lyons, and deeply imbued with the family character imparted to his disciples by the blessed presbyter of Patmos and Ephesus. But while Cyprian is the spiritual son and pupil of Tertullian, we must seek his characteristics and the key to his whole ministry in the far-off See and city where the disciples were first called Christians. Cyprian is the Ignatius of the West. We see in his works how truly historical are the writings of Ignatius, and how diffused was his simple and elementary system of organic unity. It embodies no hierarchical assumption, no "lordship over God's heritage," but is conceived in the spirit of St. Peter when he disclaimed all this, and said, "The *presbyters* who are among you I exhort, who am also a *presbyter*." Cyprian was indeed a strenuous asserter of the responsibilities of his office; but he built upon that system universally recognized by the Great Councils, which the popes and their adherents have ever labored to destroy. Nothing can be more delusive than the idea that the mediæval system derives any support from Cyprian's theory of the episcopate or of Church organization. His was the system of the universal parity and community of bishops. In his scheme, the apostolate was perpetuated in the episcopate, and the *presbyterate* was an apostolic institution, by which others were associated with bishops in all their functions as *co-presbyters*, but not in those reserved to the presidency of the churches. Feudal ideas imposed a very different system upon the simple framework of original Catholicity. But a careful study of that primitive framework, and of the history of papal development, makes evident the following propositions:—

1. That Cyprian's maxim, *Ecclesia in Episcopo*, whatever else he may have meant by it, is an aphoristic statement of the Nicene Constitutions. These were embedded in the Ignatian theory of an episcopate without a trace of a papacy; and Cyprian's maxims had to be practically destroyed in the West before it was possible to raise the portentous figure of a supreme pontiff, and to subject the Latin churches to the entirely novel principle of *Ecclesia in Papa*. To this novelty Cyprian's system is essentially antagonistic.

2. It will be seen that Cyprian, far from being the patron of ecclesiastical despotism, is the expounder of early canons and constitutions, in the spirit of order and discipline, indeed, but with the largest exemplification of that "liberty" which is manifested wherever "the

138

Spirit of the Lord" is operative. Cyprian is the patron and defender of the presbytery and of lay co-operation, as well as of the regimen of the episcopate. His letters illustrate the Catholic system as it was known to the Nicene Fathers; but, of all the Christian Fathers, he is the most clear and comprehensive in his conception of the body of Christ as an organic whole, in which every member has an honourable function. Popular government and representative government, the legitimate power and place of the laity, the organization of the Christian *plebs* into their faculty as the ἀντιλήψεις of St. Paul, the development of synods, *omni plebe adstante*,—all this is embodied in the Catholic system as Cyprian understood it.

3. The Orientals in large degree, even under their yoke of bondage and the superstitions engendered by their decay, have ever adhered to this Ignatian theory, of which Cyprian was the great expounder in the West; while the terrible schism of the ninth century, which removed the West from the Nicene basis, and placed the Latin churches upon the foundation of the forged Decretals, was effected by ignoring the Cyprianic maxims, and then by a practical pulverizing of their fundamental principle of unity. This change involved a subversion of the primitive episcopate, an annihilation of the rights of the presbytery, and a total abasement of the laity; in a word, the destruction of synodical constitutions and of constitutional freedom.

4. The constitutional *primacy*, of which Cyprian was an early promotor, had to be entirely destroyed by decretalism before the papacy could exist. Gregory the Great stood upon the Cyprianic base when he pronounced the author of a scheme for a "universal bishopric" to be a forerunner of Antichrist. It was the spirit of the Decretals to substitute the fictitious idea of a divine supremacy in one bishop and one See, for the canonical presidency of a bishop who was only *primus inter pares*.

5. Hence the Cyprianic system has ever been the great resource of the "Gallicans against the Ultramontanes" in the cruel but most interesting history of the West. From the Council of Frankfort to our own times Cyprian's spirit is reflected in Hincmar, in Gerbert, in the Gallican canonists, in De Marca, in Bossuet, in Launoy, in Dupin, in Pascal, in the Jansenists (Augustinians), and by the Old Catholics in their late uprising against the dogmatic triumph of Ultramontanism. Nobody can understand the history of Latin Christianity without mastering the system of Cyprian, and comprehending the entirely hostile and uncatholic system of the Decretals.

6. I am not anxious to conceal the fact that I profoundly sympathize with the free spirit, the true benignity, and the moral purity which are everywhere reflected in the writings of Cyprian. If ever American

Romanism becomes sufficiently enlightened and purified to comprehend this great Carthaginian Father, and to speak in his tones to the Bishop of Rome, a glorious reformation of this alien religion will be the result; and then we may comprehend the mysterious Providence which has transferred to these shores so many subjects of the despotism of the Vatican. Meanwhile the student of the *Ante-Nicene Fathers* will not be slow to perceive that he has, in the eight volumes of this series, all that is needful to disarm Romanism, to refute its pretensions, and to direct honest and truth-loving spirits in the Roman Obedience to the door of escape opened by Döllinger and his associates in the "Old Catholic" effort for the restoration of the Latin churches. Let us "speak the truth in love," and pray the Lord to bless this and every endeavour to promote and to sanctify the spirit of enlightened research after the "pattern in the mount." For "thus saith the Lord, Stand ye in the ways, and see and ask for the old paths:" τὰ ἀρχαῖα ἔθη. The following Introduction, from the Edinburgh editor, supplies further answers to inquiry, and suffices to elucidate the subjoined narrative of Pontius.

Little is known of the early history of Thascius Cyprian (born probably about 200 A.D.) until the period of his intimacy with the Carthaginian presbyter Cæcilius, which led to his conversion A.D. 246. That he was born of respectable parentage, and highly educated for the profession of a rhetorician, is all that can be said with any degree of certainty. At his baptism he assumed the name of his friend Cæcilius, and devoted himself, with all the energies of an ardent and vigorous mind, to the study and practice of Christianity.

His ordination and his elevation to the episcopate rapidly followed his conversion. With some resistance on his own part, and not without great objections on the part of older presbyters, who saw themselves superseded by his promotion, the popular urgency constrained him to accept the office of Bishop of Carthage (A.D. 248), which he held until his martyrdom (A.D. 258).

The writings of Cyprian, apart from their intrinsic worth, have a very considerable historical interest and value, as illustrating the social and religious feelings and usages that then prevailed among the members of the Christian community. Nothing can enable us more vividly to realize the intense convictions—the high-strained enthusiasm—which formed the common level of the Christian experience, than does the indignation with which the prelate denounces the evasions of those who dared not confess, or the lapses of those who shrank from martyrdom. Living in the atmosphere of persecution, and often in the immediate presence of a lingering death, the professors of Christianity were nerved up to a wonderful contempt of suffering and of worldly enjoyment, and saw every event that occurred around them in the glow of their excited imagination; so that many circumstances were sincerely believed and honestly recorded, which will not be for a moment received as true by the calm and critical reader. The account given by Cyprian in his treatise on the Lapsed may serve as an illustration. Of this Dean Milman observes: "In what a high-wrought state of enthusiasm must men have been, who could relate and believe such statements as miraculous!"[2]

Before being advanced to the episcopate, Cyprian had written his Epistle to Donatus shortly after his baptism (A.D. 246); his treatise, or fragment of a treatise, on the Vanity of Idols; and his three books of Testimonies against the Jews. In the following translation the order of Migne has been adopted, which places the letter to Donatus, as seems most natural, first among the Epistles, instead of with the Treatises.

The breaking out of the Decian persecution (a.d. 250) induced Cyprian to retire into concealment for a time; and his retreat gave occasion to a sharp attack upon his conduct, in a letter from the Roman to the Carthaginian clergy. During this year he wrote many letters from his place of concealment to the clergy and others at Rome and at Carthage, controlling, warning, directing, and exhorting, and in every way maintaining his episcopal superintendence in his absence, in all matters connected with the well-being of the Church.

The first 39 of the epistles, excepting the one to Donatus, were probably written during the period of Cyprian's retirement. He appears to have returned to his public duties early in June, 251. Then follow many letters between himself and Cornelius bishop of Rome, and others, on subjects connected with the schisms of Novatian, Novatus, and Felicissimus, and with the condition of those who had been perverted by them. The question proposed in Epistle 52 was settled in the Council that was held in May, 252; and the reference to that anticipated decision limits the date of the letter to about April in the same year. In the 53d Epistle, Cyprian is alluding to the impending persecution of Gallus, under which Cornelius was banished in July, 252. The 56th Epistle was a letter of congratulation to Cornelius on his banishment; and therefore it must have been written before September 14th in that year, the date of the death of Cornelius. Lucius, his successor, was also banished, and was congratulated on his return by Cyprian in Epistle 57, which therefore must have been written about the end of November, 252. The 59th Epistle is referred by Bishop Pearson to the beginning of the year 253.

There seems nothing to suggest the date of Epistles 60 and 61, except the probability that they were written during a time of peace; and for this reason they are referred to the beginning of Cyprian's episcopate, before the outbreak of the Decian persecution, a.d. 249. It is usual to assign

Epistle 64 to the same year, or at least to a very early period of Cyprian's official life; but it seems scarcely likely that his episcopal counsel should have been sought by a brother bishop in a matter of practice, until he had had some experience; and as it was probably written at a time of peace, when discipline had become relaxed, the date 253 seems preferable. The 68th Epistle is easily dated by the reference, on page 246, to an episcopate of six years' duration; and it must therefore have been written in a.d. 254. On the 14th September, Cyprian was banished to Curubis by the Emperor Valerian. From his place of exile he wrote Epistle 76, which was replied to in Epistles 77, 78, and 79. Doubts are entertained as to the date of Epistle 80, whether it should be referred to A.D. 250 or 257. Pamelius prefers the latter date, on the ground that the Rogatianus to whom it is inscribed was one who survived the Decian persecution, and a younger man than the one who, as he supposes, was declared to have suffered martyrdom at the date of this Epistle. This, however, seems very unsatisfactory; and the weight of authority is in favor of the earlier date. The remaining Epistles are easily limited by their contents to the period immediately preceding Cyprian's martyrdom.

For the sake of uniformity, it has been thought well to adhere to the arrangement of Migne, in the order of the Epistles as well as in their divisions. For the convenience of reference, however, the number of each Epistle in the Oxford edition is appended in a note. For a similar reason, the general form of Migne's text has been used in the following translation; but the use of other texts and of preceding translations has not been rejected in the endeavour to approximate to the sense of the author. Moreover, such various readings as might suggest different shades of meaning in doubtful passages have been given.

The Translator has only to add, that, as a rule, an exact rendering has been sought after, sometimes in preference to a version in fluent English. But, except in cases where the corruption or obscurity of the text seems insurmountable, the meaning of the writer is believed to be given fairly and intelligibly. The style of Cyprian, like that of his master Tertullian, is marked much more by vehemence than perspicuity, and it is often no easy matter to give exact expression in another language to the idea contained in the original text. Cyprian's Life, as written by his own deacon Pontius, is subjoined.[91]

---

[91] Alexander Roberts, James Donaldson, and A. Cleveland Coxe, eds., "Introductory Notice to Cyprian," in *Fathers of the Third Century: Hippolytus, Cyprian, Novatian, Appendix*, vol. 5, The Ante-Nicene Fathers (Buffalo, NY: Christian Literature Company, 1886), 263–266.

EARLY CHRISTIANITY 14 Tertullian - Defense of Christianity

[A.D. 145–220.] When our Lord repulsed the woman of Canaan (Matt. 15:22) with apparent harshness, he applied to her people the epithet *dogs*, with which the children of Israel had thought it piety to reproach them. When He accepted her faith and caused it to be recorded for our learning, He did something more: He reversed the curse of the Canaanite and showed that the Church was designed "for all people;" Catholic alike for all time and for all sorts and conditions of men.

Thus the North-African Church was loved before it was born: the Good Shepherd was gently leading those "that were with young." Here was the charter of those Christians to be a Church, who then were Canaanites in the land of their father Ham. It is remarkable indeed that among these pilgrims and strangers to the West the first elements of Latin Christianity come into view. Even at the close of the Second Century the Church in Rome is an inconsiderable, though prominent, member of the great confederation of Christian Churches which has its chief seats in Alexandria and Antioch, and of which the entire Literature is Greek. It is an African presbyter who takes from Latin Christendom the reproach of theological and literary barrenness and begins the great work in which, upon his foundations, Cyprian and Augustine built up, with incomparable genius, that Carthaginian School of Christian thought by which Latin Theology was dominated for centuries. It is important to note (1.) that providentially not one of these illustrious doctors died in Communion with the Roman See, pure though it was and venerable at that time; and (2.) that to the works of Augustine the Reformation in Germany and Continental Europe was largely due; while (3.) the *specialties* of the Anglican Reformation were, in like proportion, due to the writings of Tertullian and Cyprian. The hinges of great and controlling destinies for Western Europe and our own America are to be found in the period we are now approaching.

The merest school-boy knows much of the history of Carthage, and how the North Africans became Roman citizens. How they became Christians is not so clear. A melancholy destiny has enveloped Carthage from the outset, and its glory and greatness as a Christian See were transient indeed. It blazed out all at once in Tertullian, after about a century of missionary labours had been exerted upon its creation: and having given a Minucius Felix, an Arnobius and a Lactantius to adorn the earliest period of Western Ecclesiastical learning, in addition to its nobler luminaries, it rapidly declined. At the beginning of the Third Century, at a

143

council presided over by Agrippinus, Bishop of Carthage, there were present not less than seventy bishops of the Province. A period of cruel persecutions followed, and the African Church received a baptism of blood.

Tertullian was born a heathen, and seems to have been educated at Rome, where he probably practiced as a jurisconsult. We may, perhaps, adopt most of the ideas of Allix, as conjecturally probable, and assign his birth to A.D. 145. He became a Christian about 185, and a presbyter about 190. The period of his strict orthodoxy very nearly expires with the century. He lived to an extreme old age, and some suppose even until A.D. 240. More probably, we must adopt the date preferred by recent writers, A.D. 220.

It seems to be the fashion to treat of Tertullian as a Montanist, and only incidentally to celebrate his services to the Catholic Orthodoxy of Western Christendom. Were I his biographer I should reverse this course, as a mere act of justice, to say nothing of gratitude to a man of splendid intellect, to whom the filial spirit of Cyprian accorded the loving tribute of a disciple, and whose genius stamped itself upon the very words of Latin theology, and prepared the language for the labours of a Jerome. In creating the Vulgate, and so lifting the Western Churches into a position of intellectual equality with the East, the latter as well as St. Augustine himself were debtors to Tertullian in a degree not to be estimated by any other than the Providential Mind that inspired his brilliant career as a Christian.

In speaking of Tatian, I laid the base for what I wished to say of Tertullian. Let God only be their judge; let us gratefully recognize the debt we owe to them. Let us read them, as we read the works of King Solomon. We must, indeed, approve of the discipline of the Primitive Age, which allowed of no compromises. The Church was struggling for existence, and could not permit any man to become her master. The more brilliant the intellect, the more dangerous to the poor Church were its perversions of her Testimony. Before the heathen tribunals, and in the market-places, it would not answer to let Christianity appear double-tongued. The orthodoxy of the Church, not less than her children, was undergoing an ordeal of fire. It seems a miracle that her Testimony preserved its unity, and that heresy was branded as such by the instinct of the Faithful. Poor Tertullian was cut off by his own act. The weeping Church might bewail him as David mourned for Absalom, but like David, she could not give the Ark of God into other hands than those of the loyal and the true. I have set the writings of Tertullian in a natural and logical order, so as to aid the student, and to relieve him from the distractions of such an arrangement as one finds in Oehler's edition.

Valuable as it is, the practical use of it is irritating and confusing. The reader of that edition may turn to the slightly differing schemes of Neander and Kaye, for a theoretical order of the works; but here he will find a classification which will aid his inquiries. He will find, first, those works which connect with the Apologists of the former volumes of this series: which illustrate the Church's position toward the outside world, the Jews as well as the Gentiles. Next come those works which contend with internal differences and heresies. And then, those which reflect the morals and manners of Christians. These are classed with some reference to their degrees of freedom from the Montanistic taint, and are followed, last of all, by the few tracts which belong to the melancholy period of his lapse, and are directed against the Church's orthodoxy.

Let it be borne in mind, that if this sad close of Tertullian's career cannot be extenuated, the later history of Latin Christianity forbids us to condemn him, in the tones which proceeded from the Virgin Church with authority, and which the law of her testimony and the instinct of self-preservation forced her to utter. Let us reflect that St. Bernard and after him the Schoolmen, whom we so deservedly honour, separated themselves far more absolutely than ever Tertullian did from the orthodoxy of Primitive Christendom. The schism which withdrew the West from Communion with the original seats of Christendom, and from Nicene Catholicity, was formidable beyond all expression, in comparison with Tertullian's entanglements with a delusion which the See of Rome itself had momentarily patronized. Since the Council of Trent, not a theologian of the Latins has been free from organic heresies, compared with which the fanaticism of our author was a trifling aberration. Since the late Council of the Vatican, essential Montanism has become organized in the Latin Churches: for what are the new revelations and oracles of the pontiff but the *deliria* of another claimant to the voice and inspiration of the Paraclete? Poor Tertullian! The sad influences of his decline and folly have been fatally felt in all the subsequent history of the West, but, surely subscribers to the Modern Creed of the Vatican have reason to "speak gently of *their father's* fall" To Döllinger, with the "Old Catholic" remnant only, is left the right to name the Montanists heretics, or to upbraid Tertullian as a lapser from Catholicity.

From Dr. Holmes, I append the following Introductory Notice:

(I.) Quintus Septimius Florens Tertullianus, as our author is called in the mss. of his works, is thus noticed by Jerome in his *Catalogus Scriptorum Ecclesiasticorum:* "Tertullian, a presbyter, the first Latin writer after Victor and Apollonius, was a native of the province of Africa and city of Carthage, the son of a proconsular centurion: he was a man of a sharp and vehement temper, flourished under Severus and Antoninus

Caracalla, and wrote numerous works, which (as they are generally known) I think it unnecessary to particularize. I saw at Concordia, in Italy, an old man named Paulus. He said that when young he had met at Rome with an aged amanuensis of the blessed Cyprian, who told him that Cyprian never passed a day without reading some portion of Tertullian's works, and used frequently to say, *Give me any master*, meaning Tertullian. After remaining a presbyter of the church until he had attained the middle age of life, Tertullian was, by the envy and contumelious treatment of the Roman clergy, driven to embrace the opinions of Montanus, which he has mentioned in several of his works under the title of the New Prophecy.... He is reported to have lived to a very advanced age, and to have composed many other works which are not extant." We add Bishop Kaye's notes on this extract, in an abridged shape: "The correctness of some parts of this account has been questioned. Doubts have been entertained whether Tertullian was a presbyter, although these have solely arisen from Roman Catholic objections to a married priesthood; for it is certain that he was married, there being among his works two treatises addressed to his wife.... Another question has been raised respecting the place where Tertullian officiated as a presbyter—whether at Carthage or at Rome. That he at one time resided at Carthage may be inferred from Jerome's statement, and is rendered certain by several passages of his own writings. Allix supposes that the notion of his having been a presbyter of the Roman Church owed its rise to what Jerome said of the envy and abuse of the Roman clergy impelling him to espouse the party of Montanus. Optatus, and the author of the work *de Hæresibus*, which Sirmond edited under tile title of Prædestinatus, expressly call him a Carthaginian presbyter. Semler, however, in a dissertation inserted in his edition of Tertullian's works, contends that he was a presbyter of the Roman Church. Eusebius[6] tells us that he was accurately acquainted with the Roman laws, and on other accounts a distinguished person at Rome. Tertullian displays, moreover, a knowledge of the proceedings of the Roman Church with respect to Marcion and Valentinus, who were once members of it, which could scarcely have been obtained by one who had not himself been numbered amongst its presbyters. Semler admits that, after Tertullian seceded from the church, he left and returned to Carthage. Jerome does not inform us whether Tertullian was born of Christian parents, or was converted to Christianity. There are passages in his writings[2] which seem to imply that he had been a Gentile; yet he may perhaps mean to describe, not his own condition, but that of Gentiles in general, before their conversion. Allix and the majority of commentators understand them literally, as well as some other passages in which he speaks of his own infirmities and sinfulness. His writings show that he flourished at the period specified by Jerome—that is, during the reigns of Severus and Antoninus Caracalla, or between the years a.d. 193 and 216; but they supply no precise information respecting the date of his birth, or any of the principal occurrences of his life. Allix places his birth about 145 or 150; his conversion to Christianity about a.d. 185; his marriage about 186; his admission to the priesthood about 192; his adoption of the opinions of Montanus about 199; and his death about A.D. 220. But these dates, it must be understood, rest entirely on conjecture."

(II.) Tertullian's work against Marcion, as it happens, is, *as to its date*, the best authenticated—perhaps the only well authenticated—particular connected with the author's life. He himself mentions the fifteenth year of the reign of Severus as the time when he was writing the work: "Ad xv. jam Severi imperatoris." This agrees with Jerome's Chronicle, where occurs this note: "Anno 2223 Severi xv⁰ Tertullianus ... celebratur." This year is assigned to the year of our Lord 207;[7] but notwithstanding the certainty of this date, it is far from clear that it describes more than the time of the publication of *the first book*. On the contrary, it is nearly certain that the other books, although connected manifestly enough in the author's argument and purpose (compare the initial and the final chapters of the several books), were yet issued at separate times. Noesselt shows that between the Book i. and Books ii.–iv. Tertullian issued his *De Præscript. Hæret.*, and previous to Book v. he published his tracts, *De Carne Christi* and *De Resurrectione Carnis*. After giving the incontestable date of the xv. of Severus for the first book, he says it is a mistake to suppose that the other books were published with it. He adds: "Although we cannot undertake to determine whether Tertullian issued his Books ii., iii., iv., against Marcion, together or separately, or in what year, we yet venture to affirm that Book v. appeared apart from the rest. For the tract *De Resurr. Carnis* appears from its second chapter to have been published after the tract *De Carne Christi*, in which latter work (chap. vii.) he quotes a passage from the fourth book against Marcion. But in his Book v. against Marcion (chap. x.), he refers to his work *De Resurr. Carnis*; which circumstance makes it evident that Tertullian published his Book v. at a different time from his Book iv. In his Book i. he announces his intention (chap. i.) of some time or other completing his tract *De Præscript. Hæret.*, but in his book *De Carne Christi* (chap. ii.), he mentions how he had completed it,—a conclusive proof that his Book i. against Marcion preceded the other books."

(III.) Respecting Marcion himself, the most formidable heretic who had as yet opposed revealed truth, enough will turn up in this treatise, with the notes which we have added in explanation, to satisfy the reader. It will, however, be convenient to give here a few introductory particulars of him. Tertullian mentions Marcion as being, with Valentinus, in communion with the Church at Rome, "under the episcopate of the blessed Eleutherus." He goes on to charge them with "ever-restless curiosity, with which they infected even the brethren;" and informs us that they were more than once put out of communion—"Marcion, indeed, with the 200 sesterces which he brought into the church."[2] He goes on to say, that "being at last condemned to the banishment of a perpetual separation, they sowed abroad the poisons of their doctrines. Afterwards, when Marcion, having professed penitence, agreed to the terms offered to him, that he should receive reconciliation on condition that he brought back to the church the rest also, whom he had trained up for perdition, he was prevented by death." He was a native of Sinope in Pontus, of which city, according to an account preserved by Epiphanius, which, however, is somewhat doubtful, his father was bishop, and of high character both for his orthodoxy and exemplary practice. He came to Rome soon after the death of Hyginus, probably about A.D. 141 or 142; and soon after his arrival he adopted the heresy of Cerdon.

(IV.) It is an interesting question as to what edition of the Holy Scriptures Tertullian used in his very copious quotations. It may at once be asserted that he did not cite from the Hebrew, although some writers have claimed for him, among his varied learning, a knowledge of the sacred language. Bp. Kaye observes, page 61, n. 1, that "he sometimes speaks as if he was acquainted with Hebrew," and refers to the *Anti-Marcion* iv. 39, the *Adv. Praxeam* v., and the *Adv. Judæos* ix. Be this as it may, it is manifest that Tertullian's Scripture passages never resemble the Hebrew, but in nearly every instance the Septuagint, whenever, as is most frequently the case, that version differs from the original. In the New Testament there is, as might be expected, a tolerably close conformity to the Greek. There is, however, it must be allowed, a sufficiently frequent variation from the letter of both the Greek Testaments to justify Semler's suspicion that Tertullian always quoted from the old Latin version, whatever that might have been, which was current in the African church in the second and third centuries. The most valuable part of Semler's *Dissertatio de varia et incerta indole Librorum Q. S. F. Tertulliani* is his investigation of this very point. In section iv. he endeavours to prove this proposition: "Hic scriptor non in manibus habuit Græcos libros sacros;" and he states his conclusion thus: "Certissimum est nec Tertullianum nec Cyprianum nec ullum scriptorem e Latinis illis ecclesiasticis provocare unquam ad Græcorum librorum auctoritatem si vel maxime obscura aut contraria lectio occurreret;" and again: "Ex his satis certum est, Latinos satis diu secutos fuisse auctoritatem suorum librorum adversus Græcos, nec concessisse nisi serius, cum Augustini et Hieronymi nova auctoritas juvare videretur." It is not ignorance of Greek which is imputed to Tertullian, for he is said to have well understood that language, and even to have composed in it. He probably followed the Latin, as writers now usually quote the authorized English, as being current and best known among their readers. Independent feeling, also, would have weight with such a temper as Tertullian's, to say nothing of the suspicion which largely prevailed in the African branch of the Latin church, that the Greek copies of the Scriptures were much corrupted by the heretics, who were chiefly, if not wholly, Greeks or Greek-speaking persons.

(V.) Whatever perverting effect Tertullian's secession to the sect of Montanus may have had on his judgment in his latest writings, it did not vitiate the work against Marcion. With a few trivial exceptions, this treatise may be read by the strictest Catholic without any feeling of annoyance. His lapse to Montanism is set down conjecturally as having taken place a.d. 199. Jerome, we have seen, attributed the event to his quarrel with the Roman clergy, but this is at least doubtful; nor must it be forgotten that Tertullian's mind seems to have been peculiarly suited by nature to adopt the mystical notions and ascetic principles of Montanus. It is satisfactory to find that, on the whole, "the authority of Tertullian," as the learned Dr. Burton says, "upon great points of doctrine is considered to be little, if at all, affected by his becoming a Montanist." (*Lectures on Eccl. Hist.* vol. ii. p. 234.) Besides the different works which are expressly mentioned in the notes of this volume, recourse has been had by the translator to Dupin's *Hist. Eccl. Writers* (trans.), vol. i. pp. 69–86; Tillemont's *Mémoires Hist. Eccl.* iii. 85–103; Dr. Smith's *Greek and Roman Biography*, articles "Marcion" and "Tertullian;" Schaff's article, in Herzog's *Cyclopædia*, on "Tertullian;" Munter's *Primordia Eccl. Africanæ*, pp. 118–150; Robertson's *Church Hist.* vol. i. pp. 70–77; Dr. P. Schaff's *Hist. of Christian Church* (New York, 1859, pp. 511–519), and Archdeacon Evans' *Biography of the Early Church*, vol. i. (Lives of "Marcion," pp. 93–122, and "Tertullian," pp. 325–363). This last work, though of a popular cast, shows a good deal of research and learning, expressed in the pleasant style of the once popular author of *The Rectory of Vale Head*. The translator has mentioned these works, because they are all quite accessible to the general reader, and will give him adequate information concerning the subject treated in the present volume.

To this introduction of Dr. Holmes must be added that of Mr. Thelwall, the translator of the Third volume in the Edinburgh Series, as follows:

To arrange chronologically the works (especially if numerous) of an author whose own date is known with tolerable precision, is not always or necessarily easy: witness the controversies as to the succession of St. Paul's epistles. To do this in the case of an author whose own date is itself a matter of controversy may therefore be reasonably expected to be still less so; and such is the predicament of him who attempts to perform this task for Tertullian. I propose to give a specimen or two of the difficulties with which the task is beset; and then to lay before the reader briefly a summary of the results at which eminent scholars, who have devoted much time and thought to the subject, have arrived. Such a course, I think, will at once afford him means of judging of the absolute impossibility of arriving at definite certainty in the matter; and induce him to excuse me if I prefer furnishing him with materials from which to deduce his own conclusions, rather than venturing on an *ex cathedra* decision on so doubtful a subject.

1. The book, as Dr. Holmes has reminded us, of the date of which we seem to have the surest evidence, is *adv. Marc.* i. This book was in course of writing, as its author himself (c. 15) tells us, "in the fifteenth year of the empire of Severus." Now this date would be clear if there were no doubt as to which year of our era corresponds to Tertullian's fifteenth of Severus. Pamelius, however, says Dr. Holmes, makes it a.d. 208; Clinton, (whose authority is more recent and better,) 207.

2. Another book which promises to give some clue to its date is the *de Pallio*. The writer uses these phrases: "præsentis imperii *triplex virtus*;" "Deo *tot Augustis in unum* favente;" which show that there were at the time *three* persons unitedly bearing the title *Augusti*—not *Cæsares* only, but the still higher *Augusti*;—while the remainder of that context, as well as the opening of c. 1, indicates a time of peace of some considerable duration; a time of plenty; and a time during and previous to which great changes had taken place in the general aspect of the Roman Empire, and some particular traitor had been discovered and frustrated. Such a combination of circumstances might seem to fix the date with some degree of assurance. But unhappily, as Kaye reminds us, commentators cannot agree as to who the three Augusti are. Some say Severus, Caracalla, and *Albinus*; some say Severus, Caracalla, and *Geta*. Hence we have a difference of some twelve years or thereabouts in the computations. For Albinus was defeated by Severus in person, and fell by his own hand, in A.D. 197; and Geta, Severus' second son, brother of Caracalla, was not associated by his father with himself and his other son as *Augustus* until A.D. 208, though he had received the title of *Cæsar* ten years before, in the same year in which *Caracalla* had received that of *Augustus*. For my own part, I may perhaps be allowed to say that I should incline to agree, like Salmasius, with those who assign the later date. The limits of the present Introduction forbid my entering at large into my reasons for so doing. I am, however, supported in it by the authority of Neander.[4] In one point, though, I should hesitate to agree with Oehler, who appears to follow Salmasius and others herein,— namely, in understanding the expression "et cacto et rubo subdolæ familiaritatis convulso" of *Albinus*. It seems to me the words might with

more propriety be applied to *Plautianus*; and that in the word "familiaritatis" we may *see* (after Tertullian's fashion) a play upon the meaning, with a reference not only to the long-standing but mischievous *intimacy* which existed between Severus and his countryman (perhaps fellow-townsman) Plautianus, who for his harshness and cruelty is fitly compared to the prickly *cactus*. He alludes likewise to the alliance which this ambitious prætorian præfect had contrived to contract with the *family* of the emperor, by the marriage of his daughter Plautilla to Caracalla,—an event which, as it turned out, led to his own death. Thus in the "*rubo*" there may be a reference to the ambitious and conceited "*bramble*" of Jotham's parable, and perhaps, too, to the "thistle" of Jehoash's.[6] If this be so, the date would be at least approximately fixed, as Plautianus did not marry his daughter to Caracalla till a.d. 203, and was himself put to death in the following year, 204, while Geta, as we have seen, was made Augustus in 208.

3. The date of the *Apology*, however, is perhaps at once the most contested, and the most strikingly illustrative of the difficulties to which allusion has been made. It is not surprising that its date *should* have been more disputed than that of other pieces, inasmuch as it is the best known, and (for some reasons) the most interesting and famous, of all our author's productions. In fact, the dates assigned to it by different authorities vary from Mosheim's 198 to that suggested by the very learned Allix, who assigns it to 217.

4. Once more. In the tract *de Monogamia* (c. 3) the author says that since the date of St. Paul's first Epistle to the Corinthians "about 160 years had elapsed." Here, again, did we only know with certainty the precise date of that epistle, we could ascertain "*about*" the date of the tract. But (*a*) the date of the epistle is itself variously given, Burton giving it as early as a.d. 52, Michaelis and Mill as late as 57; and (*b*) Tertullian only says, "Armis *circiter* clx. exinde productis;" while the way in which, in the *ad Natt.*, within the short space of three chapters, he states first than 250, and then (in c. 9) that 300, years had not elapsed since the rise of the Christian name, leads us to think that here again[2] he only desires to speak in round numbers, meaning perhaps *more* than 150, but *less* than 170.

These specimens must suffice, though it might be easy to add to them. There is, however, another classification of our author's writings which has been attempted. Finding the hopelessness of strict chronological accuracy, commentators have seized on the idea that peradventure there might be found at all events some internal marks by which to determine which of them were written before, which after, the writer's secession to Montanism. It may be confessed that this attempt has been somewhat more successful than the other. Yet even here there are two formidable obstacles standing in our way. The first and greatest is, that the natural temper of Tertullian was from the first so akin to the spirit of Montanism, that, unless there occur distinct allusions to the "New Prophecy," or expressions specially connected with Montanistic phraseology, the *general tone* of any treatise is not a very safe guide. The second is, that the subject-matter of *some* of the treatises is not such as to afford much scope for the introduction of the peculiarities of a sect which professed to differ in discipline only, not doctrine, from the church at large.

Still the result of this classification seems to show one important feature of agreement between commentators, however they may differ upon details; and that is, that considerably the larger part of our author's rather voluminous productions must have been subsequent to his lamented secession. I think the best way to give the reader means for forming his own judgment will be, as I have said, to lay before him in parallel columns a tabular view of the disposition of the books by Dr. Neander and Bishop Kaye. These two modern writers, having given particular care to the subject, bringing to bear upon it all the advantages derived from wide reading, eminent abilities, and a diligent study of the works of preceding writers on the same questions,[4] have a special right to be heard upon the matter in hand; and I think, if I may be allowed to say so, that, for calm judgment, and minute acquaintance with his author, I shall not be accused of undue partiality if I express my opinion that, as far as my own observation goes, the palm must be awarded to the Bishop. In this view I am supported by the fact that the accomplished Professor Ramsay, follows Dr. Kaye's arrangement. I premise that Dr. Neander adopts a threefold division, into:

1. Writings which were occasioned by the relation of the Christians to the heathen, and refer to their vindication of Christianity against the heathen; attacks on heathenism; the sufferings and conduct of Christians under persecution; and the intercourse of Christians with heathens:

2. Writings which relate to Christian and church life, and to ecclesiastical discipline

3. The dogmatic and dogmatico-controversial treatises.

And under each head he subdivides into:

a. Pre-Montanist writings: *b*. Post-Montanist writings:

thus leaving no room for what Kaye calls "works respecting which nothing certain can be pronounced." For the sake of clearness, this order has not been followed in the table. On the other side, it will be seen that Dr. Kaye, while not assuming to speak with more than a reasonable probability, is careful so to arrange the treatises under each head as to show the *order*, so far as it is discoverable, in which the books under that head were *published*; i.e., if one book is *quoted* in another book, the book so quoted, if distinctly referred to as *already before the world*, is plainly anterior to that in which it is quoted. Thus, then, we have:

Neander	Kaye
1. *Pre-Montanist.*	1. *Pre-Montanist* (probably).
1. De Pœnitentia.	1. De Pœnitentia.
2. De Oratione.	2. De Oratione.
3. De Baptismo.	3. De Baptismo.
4. Ad Uxorem i.	4. Ad Uxorem i.
5. Ad Uxorem ii.	5. Ad Uxorem ii.
6. Ad Martyres.	6. Ad Martyres.
7. De Patientia.	7. De Patientia
8. De Spectaculis.	8. Adv. Judæos.
9. De Idololatria	9. De Præscr. Hæreticorum.
10, 11. Ad Nationes i, ii.	
12. Apologeticus.	2. *Montanist* (certainly).
13. De Testimonio Animæ.	
14. De Præscr. Hæreticorum.	10. Adv. Marc. i.
15. De Cult. Fem. i.	11. Adv. Marc. ii.
16 De Cult. Fem. ii.	12. De Anima.
	13. Adv. Marc. iii.
2. *Montanist*	14. Adv. Marc. iv.
	15. De Carne Christi.
17–21. Adv. Marc. i. ii. iii. iv.	16. De Resurrectione Carnis.
v.	17. Adv. Marc. v.
22. De Anlma.	18. Adv. Praxeam.
23. De Carne Christi.	19. Scorpiace.
24. De Res. Carn.	20. De Corona Militis.
25. De Cor. Mil.	21. De Virginibus Velandis.
26. De Virg. Vel.	22. De Exhortatione Castitatis.
27. De Ex. Cast.	23. De Fuga in Persecutione.
28. De Monog.	24. De Monogamia.
29. De Jejuniis.	25. De Jejuniis.
30. De Pudicitia.	26. De Pudicitia
31. De Pallio.	
32. Scorpiace.	3. *Montanist* (probably).
33. Ad Scapulam.	
34. Adv. Valentinianos.	27. Adv. Valentinianos.
35. Adv. Hermogenem.	28. Ad Scapulam.
36. Adv. Praxeam.	29. De Spectaculis.
37. Adv. Judæos.	30. De Idololatria.

38. De Fuga in Persecutione.	31. De Cultu Feminarum i. 32. De Cultu Feminarum ii. *4. Works respecting which nothing certain can be pronounced* 33. The Apology. 34. Ad Nationes i. 35. Ad Nationes ii. 36. De Testimonio Animæ. 37. De Pallio. 38. Adv. Hermogenem.

A comparison of these two lists will show that the difference between the two great authorities is, as Kaye remarks, "not great; and with respect to some of the tracts on which we differ, the learned author expresses himself with great diffidence." The main difference, in fact, is that which affects two tracts upon kindred subjects, the *de Spectaculis*, and *Idololatria*, the *de Cultu Feminarum* (a subject akin to the other two), and the *adv. Judæos*. With reference to all these, except the last, to which I believe the Archdeacon does not once refer, the Bishop's opinion appears to have the support of Archdeacon Evans, whose learned and interesting essay, referred to in the note, appears in a volume published in 1837. Dr. Kaye's Lectures, on which his book is founded, were delivered in 1825. Of the date of his first edition I am not aware. Dr. Neander's *Antignostikus* also first appeared in 1825. The preface to his second edition bears date July 1, 1849. As to the *adv. Judæos*, I confess I agree with Neander in thinking that, at all events from the beginning of c. 9, it is spurious. If it be urged that Jerome expressly quotes it as Tertullian's, I reply, Jerome *so* quotes it, I believe, when he is expounding *Daniel*. Now all that the *adv. Jud.* has to say about *Daniel* ends with the end of c. 8. It is therefore quite compatible with the fact thus stated to recognize the earlier half of the book as genuine, and to reject the rest, *beginning*, as it happens, just *after* the eighth chapter, as spurious. Perhaps Dr. Neander's Jewish birth and training peculiarly fit him to be heard on this question. Nor do I think Professor Ramsay (in the article above alluded to) has quite seen the force of Kaye's own remarks on Neander. What he does say is equally creditable to his candour and his accuracy; namely: "The instances alleged by Dr. Neander, in proof of this position, are undoubtedly very remarkable; but if the concluding chapters of the tract are spurious, no ground seems to be left for asserting that the genuine portion was posterior to the third Book against Marcion,[4]—and none, consequently, for asserting that it was written by a Montanist." With which remark I must draw these observations on the genuine extant works of Tertullian to a close.

The next point to which a brief reference must be made is the *lost works* of Tertullian, lists of these are given both by Oehler and by Kaye, viz.:

1. A Book on Aaron's Robes: mentioned by Jerome, Epist. 128, *ad Fabiolam de Veste Sacerdotali* (tom. ii. p. 586, Opp. ed. Bened.).

2. A Book on the Superstition of the Age.

3. A Book on the Submission of the Soul.

4. A Book on the Flesh and the Soul.

Nos. 2, 3, and 4 are known only by their titles, which are found in the Index to Tertullian's works given in the *Codex Agobardi*; but the tracts themselves are not extant in the ms., which appears to have once contained—

5. A Book on Paradise, named in the Index, and referred to in *de Anima* 55, *adv. Marc.* iii. 12; and

6. A Book on the Hope of the Faithful: also named in the Index, and referred to *adv. Marc.* iii. 24; and by Jerome in his account of Papias, and on Ezek. 36; and by Gennadius of Marseilles.[3]

7. Six Books on Ecstasy, with a seventh in reply to Apollonius: see Jerome.[5] See, too, J. A. Fabricius on the words of the unknown author whom the Jesuit Sirmond edited under the name *Prædestinatus*; who gathers thence that "Soter, pope of the City, and Apollonius, bishop[7] of the Ephesians, wrote a book against the Montanists; *in reply to whom* Tertullian, a Carthaginian presbyter, wrote." J. Pamelius thinks these seven books were originally published *in Greek*.

8. A Book in reply to the Apellesites (i.e. the followers of Apelles): referred to in *de Carne Christi*, c. 8.

9. A Book on the Origin of the Soul, in reply to Hermogenes: referred to in *de Anima*, cc. 1, 3, 22, 24.

10. A Book on Fate: referred to by Fulgentius Planciades, p. 562, Merc.; also referred to as either written, or intended to be written, by Tertullian himself, *de Anima*, c. 20. Jerome states that there was extant, or had been extant, a book on Fate under the name of Minucius Felix, written indeed by a perspicuous author, but not in the style of Minucius Felix. This, Pamelius judged, should perhaps be rather ascribed to Tertullian.

11. A Book on the Trinity. Jerome says: "Novatian wrote ... a large volume on the Trinity, *as if making an epitome of a work of Tertullian's, which most men not knowing regard it as Cyprian's.*" Novatian's book stood in Tertullian's name in the mss. of J. Gangneius, who was the first to edit it; in a Malmesbury ms. which Sig. Gelenius used; and in others.

12. A Book addressed to a Philosophic Friend on the Straits of Matrimony. Both Kaye and Oehler are in doubt whether Jerome's words,[13] by which some have been led to conclude that Tertullian wrote some book or books on this and kindred subjects, really imply as much, or whether they may not refer merely to those tracts and passages in his extant writings which touch upon such matters. Kaye hesitates to think that the "Book to a Philosophic Friend" is the same as the *de Exhortatiotne Castitatis*, because Jerome says Tertullian wrote on the subject of celibacy "*in his youth;*" but as Cave takes what Jerome elsewhere says of Tertullian's leaving the Church "*about the middle of his age*" to mean his *spiritual age*, the same sense might attach to his words here too, and thus obviate the Bishop's difficulty.

There are some other works which have been attributed to Tertullian—on Circumcision; on Animals Clean and Unclean; on the truth that God is a Judge—which Oehler likewise rejects, believing that the expressions of Jerome refer only to passages in the *Anti-Marcion* and other extant works. To Novatian Jerome does ascribe a distinct work on Circumcision, and this may (comp. 11, just above) have given rise to the view that Tertullian had written one also.

There were, moreover, three treatises at least written by Tertullian *in Greek*. They are:

1. A Book on Public Shows. See *de Cor.* c. 6.

2. A Book on Baptism. See *de Bapt.* c. 15.

3. A Book on the Veiling of Virgins. See *de V.V.* c. 1.

Oehler adds that J. Pamelius, in his epistle dedicatory to Philip II. of Spain, makes mention of a *Greek copy* of Tertullian in the library of that king. This report, however, since nothing has ever been seen or heard of the said copy from that time, Oehler judges to be erroneous.

It remains briefly to notice the confessedly spurious works which the editions of Tertullian generally have appended to them. With these Kaye does not deal. The fragment, *adv. omnes Hæreses*, Oehler attributes to Victorinus Petavionensis, i.e., Victorinus bishop of Pettaw, on the Drave, in Austrian Styria. It was once thought he ought to be called *Pictaviensis*, *i.e.* of *Poictiers*; but John Launoy has shown this to be an errors Victorinus is said by Jerome to have "understood Greek better than Latin; hence his works are excellent for the sense, but mean as to the style."[3] Cave believes him to have been a Greek by birth. Cassiodorus states him to have been once a professor of rhetoric. Jerome's statement agrees with the style of the tract in question; and Jerome distinctly says Victorinus did write *adversus omnes Hæreses*. Allix leaves the question of its authorship quite uncertain. If Victorinus be the author, the book falls clearly within the ante-Nicene period; for Victorinus fell a martyr in the Diocletian persecution, probably about a.d. 303.

The next fragment—"Of the Execrable Gods of the Heathens"—is of quite uncertain authorship. Oehler would attribute it "to some declaimer not quite ignorant of Tertullian's writings," but certainly not to Tertullian himself.

Lastly we come to the metrical fragments. Concerning these, it is perhaps impossible to assign them to their rightful owners. Oehler has not troubled himself much about them; but he seems to regard the *Jonah* as worthy of more regard than the rest, for he seems to have intended giving more labour to its editing at some future time. Whether he has ever done so, or given us his German version of Tertullian's own works, which, "si Deus adjuverit," he distinctly promises in his preface, I do not know. Perhaps the best thing to be done under the circumstances is to give the judgment of the learned Peter Allix. It may be premised that by the celebrated George Fabricius—who published his great work, *Poetarum Veterum Ecclesiasticorum Opera Christiana*, etc., in 1564—the *Five Books in Reply to Marcion*, and the *Judgment of the Lord*, are ascribed to Tertullian, the Genesis and *Sodom* to Cyprian. Pamelius likewise seems to have ascribed the *Five Books*, the *Jonah*, and the *Sodom* to Tertullian; and according to Lardner, Bishop Bull likewise attributed the *Five Books* to him. They have been generally ascribed to the Victorinus above mentioned. Tillemont, among others, thinks they may well enough be his.[8] Rigaltius is content to demonstrate that they are not Tertullian's, but leaves the real authorship without attempting to decide it. Of the others the same eminent critic says, "They seem to have been written at Carthage, at an age not far removed from Tertullian's." Allix, after observing that Pamelius is inconsistent with himself in attributing the *Genesis* and *Sodom* at one time to Tertullian, at another to Cyprian, rejects both views equally, and assigns the *Genesis* with some confidence to Salvian, a presbyter of Marseilles, whose "floruit" Cave gives *cir.* 440, a contemporary of Gennadius, and a copious author. To this it is, Allix thinks, that Gennadius alludes in his *Catalogue of Illustrious Men*, c. 77.

The *Judgment of the Lord* Allix ascribes to one Verecundus, an African bishop, whose date he finds it difficult to decide exactly. He refers to two of the name: one Bishop of Tunis, whom Victor of Tunis in his chronicle mentions as having died in exile at Chalcedon a.d. 552; the other Bishop of Noba, who visited Carthage with many others a.d. 482, at the summons of King Huneric, to answer there for their faith;—and would ascribe the poem to the former, thinking that he finds an allusion to it in the article upon that Verecundus in the *de Viris Illustribus* of Isidore of Seville. Oehler agrees with him. The *Five Books* Allix seems to hint *may* be attributed to some imitator of the Victorinus of Pettaw named above. Oehler attributes them rather to one Victorinus, or Victor, of Marseilles, a rhetorician, who died a.d. 450. He appears in G. Fabricius as Claudius Marius Victorinus, writer of a *Commentary on Genesis*, and an epistle *ad Salomonem Abbata*, both in verse, and of some considerable length.[92]

---

[92] Alexander Roberts, James Donaldson, and A. Cleveland Coxe, eds., "Introductory Note," in *Latin Christianity: Its Founder, Tertullian*, vol. 3, The Ante-Nicene Fathers (Buffalo, NY: Christian Literature Company, 1885), 3–15.

EARLY CHRISTIANITY 15 Hippolytus of Rome

[A.D. 170–236.] The first great Christian Father whose history is Roman is, nevertheless, not a Roman, but a Greek. He is the disciple of Irenæus, and the spirit of his life-work reflects that of his master. In his personal character he so much resembles Irenæus risen again, that the great Bishop of Lyons must be well studied and understood if we would do full justice to the conduct of Hippolytus. Especially did he follow his master's example in withstanding contemporary bishops of Rome, who, like Victor, "deserved to be blamed," but who, much more than any of their predecessors, merited rebuke alike for error in doctrine and viciousness of life.

In the year 1551, while some excavations were in progress near the ancient Church of St. Lawrence at Rome, on the Tiburtine Road, there was found an ancient statue, in marble, of a figure seated in a chair, and wearing over the Roman tunic the *pallium* of Tertullian's eulogy. It was in 1851, just three hundred years after its discovery, and in the year of the publication of the newly discovered *Philosophumena* at Oxford, that I saw it in the Vatican. As a specimen of early Christian art it is a most interesting work, and possesses a higher merit than almost any similar production of a period subsequent to that of the Antonines. It represents a grave personage, of noble features and a high, commanding forehead, slightly bearded, his right hand resting over his heart, while under it his left arm crosses the body to reach a book placed at his side. There is no reason to doubt that this is, indeed, the statue of Hippolytus, as is stated in the inscription of Pius IV., who calls him "Saint Hippolytus, Bishop of Portus," and states that he lived in the reign of the Emperor Alexander; i.e., Severus.

Of this there is evidence on the chair itself, which represents his episcopal *cathedra*, and has a modest symbol of lions at "the stays," as if borrowed from the throne of Solomon. It is a work of later date than the age of Severus, no doubt; but Wordsworth, who admirably illustrates the means by which such a statue may have been provided, gives us good reasons for supposing that it may have been the grateful tribute of contemporaries, and all the more trustworthy as a portrait of the man himself. The chair has carved upon it, no doubt for use in the Church, a calendar indicating the Paschal full moons for seven cycles of sixteen years each; answering, according to the science of the period, to similar tables in the Anglican Book of Common Prayer. It indicates the days on which

Easter must fall, from a.d. 222 to a.d. 333. On the back of the chair is a list of the author's works.

Not less interesting, and vastly more important, was the discovery, at Mount Athos, in 1842, of the long-lost *Philosophumena* of this author, concerning which the important facts will appear below. Its learned editor, Emmanuel Miller, published it at Oxford under the name of Origen, which was inscribed on the ms. Like the Epistle of Clement, its composition in the Greek language had given it currency among the Easterns long after it was forgotten in the West; and very naturally they had ascribed to Origen an anonymous treatise containing much in coincidence with his teachings, and supplying the place of one of his works of a similar kind. It is now sufficiently established as the work of Hippolytus, and has been providentially brought to light just when it was most needed. In fact, the statue rose from its grave as if to rebuke the reigning pontiff (Pius IV.), who just then imposed upon the Latin churches the novel "Creed" which bears his name; and now the *Philosophumena* comes forth as if to breathe a last warning to that namesake of the former Pius who, in the very teeth of its testimony, so recently forged and uttered the dogma of "papal infallibility" conferring this attribute upon himself, and retrospectively upon the very bishops of Rome whom St. Hippolytus resisted as heretics, and has transmitted to posterity, in his writings, branded with the shame alike of false doctrine and of heinous crimes. Dr. Döllinger, who for a time lent his learning and genius to an apologetic effort in behalf of the Papacy, was no doubt prepared, by this very struggle of his heart *versus* head, for that rejection of the new dogma which overloaded alike his intellect and his conscience, and made it impossible for him any longer to bear the lashes of Rehoboam in communion with modern Rome.

In the biographical *data*, which will be found below, enough is supplied for the needs of the reader of the present series, who, if he wishes further to investigate the subject, will find the fullest information in the works to which reference has been made, or which will be hereafter indicated. But this is the place to recur to the much-abused passage of Irenæus which I have discussed in a former volume.[4] Strange to say, I was forced to correct, from a Roman-Catholic writer, the very unsatisfactory rendering of our Edinburgh editors, and to elucidate at some length the palpable absurdity of attributing to Irenæus any other than a geographical and imperial reference to the importance of Rome, and its usefulness to the West, more especially, as its only see of apostolic origin. Quoting the Ninth Antiochian Canon, I gave good reasons for my conjecture that the Latin *convenire* represents συντρέχειν in the original; and now it remains to be noted how strongly the real meaning of Irenæus is illustrated in the life and services of his pupil Hippolytus.

160

1. That neither Hippolytus nor his master had any conception that the See of Rome possesses any pre-eminent authority, to which others are obliged to defer, is conspicuously evident from the history of both. Alike they convicted Roman bishops of error, and alike they rebuked them for their misconduct.

2. Hippolytus is the author of a work called the *Little Labyrinth*, which, like the recently discovered *Philosophumena*, attributes to the Roman See anything but the "infallibility" which the quotation from Irenæus is so ingeniously wrested to sustain. How he did *not* understand the passage is, therefore, sufficiently apparent. Let us next inquire what appears, from his conduct, to be the true understanding of Irenæus.

3. I have shown, in the elucidation already referred to, how Irenæus affirms that Rome is the city which everybody visits from all parts, and that Christians, resorting thither, because it is the Imperial City, *carry into it* the testimony of all other churches. Thus it becomes a competent witness to the *quod ab omnibus*, because it cannot be ignorant of what all the churches teach with one accord. This argument, therefore, reverses the modern Roman dogma; primitive Rome *received* orthodoxy instead of prescribing it. She embosomed the Catholic testimony *brought into* it from all the churches, and gave it forth as reflected light; not primarily her own, but what she faithfully preserved in coincidence with older and more learned churches than herself. Doubtless she had been planted and watered by St. Paul and St. Peter; but doubtless, also, she had been expressly warned by the former of her liability to error and to final severance from apostolic communion. Hippolytus lived at a critical moment, when this awful admonition seemed about to be realized.

4. Now, then, from Portus and from Lyons, Hippolytus brought into Rome the Catholic doctrine, and convicted two of its bishops of pernicious heresies and evil living. And thus, as Irenæus teaches, the faith was preserved in Rome by the testimony of those *from every side resorting thither*, not by any prerogative of the See itself. All this will appear clearly enough as the student proceeds in the examination of this volume.

But it is now time to avail ourselves of the information given us by the translator in his Introductory Notice, as follows:—

The entire of *The Refutation of all Heresies*, with the exception of book i., was found in a ms. brought from a convent on Mount Athos so recently as the year 1842. The discoverer of this treasure—for treasure it certainly is—was Minöides Mynas, an erudite Greek, who had visited his native country in search of ancient mss., by direction of M. Abel Villemain, Minister of Public Instruction under Louis Philippe. The French

Government have thus the credit of being instrumental in bringing to light this valuable work, while the University of Oxford shares the distinction by being its earliest publishers. *The Refutation* was printed at the Clarendon Press in 1851, under the editorship of M. Emmanuel Miller, whose labours have proved serviceable to all subsequent commentators. One generally acknowledged mistake was committed by Miller in ascribing the work to Origen. He was right in affirming that the discovered ms. was the continuation of the fragment, *The Philosophumena*, inserted in the Benedictine copy of Origen's works. In the volume, however, containing the *Philosophumena*, we have dissertations by Huet, in which he questions Origen's authorship in favour of Epiphanius. Heuman attributed the *Philosophumena* to Didymus of Alexandria, Gale to Aetius; and it, with the rest of *The Refutation*, Fessler and Baur ascribed to Caius, but the Abbe Jellabert to Tertullian. The last hypothesis is untenable, if for no other reason, because the work is in Greek. In many respects, Caius, who was a presbyter of Rome in the time of Victor and Zephyrinus, would seem the probable author; but a fatal argument—one applicable to those named above, except Epiphanius—against Caius is his not being, as the author of *The Refutation* in the *Prooemium* declares himself to be, a bishop. Epiphanius no doubt filled the episcopal office; but when we have a large work of his on the heresies, with a summary, it would seem scarcely probable that he composed likewise, on the same topic, an extended treatise like the present, with two abridgments. Whatever diversity of opinion, however, existed as to these claimants, most critics, though not all, now agree in denying the authorship of Origen. Neither the style nor tone of *The Refutation* is Origenian. Its compilatory process is foreign to Origen's plan of composition; while the subject-matter itself, for many reasons, would not be likely to have occupied the pen of the Alexandrine Father. It is almost impossible but that Origen would have made some allusions in *The Refutation* to his other writings, or in them to it. Not only, however, is there no such allusion, but the derivation of the word "Ebionites," in *The Refutation*, and an expressed belief in the (orthodox) doctrine of eternal punishment, are at variance with Origen's authorship. Again, no work answering the description is awarded to Origen in catalogues of his extant or lost writings. These arguments are strengthened by the facts, that Origen was never a bishop, and that he did not reside for any length of time at Rome. He once paid a hurried visit to the capital of the West, whereas the author of *The Refutation* asserts his presence at Rome during the occurrence of events which occupied a period of some twenty years. And not only was he a spectator, but took part in these transactions in such an official and authoritative manner as Origen could never have assumed, either at Rome or elsewhere.

In this state of the controversy, commentators turned their attention towards Hippolytus, in favour of whose authorship the majority of modern scholars have decided. The arguments that have led to this conclusion, and those alleged by others against it, could not be adequately discussed in a notice like the present. Suffice it to say, that such names as Jacobi, Gieseler, Duncker, Schneidewin, Bernays, Bunsen, Wordsworth, and Döllinger, support the claims of Hippolytus. The testimony of Dr. Döllinger, considering the extent of his theological learning, and in particular his intimate acquaintance with the apostolic period in church history, virtually, we submit, decides the question.

For a biography of Hippolytus we have not much authentic materials. There can be no reasonable doubt but that he was a bishop, and passed the greater portion of his life in Rome and its vicinity. This assertion corresponds with the conclusion adopted by Dr. Döllinger, who, however, refuses to allow that Hippolytus was, as is generally maintained, Bishop of Portus, a harbour of Rome at the northern mouth of the Tiber, opposite Ostia. However, it is satisfactory to establish, and especially upon such eminent authority as that of Dr. Döllinger, the fact of Hippolytus' connection with the Western Church, not only because it bears on the investigation of the authorship of *The Refutation*, the writer of which affirms his personal observation of what he records as occurring in his own time at Rome, but also because it overthrows the hypothesis of those who contend that there were more Hippolytuses than one—Dr. Döllinger shows that there is only one historical Hippolytus—or that the East, and not Italy, was the sphere of his episcopal labours. Thus Le Moyne, in the seventeenth century, a French writer resident in Leyden, ingeniously argues that Hippolytus was bishop of *Portus Romanorum* (Aden), in Arabia. Le Moyne's theory was adopted by some celebrities, viz., Dupin, Tillemont, Spanheim, Basnage, and our own Dr. Cave. To this position are opposed, among others, the names of Nicephorus, Syncellus, Baronius, Bellarmine, Dodwell, Beveridge, Bull, and Archbishop Ussher. The judgment and critical accuracy of Ussher is, on a point of this kind, of the highest value. Wherefore the question of Hippolytus being bishop of Portus near Rome would also appear established, for the reasons laid down in Bunsen's *Letters to Archdeacon Hare*, and Canon Wordsworth's *St. Hippolytus*. The mind of inquirers appears to have been primarily unsettled in consequence of Eusebius' mentioning Hippolytus (*Ecclesiast. Hist.*, vi. 10) in company with Beryllus (of Bostra), an Arabian, expressing at the same time his uncertainty as to where Hippolytus was bishop. This indecision is easily explained, and cannot invalidate the tradition and historical testimony which assign the bishopric of Portus near Rome to Hippolytus, a saint and martyr of the Church. Of his martyrdom, though the fact itself is certain, the details, furnished in

Prudentius' hymn, are not historic. Thus the mode of Hippolytus' death is stated by Prudentius to have been identical with that of Hippolytus the son of Theseus, who was torn limb from limb by being tied to wild horses. St. Hippolytus, however, is known on historical testimony to have been thrown into a canal and drowned; but whether the scene of his martyrdom was Sardinia, to which he was undoubtedly banished along with the Roman bishop Pontianus, or Rome, or Portus, has not as yet been definitively proved. The time of his martyrdom, however, is probably a year or two, perhaps less or more, after the commencement of the reign of Maximin the Thracian, that is, somewhere about a.d. 235–39. This enables us to determine the age of Hippolytus; and as some statements in *The Refutation* evince the work to be the composition of an old man, and as the work itself was written after the death of Callistus in a.d. 222, this would transfer the period of his birth to not very long after the last half of the second century.

The contents of *The Refutation*, as they originally stood, seem to have been arranged thus: The first book (which we have) contained an account of the different schools of ancient philosophers; the second (which is missing), the doctrines and mysteries of the Egyptians; the third (likewise missing), the Chaldean science and astrology; and the fourth (the beginning of which is missing), the system of the Chaldean horoscope, and the magical rites and incantations of the Babylonian Theurgists. Next came the portion of the work relating more immediately to the heresies of the Church, which is contained in books v.–ix. The tenth book is the *résumé* of the entire, together with the exposition of the author's own religious opinions. The heresies enumerated by Hippolytus comprehend a period starting from an age prior to the composition of St. John's Gospel, and terminating with the death of Callistus. The heresies are explained according to chronological development, and may be ranged under five leading schools: (1) The Ophites; (1) Simonists; (3) Basilidians; (4) Docetæ; (5) Noetians. Hippolytus ascends to the origin of heresy, not only in assigning heterodoxy a derivative nature from heathenism, but in pointing out in the *Gnosis* elements of abnormal opinions antecedent to the promulgation of Christianity. We have thus a most interesting account of the early heresies, which in some respects supplies many *desiderata* in the ecclesiastical history of this epoch.

We can scarcely over-estimate the value of *The Refutation*, on account of the propinquity of its author to the apostolic age. Hippolytus was a disciple of St. Irenæus, St. Irenæus of St. Polycarp, St. Polycarp of St. John. Indeed, one fact of grave importance connected with the writings of St. John, is elicited from Hippolytus' *Refutation*. The passage given out of Basilides' work, containing a quotation by the heretic from St. John 1:9, settles the period of the composition of the fourth Gospel, as of greater antiquity by at least thirty years than is allowed to it by the Tübingen school. It is therefore obvious that Basilides formed his system out of the prologue of St. John's Gospel; thus for ever setting at rest the allegation of these critics, that St. John's Gospel was written at a later date, and assigned an apostolic author, in order to silence the Basilidian Gnostics. In the case of Irenæus, too, The Refutation has restored the Greek text of much of his book Against Heresies, hitherto only known to us in a Latin version. Nor is the value of Hippolytus' work seriously impaired, even on the supposition of the authorship not being proved,—a concession, however, in no wise justified by the evidence. Whoever the writer of The Refutation be, he belonged to the early portion of the third century, formed his compilations from primitive sources, made conscientious preparation for his undertaking, delivered statements confirmed by early writers of note, and lastly, in the execution of his task, furnished indubitable marks of information and research, and of having thoroughly mastered the relations and affinities, each to other, of the various heresies of the first two and a quarter centuries. These heresies, whether deducible from attempts to Christianize the philosophy of Paganism, or to interpret the Doctrines and Life of our Lord by the tenets of Gnosticism and Oriental speculation generally, or to create a compromise with the pretensions of Judaism,—these heresies, amid all their complexity and diversity, St. Hippolytus[3] reduces to one common ground of censure—antagonism to Holy Scripture. Heresy, thus branded, he leaves to wither under the condemnatory sentence of the Church.[93]

---

[93] Alexander Roberts, James Donaldson, and A. Cleveland Coxe, eds., "Introductory Notice to Hippolytus," in Fathers of the Third Century: Hippolytus, Cyprian, Novatian, Appendix, vol. 5, The Ante-Nicene Fathers (Buffalo, NY: Christian Literature Company, 1886), 3–7.

EARLY CHRISTIANITY 16 Theophilus of Antioch - Valuable Testimony

[A.D. 115–168–181.] Eusebius praises the pastoral fidelity of the primitive pastors, in their unwearied labours to protect their flocks from the heresies with which Satan contrived to endanger the souls of believers. By exhortations and admonitions, and then again by *oral discussions* and refutations, contending with the heretics themselves, they were prompt to ward off the devouring beasts from the fold of Christ. Such is the praise due to Theophilus, in his opinion; and he cites especially his lost work against Marcion as "of no mean character." He was one of the earliest commentators upon the Gospels, if not the first; and he seems to have been the earliest Christian historian of the Church of the Old Testament. His only remaining work, here presented, seems to have originated in an "oral discussion," such as Eusebius instances. But nobody seems to accord him due praise as the founder of the science of *Biblical Chronology* among Christians, save that his great successor in modern times, Abp. Usher, has not forgotten to pay him this tribute in the *Prolegomena* of his Annals. (*Ed*. Paris, 1673.)

Theophilus occupies an interesting position, after Ignatius, in the succession of faithful men who represented Barnabas and other prophets and teachers of Antioch, in that ancient seat, from which comes our name as Christians. I cannot forbear another reference to those recent authors who have so brilliantly illustrated and depicted the Antioch of the early Christians;[3] because, if we wish to understand Autolycus, we must *feel* the state of society which at once fascinated him, and disgusted Theophilus. The Fathers are dry to those only who lack imagination to reproduce their age, or who fail to study them geographically and chronologically. Besides this, one should bring to the study of their works, that sympathy springing from a burning love to Christ, which borrows its motto, in slightly altered words, from the noble saying of the African poet: "I am a *Christian*, and nothing which concerns *Christianity* do I consider foreign to myself."

Theophilus comes down to us only as an apologist intimately allied in spirit to Justin and Irenæus; and he should have been placed with Tatian between these two, in our series, had not the inexorable laws of our compilation brought them into this volume. I need add no more to what follows from the translator, save only the expression of a hope that others will enjoy this author as I do, rating him very highly, even at the side of Athenagoras. He is severe, yet gentle too, in dealing with his antagonist; and he cannot be charged with a more sublime contempt for heathenism than St. Paul betrays in all his writings, abjuring even Plato and Socrates, and accentuating his maxim, "The world by wisdom knew not God." For him it was *Christ* to live; and I love Theophilus for this very fault, if it be such. He was of Antioch; and was content to be, simply and altogether, nothing but a Christian.

The following is the original Introductory Notice:—

Little is known of the personal history of Theophilus of Antioch. We gather from the following treatise that he was born a pagan (i. 14), and owed his conversion to Christianity to the careful study of the Holy Scriptures. Eusebius (*Hist. Eccl.*, iv. 20) declares that he was the sixth bishop of Antioch in Syria from the apostles, the names of his supposed predecessors being Eros, Cornelius, Hero, Ignatius, and Euodius. We also learn from the same writer, that Theophilus succeeded to the bishopric of Antioch in the eighth year of the reign of Marcus Aurelius, that is, in a.d. 168. He is related to have died either in a.d. 181, or in a.d. 188; some assigning him an episcopate of thirteen, and others of twenty-one, years.

Theophilus is said by Eusebius, Jerome, and others, to have written several works against the heresies which prevailed in his day. He himself refers in the following treatise (ii. 30) to another of his compositions. Commentaries on the Gospels, arranged in the form of a harmony, and on the Book of Proverbs, are also ascribed to him by Jerome; but the sole remaining specimen of his writings consists of the three books that follow, addressed to his friend Autolycus. The occasion which called these forth is somewhat doubtful. It has been thought that they were written in refutation of a work which Autolycus had published against Christianity; but the more probable opinion is, that they were drawn forth by disparaging remarks made in conversation. The language of the writer (ii. 1) leads to this conclusion.

In handling his subject, Theophilus goes over much the same ground as Justin Martyr and the rest of the early apologists. He is somewhat fond of fanciful interpretations of Scripture; but he evidently had a profound acquaintance with the inspired writings, and he powerfully exhibits their immense superiority in every respect over the heathen poetry and philosophy. The whole treatise was well fitted to lead on an intelligent pagan to the cordial acceptance of Christianity[94]

---

[94] Alexander Roberts, James Donaldson, and A. Cleveland Coxe, eds., "Introductory Note to Theophilus of Antioch," in *Fathers of the Second Century: Hermas, Tatian, Athenagoras, Theophilus, and Clement of Alexandria (Entire)*, vol. 2, The Ante-Nicene Fathers (Buffalo, NY: Christian Literature Company, 1885), 87–88.

EARLY CHRISTIANITY 17 Origen – Zealous for the Church

[A.D. 185–230–254.] The reader will remember the rise and rapid development of the great Alexandrian school, and the predominance which was imparted to it by the genius of the illustrious Clement. But in Origen, his pupil, who succeeded him at the surprising age of eighteen, a new sun was to rise upon its noontide. Truly was Alexandria "the mother and mistress of churches" in the benign sense of a nurse and instructress of Christendom, not its arrogant and usurping imperatrix.

The full details of Origen's troubled but glorious career are given by Dr. Crombie, who in my opinion deserves thanks for the kind and apologetic temper of his estimate of the man and the sublime doctor, as well as of the period of his life. Upon the fervid spirit of a confessor in an age of cruelty, lust, and heathenism, what right have we to sit in judgment? Of one whose very errors were virtues at their source, how can a Christian of our self-indulgent times presume to speak in censure? Well might the Psalmist exclaim, "Let us fall now into the hand of the Lord; for His mercies are great: let me not fall into the hand of man."

Justly has it been urged that to those whose colossal labours during the ante-Nicene period exposed them to hasty judgment, and led them into mistakes, much indulgence must be shown. The language of theology was but assuming shape under their processes, and we owe them an incalculable debt of gratitude: but it was not yet moulded into precision; nor had great councils, presided over by the Holy Ghost, as yet afforded those safeguards to freedom of thought which gradually defined the limits of orthodoxy. To no single teacher did the Church defer. Holy Scripture and the *quod ab omnibus* were the grand *prescription*, against which no individual prelate or doctor could prevail, against which no see could uplift a voice, without chastisement and subjection. Over and over again were the bishops of patriarchal and apostolic sees, including Rome, adjudged heretics, and anathematized by the inexorable law of truth, and of "the faith once delivered to the saints," which not even "an angel from heaven" might presume to change or to enlarge. But before the great Synodical period (a.d. 325 to 451), while orthodoxy is marvellously maintained and witnessed to by Origen and Tertullian themselves, their errors, however serious, have never separated them from the grateful and loving regard of those upon whom their lives of heroic sorrow and suffering have conferred blessings unspeakable. The Church cannot leave their errors uncorrected. Their persons she leaves to the Master's award: their characters she cherishes, while their faults she deplores.

The great feature of the ante-Nicene theology, even in the mistakes of the writers, is its reliance on the Holy Scripture. What wealth of Scripture they lavish in their pages! We identify the Scriptures by their aid; but, were they lost in other forms, we might almost restore them from their pages. And forever is the Church indebted to Origen for the patient and encyclopedic labour and learning which he bestowed on the Scriptures in producing his *Hexapla*. Would that, in his interpretations of the inspired text, he had more strictly adhered to the counsels of Leonides, who was of Bacon's opinion, that the meanings which flow naturally from the holy text are sweetest and best, even as that wine is best which is not crushed out and extorted from the grape, but which trickles of itself from the ripe and luscious cluster in all its purity and natural flavour. So Hooker remarks; and his view is commonly accepted by critics, that the interpretation of a text which departeth most from its natural rendering is commonly the worst.

It is too striking an illustration of the childlike simplicity of the primitive faithful to be passed by, in Origen's history, that anecdote of his father, Leonides, who was himself a confessor and martyr: how he used to strip the bosom of his almost inspired boy as he lay asleep, and imprint kisses on his naked breast, "the temple of the Holy Ghost." That blessed Spirit, he believed, was near to his own lips when he thus saluted a Christian child, "for of such is the kingdom of heaven." From a child, this other Timothy "knew the Scriptures" indeed. His own doting father imbued him with the literature of the Greeks. but, far better, he taught him to love the lively oracles of the Lord of glory; and in these he became so proficient, even from tender years, that he puzzled his parent with his "understanding and answers," like the holy Child of Nazareth when He heard the doctors in the Temple, and also "asked them questions." In will he was also a martyr from his youth, and to the genuine spirit of martyrdom we must attribute that heroic fault of his youth which he lived to condemn in riper years, and which, evil and rash as it was, enabled the Church, once and for all, to give an authoritative interpretation to the language of the Saviour, and to guard her children thenceforth from similar exploits of pious mistake. None can doubt the purity of the motive. Few draw the important inference of the nature of the Church's conflict with that intolerable prevalence of sensuality and shameless vice which so impressed her children with the import of Christ's words, "Blessed are the pure in heart: for they shall see God."

Here follows the very full account of the life of Origen by Dr. Crombie, professor of biblical criticism in St. Mary's College, St. Andrew:—

Origen, surnamed Adamantinus, was born in all probability at Alexandria, about the year 185 a.d. Notwithstanding that his name is derived from that of an Egyptian deity,[2] there seems no reason to doubt that his parents were Christian at the time of his birth. His father Leonides was probably, as has been conjectured, one of the many teachers of rhetoric or grammar who abounded in that city of Grecian culture, and appears to have been a man of decided piety. Under his superintendence, the youthful Origen was not only educated in the various branches of Grecian learning, but was also required daily to commit to memory and to repeat portions of Scripture prescribed him by his father; and while under this training, the spirit of inquiry into the meaning of Scripture, which afterwards formed so striking a feature in the literary character of the great Alexandrine, began to display itself. Eusebius[4] relates that he was not satisfied with the plain and obvious meaning of the text, but sought to penetrate into its deeper signification, and caused his father trouble by the questions which he put to him regarding the sense of particular passages of Holy Writ. Leonides, like many parents, assumed the appearance of rebuking the curiosity of the boy for inquiring into things which were beyond his youthful capacity, and recommended him to be satisfied with the simple and apparent meaning of Scripture, while he is described as inwardly rejoicing at the signs of genius exhibited by his son, and as giving thanks to God for having made him the parent of such a child. But this state of things was not to last; for in the year 202 when Origen was about seventeen years of age, the great persecution of the Christians under Septimius Severus broke out, and among the victims was his father Leonides, who was apprehended and put in prison. Origen wished to share the fate of his father, but was prevented from quitting his home by the artifice of his mother, who was obliged to conceal his clothes to prevent him from carrying out his purpose. He wrote to his father, however, a letter, exhorting him to constancy under his trials, and entreating him not to change his convictions for the sake of his family.[2] By the death of his father, whose property was confiscated to the imperial treasury, Origen was left, with his mother and six younger brothers dependent upon him for support. At this juncture, a wealthy and benevolent lady of Alexandria opened to him her house, of which he became an inmate for a short time. The society, however, which he found there was far from agreeable to the feelings of the youth. The lady had adopted as her son one Paul of Antioch, whom Eusebius terms an "advocate of the heretics then existing at Alexandria." The eloquence of the man drew crowds to hear him, although Origen could never be induced to regard him with any favour, nor even to join with him in any act of worship, giving then, as Eusebius remarks, "unmistakeable specimens of the orthodoxy of his faith."

Finding his position in his household so uncomfortable, he resolved to enter upon the career of a teacher of grammar, and to support himself by his own exertions. As he had been carefully instructed by his father in Grecian literature, and had devoted himself to study after his death, he was enabled successfully to carry out his intention. And now begins the second stadium of his career.

The diligence and ability with which Origen prosecuted his profession speedily attracted attention and brought him many pupils. Among others who sought to avail themselves of his instructions in the principles of the Christian religion, were two young men, who afterwards became distinguished in the history of the Church,—Plutarch, who died the death of martyrdom, and Heraclas, who afterwards became bishop of Alexandria. It was not, however, merely by his success as a teacher that Origen gained a reputation. The brotherly kindness and unwearied affection which he displayed to all the victims of the persecution, which at that time was raging with peculiar severity at Alexandria under the prefect Aquila, and in which many of his old pupils and friends were martyred, are described as being so marked and conspicuous, as to draw down upon him the fury of the mob, so that he was obliged on several occasions to flee from house to house to escape instant death. It is easy to understand that services of this kind could not fail to attract the attention of the heads of the Christian community at Alexandria; and partly, no doubt, because of these, but chiefly on account of his high literary reputation, Bishop Demetrius appointed him to the office of master in the Catechetical School, which was at that time vacant (by the departure of Clement, who had quitted the city on the outbreak of the persecution), although he was still a layman, and had not passed his eighteenth year. The choice of Demetrius was amply justified by the result. Origen discontinued his instructions in literature, in order to devote himself exclusively to the work of teaching in the Catechetical School. For his labours he refused all remuneration. He sold the books which he possessed,—many of them manuscripts which he himself had copied,—on condition of receiving from the purchaser four obols a day; and on this scanty pittance he subsisted, leading for many years a life of the greatest asceticism and devotion to study. After a day of labour in the school, he used to devote the greater part of the night to the investigation of Scripture, sleeping on the bare ground, and keeping frequent fasts. He carried out literally the command of the Saviour, not to possess two coats, nor wear shoes. He consummated his work of mortification of the flesh by an act of self-mutilation, springing from a perverted interpretation of our Lord's words in Matthew 19:12, and the desire to place himself beyond the reach of temptation in the intercourse which he necessarily had to hold with youthful female catechumens. This act was destined to exercise a baneful influence upon his subsequent career in the Church.

During the episcopate of Zephyrinus (201–218) Origen visited Rome, and on his return again resumed his duties in the Catechetical School, transferring the care of the younger catechumens to his friend and former pupil Heraclas, that he might devote himself with less distraction to the instruction of the more advanced, and to the more thorough investigation and exposition of Scripture. With a view to accomplish this more successfully, it is probable that about this time he set himself to acquire a knowledge of the Hebrew language, the fruit of which may be seen in the fragments which remain to us of his *magnum opus*, the *Hexapla*; and as many among the more cultured heathens, attracted by his reputation, seem to have attended his lectures, he felt it necessary to make himself more extensively acquainted with the doctrines of the Grecian schools, that he might meet his opponents upon their own ground, and for this purpose he attended the prelections of Ammonius Saccas, at that time in high repute at Alexandria as an expounder of the Neo-Platonic philosophy, of which school he has generally been considered the founder. The influence which the study of philosophical speculations exerted upon the mind of Origen may be traced in the whole course of his after development, and proved the fruitful source of many of those errors which were afterwards laid to his charge, and the controversies arising out of which disturbed the peace of the Church during the two following centuries. As was to be expected, the fame of the great Alexandrine teacher was not confined to his native city, but spread far and wide; and an evidence of this was the request made by the Roman governor of the province of Arabia to Demetrius and to the prefect of Egypt, that they would send Origen to him that he might hold an interview with one whose reputation was so great. We have no details of this visit, for all that Eusebius relates is that, "having accomplished the objects of his journey, he again returned to Alexandria." It was in the year 216 that the Emperor Caracalla visited Alexandria, and directed a bloody persecution against its inhabitants, especially the literary members of the community, in revenge for the sarcastic verses which had been composed against him for the murder of his brother Geta, a crime which he had perpetrated under circumstances of the basest treachery and cruelty.

Origen occupied too prominent a position in the literary Society of the city to be able to remain with safety, and therefore withdrew to Palestine to his friend Bishop Alexander of Jerusalem, and afterwards to Cæsarea, where he received an honourable welcome from Bishop Theoctistus. This step proved the beginning of his after troubles. These two men, filled with becoming admiration for the most learned teacher in the Church, requested him to expound the Scriptures in their presence in a public assembly of the Christians. Origen, although still a layman, and without any sacerdotal dignity in the Church, complied with the request. When this proceeding reached the ears of Demetrius, he was filled with the utmost indignation. "Such an act was never either heard or done before, that laymen should deliver discourses in the presence of the bishops," was his indignant remonstrance to the two offending bishops, and Origen received a command to return immediately to Alexandria. He obeyed, and for some years appears to have devoted himself solely to his studies in his usual spirit of self-abnegation.

It was probably during this period that the commencement of his friendship with Ambrosius is to be dated. Little is known of this individual. Eusebius states that he had formerly been an adherent of the Valentinian heresy, but had been converted by the arguments and eloquence of Origen to the orthodox faith of the Church. They became intimate friends; and as Ambrose seems to have been possessed of large means, and entertained an unbounded admiration of the learning and abilities of his friend, it was his delight to bear the expenses attending the transcription and publication of the many works which he persuaded him to give to the world. He furnished him "with more than seven amanuenses, who relieved each other at stated times, and with an equal number of transcribers, along with young girls who had been practiced in calligraphy," to make fair copies for publication of the works dictated by Origen. The literary activity of these years must have been prodigious, and probably they were among the happiest which Origen ever enjoyed. Engaged in his favourite studies, surrounded by many friends, adding yearly to his own stores of learning, and enriching the literature of the Church with treatises of the highest value in the department of sacred criticism and exegesis, it is difficult to conceive a condition of things more congenial to the mind of a true scholar. Only one incident of any importance seems to have taken place during these peaceful years,—his visit to Julia Mammæa, the pious mother of Alexander Severus. This noble lady had heard of the fame of Origen, and invited him to visit her at Antioch, sending a military escort to conduct him from Alexandria to the Syrian capital. He remained with her some time, "exhibiting innumerable illustrations of the glory of the Lord, and of the excellence of divine instruction, and then hastened back to his accustomed studies."[2]

These happy years, however, were soon to end. Origen was called to Greece, probably about the year 228, upon what Eusebius vaguely calls "the pressing need of ecclesiastical affairs."[4] But, this has generally been understood to refer to the prevalence of heretical views in the Church there, for the eradication of which the assistance of Origen was invoked. Before entering on this journey, he obtained letters of recommendation from his bishop.[6] He passed through Palestine on his way to Greece, and at Cæsarea received at the bands of his friends Alexander and Theoctistus ordination to the office of presbyter,—an honour which proved to him afterwards the source of much persecution and annoyance. No doubt the motives of his friends were of the highest kind, and among them may have been the desire to take away the ground of objection formerly raised by Demetrius against the public preaching of a mere layman in the presence of a bishop. But they little dreamed of the storm which this act of theirs was to raise, and of the consequences which it was to bring upon the head of him whom they had sought to honour. After completing his journey through Greece, Origen returned to Alexandria about the year 230. He there found his bishop greatly incensed against him for what had taken place at Cæsarea. Nor did his anger expend itself in mere objurgations and rebukes. In the year 231 a synod was summoned by Demetrius, composed of Egyptian bishops and Alexandrian presbyters, who declared Origen unworthy to hold the office of teacher, and excommunicated him from the fellowship of the Church of Alexandria. Even this did not satisfy the vindictive feeling of Demetrius. He summoned a second synod, in which the bishops alone were permitted to vote, and by their suffrages Origen was degraded from the office of presbyter, and intimation of this sentence was ordered to be made by encyclical letter to the various Churches. The validity of the sentence was recognised by all of them, with the exception of those in Palestine, Phœnicia, Arabia, and Achaia; a remarkable proof of the position of influence which was at that time held by the Church of Alexandria. Origen appears to have quitted the city before the bursting of the storm, and betook himself to Cæsarea, which henceforth became his home, and the seat of his labours for a period of nearly a quarter of a century. The motives which impelled Demetrius to this treatment of Origen have been variously stated and variously criticised. Eusebius refers his readers for a full account of all the matters involved to the treatise which he and Pamphilus composed in his defence; but this work has not come down to us,[2] although we possess a brief notice of it in the *Bibliotheca* of Photius, from which we derive our knowledge of the proceedings of the two synods. There seems little reason to doubt that jealousy of interference on the part of the bishops of another diocese was one main cause of the resentment displayed by Demetrius; while it is also possible that another alleged cause, the heterodox character of some of Origen's opinions, as made known in his already published works, among which were his *Stromata* and *De Principiis*, may have produced some effect upon the minds of the hostile bishops. Hefele[5] asserts that the act of the Palestinian bishops was contrary to the Church law of the time, and that Demetrius was justified on that ground for his procedure against him. But it may well be doubted whether there was any generally understood law or practice existing at so early a period of the Church's history. If so, it is difficult to understand how it should have been unknown to the Palestinian bishops; or, on the supposition of any such existing law or usage, it is equally difficult to conceive that either they themselves or Origen should have agreed to disregard it, knowing as they did the jealous temper of Demetrius, displayed on the occasion of Origen's preaching at Cæsarea already referred to. This had drawn from the Alexandrine bishop an indignant remonstrance, in which he had asserted that such an act was "quite unheard of before;" but, to this statement the Cæsarean bishops replied in a letter, in which they enumerated several instances of laymen who had addressed the congregation.[7] The probabilities, therefore, are in favour of there being no generally understood law or practice on the subject, and that the procedure, therefore, was dictated by hierarchical jealousy on the part of Demetrius. According to Eusebius, indeed, the act of mutilation already referred to was made a ground of accusation against Origen; and there seems no doubt that there existed an old canon of the Church,[9] based upon the words in Deuteronomy 23:1, which rendered one who had committed such an act ineligible for office in the Church. But there is no trace of this act, as disqualifying Origen for the office of presbyter, having been urged by Demetrius, so far as can be discovered from the notices of the two synods which have been preserved by Rufinus and Photius. And it seems extremely probable, as Redepenning remarks, that if Demetrius were acquainted with this act of Origen, as Eusebius says he was[11] he made no public mention of it, far less that he made it a pretence for his deposition.

Demetrius did not long survive the execution of his vengeance against his unfortunate catechist. He died about a year afterwards, and was succeeded by Heraclas, the friend and former pupil of Origen. It does not, however, appear that Heraclas made any effort to have the sentence against Origen recalled, so that he might return to the early seat of his labours. Origen devoted himself at Cæsarea chiefly to exegetical studies upon the books of Scripture, enjoying the countenance and friendship of the two bishops Alexander and Theoctistus, who are said by Eusebius "to have attended him the whole time as pupils do their master." He speedily raised the theological school of that city to a degree of reputation which attracted many pupils. Among those who placed themselves under his instructions were two young Cappadocians, who had come to Cæsarea with other intentions, but who were so attracted by the whole character and personality of Origen, that they immediately became his pupils. The former of these, afterwards Gregory Thaumaturgus, Bishop of New Cæsarea, has left us, in the panegyric which he wrote after a discipleship of five years, a full and admiring account of the method of his great master.

The persecution under the Emperor Maximin obliged Origen to take refuge in Cæsarea in Cappadocia, where he remained in concealment about two years in the house of a Christian lady named Juliana, who was the heiress of Symmachus, the Ebionite translator of the Septuagint, and from whom he obtained several mss. which had belonged to Symmachus. Here, also, he composed his *Exhortation to Martyrdom*, which was expressly written for the sake of his friends Ambrosius and Protoctetus, who had been imprisoned on account of their Christian profession, but who recovered their freedom after the death of Maximin,—an event which allowed Origen to return to the Palestinian Cæsarea and to the prosecution of his labours. A visit to Athens, where he seems to have remained some time, and to Bostra in Arabia, in order to bring back to the true faith Bishop Beryllus, who had expressed heterodox opinions upon the subject of the divinity of Christ, (in which attempt he proved successful,) were the chief events of his life during the next five years. On the outbreak of the Decian persecution, however, in 249, he was imprisoned at Tyre, to which city he had gone from Cæsarea for some unknown reason, and was made to suffer great cruelties by his persecutors. The effect of these upon a frame worn out by ascetic labours may be easily conceived. Although he survived his imprisonment, his body was so weakened by his sufferings, that he died at Tyre in 254, in the seventieth year of his age.

The character of Origen is singularly pure and noble; for his moral qualities are as remarkable as his intellectual gifts. The history of the Church records the names of few whose patience and meekness under unmerited suffering were more conspicuous than his. How very differently would Jerome have acted under circumstances like those which led to Origen's banishment from Alexandria! And what a favourable contrast is presented by the self-denying asceticism of his whole life, to the sins which stained the early years of Augustine, prior to his conversion! The impression which his whole personality made upon those who came within the sphere of his influence is evidenced in a remarkable degree by the admiring affection displayed towards him by his friend Ambrose and his pupil Gregory. Nor was it friends alone that he so impressed. To him belongs the rare honour of convincing heretics of their errors, and of leading them back to the Church; a result which must have been due as much to the gentleness and earnestness of his Christian character, as to the prodigious learning, marvellous acuteness, and logical power, which entitle him to be regarded as the greatest of the Fathers. It is singular, indeed, that a charge of heresy should have been brought, not only after his death, but even during his life, against one who rendered such eminent services to the cause of orthodox Christianity. But this charge must be considered in reference to the times when he lived and wrote.

No General Council had yet been held to settle authoritatively the doctrine of the Church upon any of those great questions, the discussion of which convulsed the Christian world during the two following centuries; and in these circumstances greater latitude was naturally permissible than would have been justifiable at a later period. Moreover, a mind so speculative as that of Origen, and so engrossed with the deepest and most difficult problems of human thought, must sometimes have expressed itself in a way liable to be misunderstood. But no doubt the chief cause of his being regarded as a heretic is to be found in the haste with which he allowed many of his writings to be published. Had he considered more carefully what he intended to bring before the public eye, less occasion would have been furnished to objectors, and the memory of one of the greatest scholars and most devoted Christians that the world has ever seen would have been freed, to a great extent at least, from the reproach of heresy.

Origen was a very voluminous author. Jerome says that he wrote more than any individual could read; and Epiphanius relates that his writings amounted to 6,000 volumes, by which statement we are probably to understand that every individual treatise, large or small, including each of the numerous homilies, was counted as a separate volume. The admiration entertained for him by his friend Ambrosius, and the readiness with which the latter bore all the expenses of transcription and publication, led Origen to give to the world much which otherwise would never have seen the light.

The works of the great Adamantinus may be classed under the following divisions:—

(1) exegetical works

These comprise Σχόλια, brief notes on Scripture, of which only fragments remain: Τόμοι, Commentaries, lengthened expositions, of which we possess considerable portions, including those on Matthew, John, and Epistle to the Romans; and about 200 Homilies, upon the principal books of the Old and New Testaments, a full list of which may be seen in Migne's edition. In these works his peculiar system of interpretation found ample scope for exercise; and although he carried out his principle of allegorizing many things, which in their historical and literal signification offended his exegetical sense, he nevertheless maintains that "the passages which hold good in their historical acceptation are much more numerous than those which contain a purely spiritual meaning." The student will find much that is striking and suggestive in his remarks upon the various passages which he brings under review. For an account of his method of interpreting Scripture, and the grounds on which he based it, the reader may consult the fourth book of the treatise *On the Principles*.

(2) critical works

The great critical work of Origen was the Hexapla or Six-columned Bible; an attempt to provide a revised text of the Septuagint translation of Old Testament Scripture. On this undertaking he is said to have spent eight-and-twenty years of his life, and to have acquired a knowledge of Hebrew in order to qualify himself for the task. Each page of this work consisted, with the exception to be noticed immediately, of six columns. In the first was placed the current Hebrew text; in the second, the same represented in *Greek* letters; in the third, the version of Aquila; in the fourth, that of Symmachus; in the fifth, the text of the LXX., as it existed at the time; and in the sixth, the version of Theodotion. Having come into possession also of certain other Greek translations of some of the books of Scripture, he added these in their appropriate place, so that the work presented in some parts the appearance of seven, eight, or nine columns, and was termed Heptapla, Octopla, or Enneapla, in consequence. He inserted critical marks in the text of the LXX., an asterisk to denote what ought to be added, and an obelus to denote what ought to be omitted; taking the additions chiefly from the version of Theodotion. The work, with the omission of the Hebrew column, and that representing the Hebrew in Greek letters, was termed Tetrapla; and with regard to it, it is uncertain whether it is to be considered a preliminary work on the part of Origen, undertaken by way of preparation for the larger, or merely as an excerpt from the latter. The whole extended, it is said, to nearly fifty volumes, and was, of course, far too bulky for common use, and too costly for transcription. It was placed in some repository in the city of Tyre, from which it was removed after Origen's death to the library at Cæsarea, founded by Pamphilus, the friend of Eusebius. It is supposed to have been burnt at the capture of Cæsarea by the Arabs in 653 a.d. The column, however, containing the version of the LXX. had been copied by Pamphilus and Eusebius, along with the critical marks of Origen, although, owing to carelessness on the part of subsequent transcribers, the text was soon again corrupted. The remains of this work were published by Montfaucon at Paris, 1713, 2 vols. folio; by Bahrdt at Leipsic in 1769; and is at present again in course of publication from the Clarendon press, Oxford, under the editorship of Mr. Field, who has made use of the Syriac-Hexaplar version, and has added various fragments not contained in prior editions. (For a full and critical account of this work, the English reader is referred to Dr. Sam. Davidson's *Biblical Criticism*, vol. i. ch. xii., which has been made use of for the above notice.)

(3) apologetical works

His great apologetical work was the treatise undertaken at the special request of his friend Ambrosius, in answer to the attack of the heathen philosopher Celsus on the Christian religion, in a work which he entitled Λόγος ἀληθής, or *A True Discourse*. Origen states that he had heard that there were two individuals of this name, both of them Epicureans, the earlier of the two having lived in the time of Nero, and the other in the time of Adrian, or later. Redepenning is of opinion that Celsus must have composed his work in the time of Marcus Aurelius (161–180 a.d.), on account of his supposed mention of the Marcionites (whose leader did not make his appearance at Rome before 142 a.d.), and of the Marcellians (followers of the Carpocratian Marcellina), a sect which was founded after the year 155 a.d. under Bishop Anicetus. Origen believed his opponent to be an Epicurean, but to have adopted other doctrines than those of Epicurus, because he thought that by so doing he could assail Christianity to greater advantage.[3] The work which Origen composed in answer to the so-styled *True Discourse* consists of eight books, and belongs to the latest years of his life. It has always been regarded as the great apologetic work of antiquity; and no one can peruse it without being struck by the multifarious reading, wonderful acuteness, and rare subtlety of mind which it displays. But the rule which Origen prescribed to himself, of not allowing a single objection of his opponent to remain unanswered, leads him into a minuteness of detail, and into numerous repetitions, which fatigue the reader, and detract from the interest and unity of the work. He himself confesses that he began it on one plan, and carried it out on another. No doubt, had he lived to re-write and condense it, it would have been more worthy of his reputation. But with all its defects, it is a great work, and well deserves the notice of the students of Apologetics. The table of contents subjoined to the translation will convey a better idea of its nature than any description which our limits would permit us to give.

(4) dogmatic works

These include the Στρωματεῖς, a work composed in imitation of the treatise of Clement of the same name, and consisting originally of ten books, of which only three fragments exist in a Latin version by Jerome; a treatise on the Resurrection, of which four fragments remain;[6] and the treatise Περὶ Ἀρχῶν, *De Principiis*, which contains Origen's views on various questions of systematic theology. The work has come down to us in the Latin translation of his admirer Rufinus; but, from a comparison of the few fragments of the original Greek which have been preserved, we see that Rufinus was justly chargeable with altering many of Origen's expressions, in order to bring his doctrine on certain points more into harmony with the orthodox views of the time. The *De Principiis* consists of four books, and is the first of the works of Origen in this series, to which we refer the reader.

(5) Practical Works

Under this head we place the little treatise Περὶ Εὐχῆς, *On Prayer*, written at the instance of his friend Ambrose, and which contains an exposition of the Lord's Prayer; the Λόγος προτρεπτικὸς εἰς μαρτύριον, *Exhortation to Martyrdom*, composed at the outbreak of the persecution by Maximian, when his friends Ambrose and Protoctetus were imprisoned. Of his numerous letters only two have come down entire, viz., that which was addressed to Julius Africanus, who had questioned the genuineness of the history of Susanna in the apocryphal additions to the book of Daniel, and that to Gregory Thaumaturgus on the use of Greek philosophy in the explanation of Scripture, although, from the brevity of the latter, it is questionable whether it is more than a fragment of the original. The Φιλοκαλία, *Philocalia*, was a compilation from the writings of Origen, intended to explain the difficult passages of Scripture, and executed by Basil the Great and Gregory of Nazianzum; large extracts of which have been preserved, especially of that part which was taken from the treatise against Celsus. The remains were first printed at Paris in 1618, and again at Cambridge in 1676, in the reprint of Spencer's edition of the *Contra Celsum*. In the Benedictine edition, and in Migne's reprint, the various portions are quoted in foot-notes under the respective passages of Origen's writings.

(6) Editions of Origin

The first published works of Origen were his Homilies, which appeared in 1475, although neither the name of the publisher nor the place of publication is given. These were followed by the treatise against Celsus in the translation of Christopher Persana, which appeared at Rome in 1481; and this, again, by an edition of the Homilies at Venice in 1503, containing those on the first four books of Moses, Joshua, and Judges. The first collective edition of the whole works was given to the world in a Latin translation by James Merlin, and was published in two folio volumes, first at Paris in 1512 and 1519, and afterwards at Paris in 1522 and 1530. A revision of Merlin's edition was begun by Erasmus, and completed, after his death, by Beatus Rhenanus. This appeared at Basle in 1536 in two folio volumes, and again in 1557 and 1571. A much better and more complete edition was undertaken by the Benedictine Gilbertus Genebrardus, which was published also in two volumes folio at Paris in 1574, and again in 1604 and 1619. Hoeschel published the treatise against Celsus at Augsburg in 1605; Spencer, at Cambridge in 1658 and 1677, to which was added the *Philocalia*, which had first appeared in a Latin translation by Genebrardus, and afterwards in Greek by Tarinus at Paris in 1618 and 1624, in quarto. Huet, Bishop of Avranches, published the exegetical writings in Greek, including the Commentaries on Matthew and John, in two volumes folio, of which the one appeared at Rouen in 1668, and the other at Paris in 1679. The great edition by the two learned Benedictines of St. Maur—Charles de la Rue, and his nephew Vincent de la Rue—was published at Paris between the years 1733 and 1759. This is a work of immense industry and labour, and remains the standard to the present time. It has been reprinted by Migne in his series of the Greek Fathers, in nine volumes, large 8vo. In Oberthür's series of the Greek Fathers, seven volumes contain the chief portion of Origen's writings; while Lommatzsch has published the whole in twenty-five small volumes, Berlin, 1831–48, containing the Greek text alone.

For further information upon the life and opinions of Origen, the reader may consult Redepenning's *Origenes*, 2 vols., Bonn, 1841, 1846; the articles in Herzog's *Encyclopädie* and Wetzer's and Wette's *Kirchen-Lexikon*, by Kling and Hefele respectively; the brilliant sketch by Pressensé in his *Martyrs and Apologists*; and the learned compilation of Huet, entitled *Origeniana*, to be found in the ninth volume of Migne's edition.

[In the Edinburgh series the foregoing Life was delayed till the appearance of the second volume. The earlier volume appeared with a preface, as follows:]—

The name of the illustrious Origen comes before us in this series in connection with his works *De Principiis*, *Epistola ad Africanum*, *Epistola ad Gregorium*, and the treatise *Contra Celsum*.

It is in his treatise Περὶ Ἀρχῶν, or, as it is commonly known under the Latin title, *De Principiis*, that Origen most fully develops his system, and brings out his peculiar principles. None of his works exposed him to so much animadversion in the ancient Church as this. On it chiefly was based the charge of heresy which some vehemently pressed against him,— a charge from which even his firmest friends felt it no easy matter absolutely to defend him. The points on which it was held that he had plainly departed from the orthodox faith, were the four following: *First*, That the souls of men had existed in a previous state, and that their imprisonment in material bodies was a punishment for sins which they had then committed. *Second*, That the human soul of Christ had also previously existed, and been united to the Divine nature before that incarnation of the Son of God which is related in the Gospels. *Third*, That our material bodies shall be transformed into absolutely ethereal ones at the resurrection; and *Fourth*, That all men, and even devils, shall be finally restored through the mediation of Christ. His principles of interpreting Scripture are also brought out in this treatise; and while not a little ingenuity is displayed in illustrating and maintaining them, the serious errors into which they might too easily lead will be at once perceived by the reader.

It is much to be regretted that the original Greek of the *De Principiis* has for the most part perished. We possess it chiefly in a Latin translation by Rufinus. And there can be no doubt that he often took great liberties with his author. So much was this felt to be the case, that Jerome undertook a new translation of the work; but only small portions of his version have reached our day. He strongly accuses Rufinus of unfaithfulness as an interpreter, while he also inveighs bitterly against Origen himself, as having departed from the Catholic Faith, specially in regard to the doctrine of the Trinity. There seems, however, after all, no adequate reason to doubt the substantial orthodoxy of our author, although the bent of his mind and the nature of his studies led him to indulge in many vain and unauthorized speculations.

The *Epistle to Africanus* was drawn forth by a letter which that learned writer had addressed to Origen respecting the story of Susanna appended to the book of Daniel. Africanus had grave doubts as to the canonical authority of the account. Origen replies to his objections, and seeks to uphold the story as both useful in itself, and a genuine portion of the ancient prophetical writings.

The treatise of Origen *Against Celsus* is, of all his works, the most interesting to the modern reader. It is a defence of Christianity in opposition to a Greek philosopher named Celsus, who had attacked it in a work entitled Ἀληθὴς Λόγος, that is, *The True Word*, or *The True Discourse*. Of this work we know nothing, except from the quotations contained in the answer given to it by Origen. Nor has anything very certain been ascertained respecting its author. According to Origen, he was a follower of Epicurus, but others have regarded him as a Platonist. If we may judge of the work by those specimens of it preserved in the reply of Origen, it was little better than a compound of sophistry and slander. But there is reason to be grateful for it, as having called forth the admirable answer of Origen. This work was written in the old age of our author, and is composed with great care; while it abounds with proofs of the widest erudition. It is also perfectly orthodox; and, as Bishop Bull has remarked, it is only fair that we should judge from a work written with the view of being considered by the world at large, and with the most elaborate care, as to the mature and finally accepted views of the author.

The best edition of Origen's works is that superintended by Charles and Charles Vincent de la Rue, Paris, 1783, 4 vols. for., which is reprinted by Migne. There is also an edition in 25 volumes, based upon that of De la Rue, but without the Latin translation, by Lommatzsch, Berlin, 1831–

1848. The *De Principiis* has been separately edited by Redepenning, Leipzig, 1836. Spencer edited the *Contra Celsum*, Cambridge, 1677.

[Professor Crombie was assisted in the *Contra Celsum* by the Rev. W. H. Cairns, M.A., Rector of the Dumfries Academy. Mr. Cairns (since deceased) was the translator of Books VII. and VIII. of that work.]

[The Works of Origen included in this volume having been placed in my hands by the Right Reverend Editor of the present series (who restricts himself to a limited task of supervision), I have endeavoured to do for them that which seemed needful in the circumstances. The temptation was strong to enter upon annotations, for which no one of the authors among the Ante-Nicene Fathers offers larger room, and to insert corrections of various sorts, based upon modern progress and research. But, in accordance with the plan of this series, I have been forced to resist this temptation, and have striven only to be useful in matters which, though of great moment, are toilsome, and in no wise flattering to editorial vanity or conceit.

I have silently corrected numerous typographical errors which exist in the Edinburgh edition, and have sought to secure uniformity in the details of reproducing the work, and, above all, accuracy in all its parts. Particularly, I may mention that the Scripture references needed correction to the extent of more than a hundred places, and that references to classical and other writers were often quite astray. A very few notes, enclosed in brackets, are all that I have deemed it expedient or proper, on my part, to add.

While no one who is aware of human infirmity will ever dare to claim perfection in the typography of a book which has passed through the press under his hands, yet in the present case I venture to assure the student and reader that no pains or effort have been spared in order to make the volume as accurate as possible in this respect. Much experience and training incline me to hope and believe that success has attended my efforts. S.]

PREFATORY NOTICE TO ORIGEN'S WORKS

[The great biblical scholar and critic of the first half of the third century deserves a more cordial recognition and appreciation than have always been accorded to him. While it is true that in various matters he has strange, even wild, fancies, and gives utterance to expressions which can hardly, if at all, be justified; while it is also true that he indulges beyond all reason (as it appears to us of the present age) in utterly useless speculations, and carries to excess his great love of allegorizing,—yet these are rather of the nature of possible guesses and surmises on numerous topics, of more or less interest, than deliberate, systematic teaching as matters of faith. He frequently speaks of them in this wise, and does not claim for these guesses and speculations any more credit than they may appear to his readers to be worth. In the great fundamentals of the Christian creed Origen is unquestionably sound and true. He does not always express himself in accordance with the exact definitions which the Church Catholic secured in the century after his decease, as a necessary result of the struggle with Arian and other deadly heresies; but surely, in fairness, he is not to be too severely judged for this. Some writers (e.g., J. M. Neale, in his *History of the Patriarchate of Alexandria*) give an unfavorable and condemnatory view of Origen and his career, but I am of opinion that Neale and others push their objections much too far. I hold that Bishop Bull, and men like him, are nearer to truth and justice in defending Origen and his lifelong labors in the cause of the Master.

The Περὶ Ἀρχῶν, which has come to us through the professedly paraphrastic but really unsatisfactory version of Rufinus, is the work which has given chief offence, and brought much odium upon Origen; but as this was written in early life, and it is doubtful in how far Origen is responsible for many things that are in it, it is only fair and just to judge him by such works as the Κατὰ Κέλσον and his valuable *Homilies* on various books of Holy Scripture. These go far to prove clearly that he, whom Dr. Barrow designates as "the father of interpreters," is worthy the high estimate which ancient as well as modern defenders of his good name have fully set forth, and to justify the conviction, that, if we possessed more out of the numerous works of his which have entirely perished, we should rank him even more highly than is done by Bishop Bull in his *Defensio Fidei Nicenæ*.[2]

In conclusion, I give a paragraph from the very valuable *Introduction to the Criticism of the New Testament*, by Dr. F. H. Scrivener, one of the ablest of living biblical scholars and critics:—

"Origen is the most celebrated biblical critic of antiquity. His is the highest name among the critics and expositors of the early Church. He is perpetually engaged in the discussion of various readings of the New Testament, and employs language, in describing the then existing state of the text, which would be deemed strong if applied even to its present condition, after the changes which sixteen more centuries must needs have produced.... Seldom have such warmth of fancy and so bold a grasp of mind been united with the lifelong, patient industry which procured for this famous man the honourable appellation of *Adamantius*." S.][95]

[95] Alexander Roberts, James Donaldson, and A. Cleveland Coxe, eds., "Introductory Note to the Works of Origen," in *Fathers of the Third Century: Tertullian, Part Fourth; Minucius Felix; Commodian; Origen, Parts First and Second*, vol. 4, The Ante-Nicene Fathers (Buffalo, NY: Christian Literature Company, 1885), 223–235.

EARLY CHRISTIANITY 18 Constantine the Great – A Defender of Christianity?

[A.D. 272 – 337.] Many Christian scholars have given Roman Emperor Constantine the expressions "saint," "thirteenth apostle," "holy equal of the apostles"; while others describe Constantine as "bloodstained, stigmatized by countless enormities and full of deceit, . . . a hideous tyrant, guilty of horrid crimes."

Numerous confessing Christians have long thought of Constantine the Great as the supreme advocate, who, in essence, was the savior of Christianity. It is to this man that most of today's Christian body attributes the delivery of Christianity from Roman persecution, releasing them from the bondage of being the outlaw religion, bringing them freedom from oppression.

Additionally, it is commonly thought that he was faithful and followed a life course as a follower of Jesus Christ with a resilient desire to spread the Christian cause. The Eastern Orthodox Church and the Coptic Church have avowed both Constantine and Helena, his mother, "saints."

Who was Constantine the Great? What role did he play in the growth of post apostolic Christianity? We will allow history and the historians to answer these questions.

In short, the reader will find that there is some truth and some untruth when it comes to Constantine the Great. It is true that he was a consummate benefactor of Christianity, but it is also untrue that he was a Christian. It is true that he was a zealous defender of Christianity, but it is also untrue that his life course was anything near reflective of being Christlike. We will allow the historical evidence and common sense to be the advocates of what is true, and what is untrue.

The Constantine of History

In Naissus, in Serbia about the year 275 C.E., there was a son born to Constantius Chlorus, whose name would be infamously known the world over as Constantine the Great. His father would become emperor of the western provinces of Rome in 293 C.E., at which time; Constantine was fighting on the Danube under the order of Emperor Galerius. In the year of 306 C.E., Constantine would have to return to his father's dying side in Britain, at which time the army raised him to the status of the emperor.

 At that point, there were five others laying hold of the title Agusti (Agustus singular). Between 306 and 324 C.E., subsequently, Constantine became lone imperator, which was a time of incessant civil war. Constantine would have two substantial victories in two sets of campaigns, placing himself in world history, making him the sole emperor of the Roman Empire.

In 312 C.E., Constantine conquered his adversary Maxentius in the battle of the Milvian Bridge outside Rome. The Christian apologist assert that throughout that battle, there appeared under the sun a flaming cross carrying the Latin words In hoc signo vinces, meaning "In this sign conquer." Some also argue that in a dream, Constantine was commanded to paint the first two letters of Christ's name in Greek on the troop's shields. However, the story suffers from numerous chronological errors. The book A History of Christianity states: "There is a conflict of evidence about the exact time, place and details of this vision." (Johnson 1976, 167) Back in Rome, the pagan Senate, received Constantine openheartedly, who declared him, chief Augustus and Pontifex Maximus, that is, high priest of the pagan religion of the Roman Empire.

Constantine organized a relationship with Emperor Licinius, ruler of the eastern provinces, in 313 C.E. By way of the Edict of Milan, the two allowed all groups to worship freely, each having equal rights. However, numerous historians soften the meaning of this document, suggesting that it was no imperial document indicating a modification of procedure toward Christianity; rather, it was simply a routine official letter.

By 323 C.E., Constantine crushed his final lingering opponent, Licinius, and became the unquestionable ruler of the Roman world. Still unbaptized, in 325 C.E., he was the head of the first great ecumenical council of the "Christian" church, which judged Arianism as heresy and penned a statement of crucial beliefs called the Nicene Creed.

In the spring of 337 C.E., Constantine fell sick. It is at this point that he chose to be baptized, and then he died that 22nd of May. The Senate placed him among the Roman gods after his death.

Constantine's Strategic use of Religion

There was a distinct attitude of the third and fourth century Roman Emperors. These ones may not have held the same position of the religion of the day, but they were politician enough to surrender to the mood of the times. Many times, they would bow to the religious movement ahead of their own agenda, giving the impression, regardless of how small, that they too were religious. Moreover, there is no doubt that Constantine was a man of his day. At the start of making his mark, he needed some divine support, which would not come from the Roman gods, who were on their way out, as an influential agent.

The Roman Empire was on the brink of full deterioration. What it needed was a new breath of life, and what better than Christianity, which gave credence to his victory, but to a new empire that was just ahead. The Christian churches throughout the empire were now what held the empire together, looking to the bishops, requesting they keep the unity.

Constantine recognized Christianity for its worth, albeit divided amongst themselves, if he could effectively solve their differences, the empire could be revitalized and united into a new force, for his will and purposes. He decided to unite the people under one "catholic," or universal, religion. Pagan customs and festivals were given "Christian" names. In addition, "Christian" religious leaders were given position, salary, and dominant influence of pagan priests. (Durant 1980, 616)

Looking for a religious accord for political motives, Constantine rapidly stamped out any nonconforming expressions, not based on Biblical truth, but based on majority agreement. The deep religious differences within the seriously divided Christian church afforded him the occasion to arbitrate as a God-sent negotiator.

By way of his relations with the Donatists in North Africa and the supporters of Arius in the eastern portion of the empire, he swiftly learned that persuading was not sufficient to establish a firm, unified reliance. The first ecumenical council in the history of the church came about by his attempt to resolve the Arian controversy.

Historian Paul Johnson has this to say concerning Constantine, "One of his main reasons for tolerating Christianity may have been that it gave himself and the State the opportunity to control the Church's policy on orthodoxy and the treatment of heterodoxy." (Johnson 1976, 87)

The Council of Nicaea and Constantine

The question is, what part did the unbaptized Constantine have at the Council of Nicaea? The Later Roman Empire states: "Constantine himself presided, actively guiding the discussions . . . Overawed by the emperor, the bishops, with two exceptions only, signed the creed, many of them much against their inclination." (Jones 1986, 87) For two months the religious debates went on before this pagan emperor stepped in and determined that those who favored homoousion (of one substance). Why? "Constantine had basically no understanding whatsoever of the questions that were being asked in Greek theology," says A Short History of Christian Doctrine. (Lohse 1978, 51)

A Case for Hope states, "Constantine, who was not a member of the church, presided at the council and said in effect, 'I really don't care what you decide, but decide you will, and then I will make certain that the decision is enforced.'" (Kerby 2001, 73) Obviously, Constantine did understand that a religiously divided empire was a threat to the solidarity he was searching for, unity. "What religion he had, many argue, was at best a blend of paganism and Christianity for purely political purposes." (Galli and Olsen 2000, 306)

Constantine Became a Christian?

Johnson notes: "Constantine never abandoned sun-worship and kept the sun on his coins." (Johnson 1976, 87) Forgery in Christianity observes, "Constantine showed equal favor to both religions. As pontifex maximus he watched over the heathen worship and protected its rights." (Wheless 2007, 30) "First, Constantine never became a Christian himself until he was baptized on his death bed. Furthermore, his behavior as emperor was the antithesis of Christian principles." (Kerby 2001, 72) In fact, the day before his death, his being the Pontifex Maximus, Constantine made a sacrifice to Zeus. Therefore, it is only fair to ask concerning his baptism, 'was it preceded by sincere repentance and a turning around from his former way, as is required by Scripture. —Acts 2:38, 40, 41.

Family Murders

Under Constantine, Crispus and Fausta heading, Michael Grant describes what one could call repulsive domestic crimes committed by Constantine:

Eutropius declared that Constantine was responsible for many murders of his 'friends.' And this was unmistakably true. There was a long list of victims. . . . Constantine's behavior is inexcusable by any standards and casts a blot on his reputation. Being an absolute autocrat, he believed that he could kill anyone. (Grant 2009, 109)

Not long after Constantine's dynasty was under way, he lost the ability at enjoying his accomplishments, as he was soon all too aware of the dangers that surrounded him. He was suspicious to start with, coupled further by those seeking to curry favor with him, nothing but disaster lay ahead. Suspicion came over his nephew Licinianus first. He had already executed Licinianus' father, who had been the co-Augustus. After Licinianus' murder, Constantine actually had his own firstborn son murdered, Crispus. It was Crispus' stepmother, who executed him because he seemed to be in the way of her own offspring.

Fausta's plot was short lived, as this act sealed her own fate. Constantine's mother, Augusta Helena, murdered Fausta or at least was involved in it. The irrational feelings that often exacted Constantine likewise contributed to the flood of executions of numerous friends and associates. The book An Introduction to Medieval Europe concludes: "The execution—not to say murder—of his own son and his wife indicates that he was untouched by any spiritual influence in Christianity." (Thompson and Johnson 1965, 32)

A "Saint"?

Philip Schaff states: "Constantine was entitled to be called Great in virtue rather of what he did than what he was. Tested by character, indeed, he stands among the lowest of all those to whom the epithet [Great] has in ancient or modern times been applied." (Schaff 1997, 18) And the book A History of Christianity informs us: "There were early reports of his violent temper and his cruelty in anger. . . . He had no respect for human life . . . His private life became monstrous as he aged." (Johnson 1976, 47)

Obviously, Constantine had grave disposition problems. His unpredictable personality was frequently the cause of his committing crimes. Constantine certainly was not a Christian by nature. The evidence do not portray him as a real Christian who had put on "the new person" and who demonstrated that he had the fruitage of the Spirit—"love, joy, peace, patience, kindness, goodness, faithfulness, gentleness, self-control."[96]—Colossians 3:9, 10; Galatians 5:22, 23.

The Consequences of His Efforts

As Pontifex Maximus—and consequently, the religious head of the Roman Empire—Constantine attempted to persuade the bishops of a church that had now fallen away. Christianity was now entering the realms of position, power, and wealth for its leaders, by means of Constantine. While they were not the state religion at this point, it was certainly heading in that direction. Soon the church was ready to bestow titles on the man that had rained splendor down on them, the angel of

---

[96] W. Hall Harris, III, The Lexham English Bible (Logos Research Systems, Inc., 2010), Ga 5:21–23

God, a sacred being, and looking to him as the Son of God, who would reign in heaven.

This Christianity was not the Christianity of the first and second century of our common era. It had chosen to become a part of the world, to such an extent, there was no difference. It had left the love it had at first, the teachings of Christ. (John 15:19; 17:14, 16; Revelation 17:1, 2) As a result, Christianity was fused with the world of government and paganism, as well as Neoplatonist.—Compare 2 Corinthians 6:14-18.

The church too would become authoritarian, by way of Constantine's early influence. The gospel was set aside for arrogant rites, and ceremonies presented, with worldly honors and monetary payments for every priestly function. Moreover, the Kingdom of Christ was moved into becoming a kingdom of this world.

EARLY CHRISTIANITY 19 Jerome - The Forerunner in Bible Translation

[A.D. 346 - 420] The Catholic Church Sacred Tradition in support of the Vulgate's magisterial authority:

> Moreover, this sacred and holy Synod,—considering that no small utility may accrue to the Church of God, if it be made known which out of all the Latin editions, now in circulation, of the sacred books, is to be held as authentic,—ordains and declares, that the said old and vulgate edition, which, by the lengthened usage of so many years, has been approved of in the Church, be, in public lectures, disputations, sermons and expositions, held as authentic; and that no one is to dare, or presume to reject it under any pretext whatever.[97]

ON April 8, 1546, the Latin Vulgate was given an approved capacity by the Council of Trent (1545–1563) as the standard of the Biblical canon regarding which parts of books are canonical. The Vulgate had been completed for over a thousand years, yet Jerome and his translation had been the center of debate throughout. Who was Jerome? Why was his translation of the Hebrew and Greek Scriptures into Latin, as well as himself debated? What impact has this work had on the field of Bible translation?

Jerome Becomes a Scholar

Jerome ([c. 346–420 C.E.] Latin: Eusebius Hieronymus) was a Roman Christian priest, confessor, theologian and historian, who became a Doctor of the Church. He was the son of Eusebius, of the city of Stridon, which was on the border of Dalmatia and Pannonia. His parents were reasonably well-off, and he felt the benefits of money at an early age, receiving an education in Rome under the well-known grammarian Donatus. Jerome demonstrated himself to be an exceptional student of grammar, rhetoric, and philosophy. Throughout this period he also began to study Greek. He is most famously known for his translation of the Bible from the original languages of Hebrew (OT) and Greek) (NT) into Latin (the Vulgate), and his list of writings is extensive.

Jerome was born at Stridon about 346 C.E. However, he was not baptized until sometime after close to 366 C.E., and shortly after that, he

---

[97] Canons and Decrees of the Council of Trent, The Fourth Session, 1546.

and his friend Bonosus headed for Rome. However, they became wanderers for a time, and then finally ended up in Aquileia, Italy, where Jerome was introduced to the idea of asceticism.[98] He became attracted to this extreme way of life, so he and a group of his friends spent a number of years cultivating an ascetic way of life.

In 373 C.E., some unnamed trouble contributed to the groups going their separate ways. Let down, Jerome traveled without a purpose and without a known destination eastward across Bithynia, Galatia, and Cilicia and eventually arrived in Antioch, Syria.

Even though he was only in his late 20's at this point, Jerome's health was damaged by a fever, and he grew very ill during his journey. "Oh, if only the Lord Jesus Christ would suddenly transport me to you," he said, writing to a friend, Rufinus. "My poor body, weak even when well, has been shattered by frequent illnesses."[99]

Jerome had already coped with sickness, seclusion, and inner turmoil; he was now thrust into a spiritual crisis. In a dream, he was ...

Suddenly I was caught up in the spirit and dragged before the judgment seat of the Judge, and here the light was so bright, and those who stood around were so radiant, that I cast myself upon the ground and did not dare to look up. Asked who and what I was I replied 'I am a Christian.' But He who presided said: 'Thou liest; thou art a follower of Cicero and not of Christ. For where thy treasure is there will thy heart be also.' Instantly I became dumb, and amid the strokes of the lash—for He had ordered me to be scourged—I was tortured more severely still by the fire of conscience, considering with myself that verse 'In the grave, who shall give thee thanks?' Yet for all that I began to cry and to bewail myself saying: 'Have mercy upon me, O Lord; have mercy upon me.' Amid the sound of the scourges, this cry still made itself heard. At last the bystanders, falling down before the knees of Him who presided, prayed that He would have pity on my youth and that He would give me space to repent of my error. He might. Still, they urged, inflict torture upon me, should I ever again read the works of the Gentiles. Under the stress of that awful moment, I should have been ready to make even still larger promises than these. Accordingly, I made oath and called upon His name, saying 'Lord, if ever again I possess worldly books, or if ever again I read

---

[98] self-denying way of life: austerity and self-denial, especially as a principled way of life

[99] Jerome, "The Letters of St. Jerome", Volume VI: St. Jerome: Letters and Select Works, ed. Philip Schaff and Henry Wace (New York: Christian Literature Company, 1893), 4.

such, I have denied thee.' On taking this oath, I was dismissed and returned to the upper world.[100]

Sometime later would sidestep his pledge that he had made in the dream, and said that he should not be held answerable for a solemn promise made in a dream. However, Jerome felt somewhat obligated to his vow, so he left Antioch and searched for solitude in Chalcis in the Syrian Desert. Living as a recluse, he submerged himself in a study of the Bible and theological literature. Jerome said, "I read the books of God with a zeal greater than I had previously given to the books of men."[101] He likewise learned the local Syriac tongue and started studying Hebrew with the help of a Jew who had become a Christian.

Jerome Receives an Assignment from the Pope

After about five years of living an ascetic life, Jerome returned to Antioch in 378 or 379 C.E. His return to civilization was met with disappointment, as the church was profoundly divided. While he had still been in the desert, Jerome had written to the Pope, saying "The Church is rent into three factions, and each of these is eager to seize me for its own."[102]

Jerome eventually decided that he would take the side of Bishop Paulinus, one of three men that claimed that title of Antioch. Jerome unwilling accepted his being ordained, but demanded (1) that he not be held back from being able to continue his ascetic life, and (2) he would remain freed from any priestly duties to minister to a specific church.

Jerome went with Paulinus to the Council of Constantinople and afterward continued on with him to Rome in 381 C.E. Pope Damasus swiftly appreciated Jerome's learning and linguistic expertise. Inside of a year Jerome was raised to the important position of personal secretary to Damasus.

---

[100] Rufinus of Aquileia, "The Apology of Rufinus", trans. William Henry Fremantle In , in A Select Library of the Nicene and Post-Nicene Fathers of the Christian Church, Second Series, Volume III: Theodoret, Jerome, Gennadius, Rufinus: Historial Writings, Etc., ed. Philip Schaff and Henry Wace (New York: Christian Literature Company, 1892), 462-63.

[101] Jerome, "The Letters of St. Jerome", Volume VI: St. Jerome: Letters and Select Works, ed. Philip Schaff and Henry Wace (New York: Christian Literature Company, 1893), 36.

[102] Jerome, "The Letters of St. Jerome", Volume VI: St. Jerome: Letters and Select Works, ed. Philip Schaff and Henry Wace (New York: Christian Literature Company, 1893), 20.

Once in the position of personal secretary, Jerome seemed to attract controversy at every turn. For example, even though he lived in a luxurious papal court, he continued in his ascetic lifestyle. This was not only frowned upon, but he even went a step further and spoke out against the excessive lifestyle of the worldly clergy, creating numerous enemies.

Regardless of those who despised him, Jerome had the complete backing of Pope Damasus. Of course, the pope had very good reasons for seeing that Jerome continued in his Bible research. The Latin Bible version were really in numerous forms; as many of them had been carelessly translated, filled with errors. Another problem that Damasus faced was the division of his church, the East, and the West. Few in the Eastern portion of the church knew Latin, and fewer still in the Western portion knew Greek.

Therefore, it was Pope Damasus' intention to have Jerome create a standard Latin text of the Gospels. Damasus desired a translation that would be a mirror image of the original language Greek texts, yet at the same time, be moving, stirring and powerful, as well as clear in the Latin. Jerome and only a handful of other scholar were up to such a task. He was fluent in Greek, Latin, and Syriac and possessed a fundamental knowledge of Hebrew, making him well suited for the job. Therefore, Jerome was commissioned into a project by Damasus that would not be completed for the next 20 years of his life.

Greater Controversies Lie Ahead

Jerome was a translator with a mission, and it showed with the speed for which he was accomplishing his task. Jerome exhibited a clear, technique that would be used by the translator and textual scholars over a millennium later. One of the leading textual scholars of the 20th century, the late Dr. Bruce M. Metzger had this to say about Jerome's method:

Within a year or so Jerome was able to present Damasus with the first-fruits of his work—a revision of the text of the four Gospels, where the variations had been extreme. In a covering letter, he explained the principles which he followed: he used a relatively good Latin text as the basis for his revision, and compared it with some old Greek manuscripts. He emphasized that he treated the current Latin text [of his day] as conservatively as possible, and changed it only where the meaning was distorted. Though we do not have the Latin manuscripts which Jerome chose as the basis of his work, it appears that they belonged to the European form of the Old Latin (perhaps they were similar to manuscript *b*). The Greek manuscripts apparently belonged to the Alexandrian type of text. (Metzger 1964, 1968, 1992, 76)

Initially, the Jerome Latin translation was well received. However, the critics came out of the woodwork to complain about the supposed liberties that he took in making his translation.

After I had written my former letter, containing a few remarks on some Hebrew words, a report suddenly reached me that certain contemptible creatures were deliberately assailing me with the charge that I had endeavored to correct passages in the Gospels, against the authority of the ancients and the opinion of the whole world.[103]

These condemnations only grew in intensity after the death of Pope Damasus in 384 C.E. The new pope and Jerome did not have a working relationship like he had shared with Damasus, so he made the decision to leave Rome. Once again, Jerome was wandering toward the east.

Jerome Becomes a Hebrew Scholar

In 386 C.E., Jerome had found his way to Bethlehem, where he would spend the rest of his life. He was traveling with a few of those who had remained loyal to him, as well as Paula, a well-off woman of nobility from Rome. Paula had grown attracted to the plain and simple way of life without luxury, as a result of Jerome's influence. However, here financial wealth was used to establish a monastery under the direction of Jerome. It would be here that he would take his scholarly pursuits to a whole new level, completing the ultimate work of his life.

As you likely remember, Jerome's understanding of Hebrew was only functional, so this new life in Bethlehem was going to offer him the opportunity at becoming an extraordinary Hebrew scholar. Here again, Paula was able to help him afford several different Jewish tutors, who helped him fully grasp a number of the more difficult characteristics of the language. Concerning one teacher, Jerome said:

> What trouble and expense it cost me to get Baraninas to teach me under cover of night. For by his fear of the Jews he presented to me in his own person the second edition of Nicodemus.[104]

---

[103] Jerome, "The Letters of St. Jerome", Volume VI: St. Jerome: Letters and Select Works, ed. Philip Schaff and Henry Wace (New York: Christian Literature Company, 1893), 43-44.

[104] John 3:2; Ibid, Volume VI, 176.

The Jews of Jerome's day were not too receptive to Gentiles for their failure to pronounce the guttural sounds properly. This did not dissuade Jerome though, as he simply put more effort into his studies, and was eventually able to master these sounds. In addition, Jerome transliterated numerous Hebrew words into Latin.[105] This method not only assisted him in remembering the words but also preserved the Hebrew pronunciation of that time.

The Greatest Controversy of Jerome

We are not sure how much of the Bible that Damasus wanted Jerome to translate. However, we are well aware of how much Jerome intended to accomplish. Jerome was very attentive and resolute. Jerome was determined to make available a revised Latin translation of the whole Bible.

Therefore, I beseech you, Paula and Eustochium, to pour out your supplications for me to the Lord, that so long as I am in this poor body, I may write something pleasing to you, useful to the Church, worthy of posterity. As for my contemporaries, I am indifferent to their opinions, for they pass from side to side as they are moved by love or hatred.[106]

The basis for the Old Testament was the Greek Septuagint (LXX).[107] The Septuagint was viewed by the Christians of the time as though it too were inspired by God.[108] It functioned as Scripture for the Greek-speaking Jews and was used by a large amount of Christians down to the time of Jesus and his apostles, as well up unto the time of Jerome. In the Greek New Testament, most of the 320 direct quotations and the collective total of perhaps 890 quotations and references to the Hebrew Old Testament are from the Septuagint.

---

[105] Transliterated means to represent letters or words written in one alphabet using the corresponding letters of another.

[106] Jerome, "Prefaces to the Books of the Vulgate Version of the Old Testament", Second Series, Volume VI: St. Jerome: Letters and Select Works, ed. Philip Schaff and Henry Wace (New York: Christian Literature Company, 1893), 493.

[107] A Greek translation of the Hebrew Bible made 280 and 150 B.C.E. to meet the needs of Greek-speaking Jews outside Palestine. The Septuagint contains some books not in the Hebrew canon. The roman numerals LXX stand for seventy, and according to tradition, The Septuagint was made by 72 Jewish scholars of Alexandria, Egypt. Later, the number 70 somehow came to be used, and thus the version was called the Septuagint.

[108] We need to offer a word of caution here, because the Greek Septuagint was not inspired. Moreover, there were a number of Greek translations made, which was not a carefully guard text, nor unified. Thus, there are considerable differences between the Greek and the Hebrew Old Testament.

As Jerome got involved in the work of translating the Old Testament, he was again met with discrepancies, like had been the case with the different Latin manuscripts, and now between the different Greek manuscripts, he was using. One can only imagine the feeling of disappointment, exasperation, or weariness of this man as he realized the work that would be involved in translating, as well as making textual decisions too. In the end, Jerome simply decided that it would be more practical to scrap his plan of using the Greek manuscripts, and even the revered Septuagint, and to go with the Hebrew text as his basis for the translation.

Here is where Jerome finds himself being falsely accused as a forger of the text, a man who was disrespectful of God, deserting the traditions of the church in favor of the Jews. Even the leading theologian of Jerome's day, Augustine, begged him to drop the Hebrew text and return to the use of the Septuagint as the basis for his Latin translation, saying: "If your translation begins to be more generally read in many churches, it will be a grievous thing that, in the reading of Scripture, differences must arise between the Latin Churches and the Greek Churches."[109]

As you can see the fear that dwelled within Augustine, was the church to become even further divided? He feared that the Western churches would be using Jerome's Latin text based on the Hebrew text, while the Eastern Greek churches would be using the Greek Septuagint. Moreover, Augustine was concerned about setting aside the Greek Septuagint, for a translation that only Jerome would be able to defend.

What was Jerome's reaction to all of these critics? He chose to stay true to himself, he simply ignored them. He stayed with the Hebrew text as the basis for his Latin translation of the Old Testament, and brought the whole Latin Bible to complete in 405 C.E. It would be labeled the Vulgate some years later, which is a reference to a commonly received version (the Latin vulgatus meaning "common, that which is popular").

The Accomplishment of Jerome

The Old Testament portion of the Latin translation that Jerome produced was not just a revision of the current Latin texts. It was the beginning of something far greater; a course change in the way the Bible was studied and translated. "The Vulgate," said historian Will Durant,

---

[109] Augustine of Hippo, "Letters of St. Augustin", trans. J. G. Cunningham In , in A Select Library of the Nicene and Post-Nicene Fathers of the Christian Church, First Series, Volume I: The Confessions and Letters of St. Augustin With a Sketch of His Life and Work, ed. Philip Schaff (Buffalo, NY: Christian Literature Company, 1886), 327.

"remains as the greatest and most influential literary accomplishment of the fourth century." (Durant 1950, 54)

Granted Jerome possessed a bitter or critical manner of speaking and a combative temperament, he by himself transmitted Bible research back to the inspired Hebrew text. With a sharp eye, he pored over and compared ancient Hebrew and Greek manuscripts of the Bible that are no longer accessible to us today. Jerome's monumental work was also accomplished before that of the Jewish Masoretes.[110] Therefore, the Vulgate is a treasured reference tool for comparing alternate renderings of Bible texts.

---

[110] The Masoretes were early Jewish scholars: any of the scholars who produced the Masoretic Text. The Masoretic Text was the Hebrew Bible: revised and annotated by Jewish scholars between the 6th and 10th centuries C.E.

Bibliography

Abbot, Nabia. *STUDIES IN ANCIENT ORIENTAL CIVILIZATIONS.* Chocago: The University of Chicago Press, 1938.

Akin, Daniel L. *The New American Commentary: 1, 2, 3 John.* Nashville, TN: Broadman & Holman , 2001.

Aland, Kurt and Barbara. *The Text of the New Testament.* Grand Rapids: Eerdmans, 1987.

Aland, Kurt, and Barbara Aland. *The Text of the New Testament.* Grand Rapids: Eerdmans, 1995.

—. *The Text of the New Testament.* Grand Rapids: Eerdmans, 1987.

Aland, Kurt, Matthew Black, and Carlo M. Martini. *The Greek New Testament, Fourth Revised Edition (Interlinear With Morphology).* Deutsche Bibelgesellschaft: United Bible Society, 1993; 2006.

Alden, Robert L. *Job, The New American Commentary, vol. 11 .* Nashville: Broadman & Holman Publishers, 2001.

Anders, Max. *Holman New Testament Commentary: vol. 8, Galatians, Ephesians, Philippians, Colossians.* Nashville, TN: Broadman & Holman Publishers, 1999.

—. *Holman Old Testament Commentary - Proverbs .* Nashville: B&H Publishing, 2005.

Anders, Max, and Trent Butler. *Holman Old Testament Commentary: Isaiah.* Nashiville, TN: B&H Publishing, 2002.

Andrews, Edward D. *The Text of the New Testament: A Beginner's Guide to New Testament Textual Criticism.* Cambridge, OH: Bible-Translation.Net Books, 2012.

Andrews, Stephen J, and Robert D Bergen. *Holman Old Testament Commentary: 1-2 Samuel.* Nashville: Broadman & Holman, 2009.

Arndt, William, Frederick W. Danker, and Walter Bauer. *A Greek-English Lexicon of the New Testament and Other Early Christian Literature. 3rd ed. .* Chicago: University of Chicago Press, 2000.

Arnold, Clinton E. *Zondervan Illustrated Bible Backgrounds Commentary Volume 2: John, Acts. .* Grand Rapids, MI: Zondervan, 2002.

—. *Zondervan Illustrated Bible Backgrounds Commentary Volume 3: Romans to Philemon.* Grand Rapids: Zondervan, 2002.

—. *Zondervan Illustrated Bible Backgrounds Commentary Volume 4: Hebrews to Revelation.* Grand Rapids, MI: Zondervan, 2002.

—. *Zondervan Illustrated Bible Backgrounds Commentary: Matthew, Mark, Luke, vol. 1.* Grand Rapids, MI: Zondervan, 2002.

Baer, Daniel. *The Unquenchable Fire.* Maitland, FL: Xulon Press, 2007.

Bagnall, Roger S. *The Oxford Handbook of Papyrology (Oxford Handbooks).* Oxford: Oxford University Press, 2009.

Balz, Horst, and Gerhard Schneider. *Exegetical Dictionary of the New Testament.* Edinburgh: T & T Clark Ltd, 1978.

Barclay, William. *The Letter to the Hebrews (New Daily Study Bible).* Louisville, KY: Westminster John Knox Press, 2002.

Barker, Kenneth L., and Waylon Bailey. *The New American Commentary: vol. 20, Micah, Nahum, Habakkuk, Zephaniah.* Nashville, TN: Broadman & Holman Publishers, 2001.

Barnett, Paul. *Jesus & the rise of early Christianity: a history of New Testament times.* Downer Groves: InterVarsity Press, 1999.

—. *PAUL Missionary of Jesus.* Grand Rapids: William B. Eerdmans Publishing Company, 2008.

—. *The Birth of Christianity: The First Twenty Years (After Jesus, Vol. 1) .* Grand Rapids, MI: Wm. B. Eerdmans , 2005.

Bercot, David W. *A Dictionary of Early Christian Beliefs.* Peabody: Hendrickson, 1998.

Bergen, Robert D. *The New American Commentary: 1-2 Samuel.* Nashville: Broadman & Holman, 1996.

Black, David Alan. *New Testament Textual Criticism: A Concise Guide.* Grand Rapids, MI: Baker Books, 1994.

—. *Rethinking New Testament Textual Criticism.* Grand Rapids: Baker Books, 2002.

Bland, Dave. *The College Press NIV Commentary: Proverbs, Ecclesiastes & Song of Songs, .* Joplin: College Press Pub. Co., 2002.

Blenkinsopp, Joseph. *Isaiah 56-66: A New Translation with Introduction and Commentary.* New York: Anchor Bible, 2003.

Blomberg, Craig L., Mariam J. Kamell, and Clinton E. Arnold. *Zondervan Exegetical Commentary on the New Testament: James.* Grand Rapids: Zondervan, 2009.

Blomberg, Craig. *The New American Commentary: Matthew* . Nashville, TN : Broadman & Holman Publishers, 2001.

Boa, Kenneth, and Kruidenier. *Holman New Testament Commentary: Romans*. Nashville: Broadman & Holman, 2000.

Bock, Darrell L. *Baker Exegetical Commentary on the New Testament: Acts*. Grand Rapids: Baker Academic, 2007.

—. *Baker Exegetical Commentary on the New Testament: Luke Volume 1: 1:1-9:50*. Grand Rapids, Mich: Baker Books, 1994.

Bock, Darrell L, and Daniel B Wallace. *Dethroning Jesus: Exposing Popular Culture's Quest to Unseat the Biblical Christ*. Nashville: Thomas Nelson, 2007.

Boles, Kenneth L. *The College Press NIV commentary: Galatians & Ephesians*. Joplin, MO: College Press, 1993.

Borchert, Gerald L. *The New American Commentary: John 1-11* . Nashville, TN: Broadman & Holman Publishers, 2001.

Borchert, Gerald L. *The New American Commentary vol. 25B, John 12–21*. Nashville: Broadman & Holman Publishers, 2002.

Borgen, Peder. *Philo of Alexandria: An Exegete for His Time*. Leiden, Boston: Brill, 1997.

Brand, Chad, Charles Draper, and England Archie. *Holman Illustrated Bible Dictionary: Revised, Updated and Expanded*. Nashville, TN: Holman, 2003.

Briley, Terry R. *The College Press NIV Commentary: Isaiah*. Joplin, MO: ollege Press Pub, 2000.

Bromiley, Geoffrey W. *The International Standard Bible Encyclopedia*. Grand Rapids, MI: William B. Eerdmans Publishing Co., 1986.

Bruce, F. F. *The Book of Acts (New International Commentary on the New Testament)* . Grand Rapids: William B. Eerdmans, 1988.

—. *The Epistle to the Galatians : A Commentary on the Greek Text* . Grand Rapids, Mich.: W.B. Eerdmans Pub. Co., 1982.

—. *The New International Commentary on the New Testament: The Epistle to the Hebrew (Revised)*. Grand Rapids: Eerdmans, 1990.

Bruce, F. F. *The New International Commentary on the New Testament: The Epistle to the Hebrews (Revised)*. Grand Rapids, MI: William B. Eermans Publishing Company, 1990.

Buter, Trent C. *Holman New Testament Commentary: Luke.* Nashville, TN: Broadman & Holman Publishers, 2000.

Cabal, Ted. "Notable Christian Apologist: Origen." In *The Apologetics Study Bibe: Real Questions, Straight Answers, Stronger Faith*, by Ted, Chad O. Brand, E. Ray Clendenen et. al Cabal, 1387. Nashville, TN: Holman Bible Publishers, 2007.

Cabaniss, A. "Origen (Origenes Adamantius)." In *Who's Who in Christian History*, by J.D., and Philip W. Comfort Douglas, 522. Wheaton, IL: Tyndale House, 1992.

Capes, David B, Rodney Reeves, and E. Randolph Richards. *Rediscovering Paul: An Introduction to His World, Letters and Theology* . Downers Grove: IVP Academic, 2007.

Carson, D. A, and Douglas J Moo. *An Introduction to the New Testament.* Grand Rapids, MI: Zondervan, 2005.

Carson, D. A. *New Bible Commentary: 21st Century Edition.* 4th ed. Downers Grove: Inter-Varisity Press, 1994.

Clayton, Joseph. *Luther and His Work.* Whitefish: Kessinger Publishing, 2006.

Colwell, E. C. *Methods in Evaluating Scribal Habits: A Study of P45, P66, P75, in Studies in Methodology in Textual Criticism of the New Testament.* Leiden and Boston: Brill, 1969.

Colwell, Ernest C. *Scribal Habits in Early Papyri: A Study in the Corruption of the Text.* Grand Rapids: Eerdmans, 1965.

Comfort, Philip. *Encountering the Manuscripts: An Introduction to New Testament Paleography and Textual Criticism.* Nashville: Broadman & Holman, 2005.

—. *Encountering the Manuscripts: An Introduction to New Testament Paleography and Textual Criticism.* Nashville: Broadman & Holman, 2005.

—. *Encounterring the Manuscripts: An Introduction to New Testament Paleography and Textual Criticism.* Nashville: Broadman & Holman, 2005.

Comfort, Philip W. *New Testament Text and Translation Commentary.* Carol Stream: Tyndale House Publishers, 2008.

Comfort, Philip Wesley. *A COMMENTARY ON THE MANUSCRIPTS AND TEXT OF THE NEW TESTAMENT.* Grand Rapids: Kregel Publications, 2015.

—. *The Quest for the Original Text of the New Testament.* Eugene: Wipf and Stock, 1992.

Comfort, Philip, and David Barret. *The Text of the Earliest New Testament Greek Manuscripts.* Wheaton: Tyndale House Publishers, 2001.

Cottrell, Peter, and Maxwell Turner. *Linguistics and Biblical Interpretation.* Downers Grove: InterVarsity Press, 1989.

Cruse, C. F. *Eusebius' Eccliatical History.* Peabody, MA: Hendrickson, 1998.

Deissmann, Adolf. *LIGHT FROM THE ANCIENT EAST: The New Testament Illustrated by Recently Discovered Texts of the Graeco-Roman World.* New York and London: Hodder and Stoughton, 1910.

Durant, Will & Ariel. *The Story of Civilization: Part III—Caesar and Christ.* New York, NY: Simon & Schuster , 1980.

—. *The Story of Civilization: Part IV—The Age of Faith.* New York, NY: Simon & Schuster, 1950.

Easley, Kendell H. *Holman New Testament Commentary, vol. 12, Revelation.* (Nashville, TN: Broadman & Holman Publishers, 1998.

Easton, M. G. *Easton's Bible Dictionary.* Oak Harbor, WA: Logos Research Systems, 1996, c1897.

Ehrman, Bart D. *Misquoting Jesus: The Story Behind Who Changed the Bible and Why.* New York: Harper One, 2005.

—. *Peter, Paul and Mary Magdalene: The Followers of Jesus in History and Legend.* Oxford: Oxford University Press, 2006.

Ehrman, Bart D, and Michael W. Holmes. *The Text of the New Testament in Contemporary Research: Essays on the Status Quaestionis. Second Edition.* Leiden and Boston: Brill, 2012.

Ehrman, Bart D. Holmes, Michael W. *The Text of the New Testament in Contemporary Research: Essays on the Status Quaestionis .* Grand Rapids, MI: Eerdmans, 1995.

Ehrman, Bart D. *Lost Christianities: The Battles for Scripture and the Faiths We Never Knew .* New York: Oxford University Press, 2003.

Eliade, Mircea, and Charles J Adams. *The Encyclopedia of Religion (Vol. 7).* New York: Macmillan Publishing Company, 1987.

Ellingworth, Paul. *The Epistle to the Hebrews: A Commentary on the Greek Text.* Grand Rapids, MI: W.B. Eerdmans, 1993.

Elwell, Walter A. *Baker Encyclopedia of the Bible.* Grand Rapids: Baker Book House, 1988.

—. *Evangelical Dictionary of Theology (Second Edition).* Grand Rapids: Baker Academic, 2001.

Elwell, Walter A, and Philip Wesley Comfort. *Tyndale Bible Dictionary.* Wheaton, Ill: Tyndale House Publishers, 2001.

Epp, Eldon J. *Studies in the Theory and Method of New Testament Textual Criticism.* Grand Rapids: Wm. B. Eerdmans Publishing Co., 1993.

—. *Textual Criticism.* Atlanta: Scholars Press, 1989.

Evans, Craig A. *Fabricating Jesus: How Modern Scholars Distort the Gospels.* Downers Grove, IL: InterVaristy Press, 2002.

—. *Jesus and His World: The Archaeological Evidence.* Louisville: Westminster John Knox Press, 2012.

Fahlbusch, Erwin (Editor), Jan Milic (Editor) Lochman, John (Editor) Mbiti, Jaroslav (Editor) Pelikan, and Lukas (Editor) Vischer. *The Encyclopedia of Christianity (Vol. 1-3).* Grand Rapids: Eerdmans Publishing Company and Koninklijke Brill NV, German 1986, 1989, 1992, 1996, 1997; English 1999, 2001, 2003, 2005.

Fahlbusch, Erwin, and Geoffrey William Bromiley. *The Encyclopedia of Christianity.* Grand Rapids: Wm. B. Eerdmans, 1999-2003.

Farrar, Frederic William. *History of Interpretation.* London: Macmillan and Co., 1886.

Fee, Gordon D. *P75, P66, and Origen: The Myth of Early Textual Recension in Alexandria, in: E. J. Epp & G. D. Fee, Studies in the Theory & Method of NT Textual Criticism.* Grand Rapids: Wm. Eerdmans, 1993.

Fee, Gordon D. *P75, P66, and Origen: The Myth of the Early Textual Recension in Alexandria.* Grand Rapids: Zondervan, 1974.

—. *The Textual Criticism of the New Testament.* Grand Rapids: Zondervan, 1979.

Ferguson, Everett. *Backgrounds of Early Christianity.* Grand Rapids, MI: Wm. B. Eerdmans, 2003.

—. *CHURCH HISTORY VOLUME ONE: From Christ to Pre-Reformation.* Grand Rapids: Zondervan, 2005.

Freeman, James M. *THE NEW MANNERS & CUSTOMS OF THE BIBLE.* Gainesville: Bridge-Logos, 1998.

Gaertner, Dennis. *The College Press NIV commentary: Acts* . Joplin, Mo: College Press, 1993.

Galli, Mark and Ted Olsen. *131 Christians Everyone Should Know.* Nashville, TN: Christianity Today, Inc., 2000.

Gamble, Henry Y. *Books and Readers in the Early Church: A History of Early Christian Texts.* New Haven: New Haven University Press, 1995.

Gangel, Kenneth O. *Holman New Testament Commentary: Acts.* Nashville, TN: Broadman & Holman Publishers, 1998.

Gangel, Kenneth O. *Holman New Testament Commentary, vol. 4, John* . Nashville, TN: Broadman & Holman Publishers, 2000.

—. *Holman Old Testament Commentary: Daniel.* Nashville: Broadman & Holman Publishers, 2001.

Gardner, Lynn, and Kenneth S Kantzer. *Christianity Stands True: A Common Sense Look At the Evidence.* Joplin: College Press Publishing, 1994.

Garland, David E. *1 Corinthians, Baker Exegetical Commentary on the New Testament.* Grand Rapids, MI: : Baker Academic, 2003.

Geisler, Norman L, and William E Nix. *A General Introduction to the Bible.* Chicago: Moody Press, 1996.

Geisler, Norman, and David Geisler. *CONVERSATION EVANGELISM: How to Listen and Speak So You Can Be Heard.* Eugene: Harvest House Publishers, 2009.

George, Timothy. *The New American Commentary: Galatians* . Nashville, TN: Broadman & Holman Publishers, 2001.

Gohl, Justin M. "Origen." In *The Lexham Bible Dictionary*, by ed. John D. Barry. Bellingham, WA: Logos Bible Software, 2012.

Gonzalez, Just L. *The Story of Christianity (Volume 2) The Reformation to the Present Day.* New York: HarperCollins, 1985.

Green, Joel B, Scot McKnight, and Howard Marshall. *Dictionary of Jesus and the Gospels.* Downers Grove, IL: InterVarsity Press, 1992.

Greenlee, J Harold. *Introduction to New Testament Textual Criticism.* Peabody: Hendrickson, 1995.

—. *The Text of the New Testament.* Peabody: Henrickson, 2008.

Guthrie, Donald. *Introduction to the New Testament (Revised and Expanded).* Downers Grove, IL: InterVarsity Press, 1990.

Guthrie, George H. *The NIV Application Commentary: Hebrews*. Grand Rapids, MI: Zondervan, 1998.

Hatch, William Henry Paine. "A Recently Discovered Fragmrnt of the Epistle to the Romans." *Harvard Theological Review*, 45: 81-85.

Head, Peter M. "The Habits of New Testament Copyists Singular Readings in the Early Fragmentary Papyri of John." *Biblica, Vol. 85, No. 3*, 2004: 399-408.

Hendriksen, William, and Simon J. Kistemaker. *New Testament Commentary: Exposition of the Gospel According to John, vol. 1-2*. Grand Rapids, MI: Baker Book House, 1953-2001.

—. *Exposition of the Pastoral Epistles, New Testament Commentary, vol. 4*. Grand Rapids: Baker Book House, 1953-2001.

Hill, Charles E., and Michael J. Kruger. *The Early Text of the New Testament*. Oxford: Oxford University Press, 2012.

Hill, Jonathan. *Zondervan Handbook to the History of Christianity*. Oxford: Lion, 2006.

Holloway, Gary. *The College NIV Commentary: James & Jude*. Joplin: College Press Publishing Company, 1996.

Holmes, Michael W. *New Testament Textual Criticism*. Grand Rapids: Baker, 1989.

—. *The Apostolic Fathers: Greek Texts and English Translations*. Grand Rapids: Baker Academics, 2007.

House, Paul R. *The New American Commentary: 2 Kings* . Nashville: Broadman & Holman Publishers, 2001.

Hurtado, Larry. "The Origin of the Nominal Sacra." *Journal of Biblical Literature*, 1998: 655-673.

Jerome. "Lives of Illustrious Men." In *A Select Library of the Nicene and Post-Nicene Fathers of the Christian Church, Second Series Volume III*, by Philip and Henry Wace Schaff, 349-385. New York: Christian Literature Company, 1892.

Johnson, Paul. *A History of Christianity*. New York: Atheneum, 1976.

Johnson, William A, and Holt N Parker. *Ancient Literacies: The Culture of Reading in Greece and Rome*. Oxford: Oxford University Press, 2011.

Jones, Timothy Paul. *Misquoting Truth: A Guide to the Fallacies of Bart Ehrman's Misquoting Jesus.* Downer Groves: InterVarsity Press, 2007.

Keil, Carl Friedrich, and Franz Delitzsch. *Commentary on the Old Testament.* Peabody, MA: Hendrickson, 2002.

Kistemaker, Simon J, and William Hendriksen. *New Testament Commentary: Exposition of the Acts of the Apostles* . Grand Rapids, MI: Baker Book House, 1953-2001.

—. *New Testament Commentary: Exposition of the Pastoral Epistles, New Testament Commentary* . Grand Rapids: Baker Book House, 1953-2001).

—. *New Testament Commentary : Exposition of Ephesians* . Grand Rapids: Baker Book House, 1953-2001.

—. *New Testament Commentary: vol. 15, Exposition of Hebrews.* Grand Rapids: Baker Book House, 1953-2001.

Kistemaker, Simon J., and William Hendriksen. *Exposition of the First Epistle to the Corinthians, vol. 18, New Testament Commentary.* Grand Rapids, MI: Baker Book House, 1953–2001.

Kittel, Gerhard, Gerhard Friedrich, and Geoffrey William Bromiley. *Theological Dictionary of the New Testament.* Grand Rapids: Eerdmans, 1995, c1985.

Komoszewski, J. Ed, James M. Sawyer, and Daniel Wallace. *Reinventing Jesus* . Grand Rapids, MI: Kregel Publications, 2006.

Lane Fox, Robin. *Pagans and Christians: In the Mediterranean World from the Second Century AD to the Conversion of Constantine.* City of Westminster, London: Penguin, 2006.

Larson, Knute. *Holman New Testament Commentary, vol. 9, I & II Thessalonians, I & II Timothy, Titus, Philemon.* Nashville, TN: Broadman & Holman Publishers, 2000.

Lea, Thomas D. *Holman New Testament Commentary: Hebrews, James.* Nashville, TN: Broadman & Holman Publishers, 1999.

Lea, Thomas D., and Hayne P. Griffin. *The New American Commentary, vol. 34, 1, 2 Timothy, Titus.* Nashville: Broadman & Holman Publishers, 1992.

Lightfoot, Joseph Barber, and J. R Harmer. *The Apostolic Fathers.* London: Macmillan and Co., 1891.

Lightfoot, Neil R. *How We Got the Bible.* Grand Rapids, MI: Baker Books, 1963, 1988, 2003.

McCarthy, Dan, and Charles Clayton. *Let the Reader Understand: A guide to Interpreting and Applying the Bible.* Wheaton, Illinois: BridgePoint, 1994.

McKenzie, John L. *Light on the Epistles: A Reader's Guide.* Chicago, IL: Thomas More Press, 1975.

McRay, John. *Paul: His Life and Teaching.* Grand Rapids: Baker Academics, 2003.

Metzger, Bruce M. *The Text of the New Testament: Its Transmission, Corruption, and Transmission.* New York: Oxford University Press, 1964, 1968, 1992.

Metzger, Bruce M. *A Textual Commentary on the Greek New Testament.* New York: United Bible Society, 1994.

Metzger, Bruce M., and Bart D. Ehrman. *The Text of the New Testament: Its Transmission, Corruption, and Restoration (4th Edition).* New York: Oxford University Press, 2005.

Metzger, Bruce. *Manuscripts of the Greek Bible: An Introduction to Palaeography .* New York, NY: Oxford University Press, 1981.

Mirriam-Webster, Inc. *Mirriam-Webster's Collegiate Dictionary. Eleventh Edition.* Springfield: Mirriam-Webster, Inc., 2003.

Mounce, Robert H. *The New American Commentary.* Nashville, TN: Broadman & Holman Publishers, 2001.

Mounce, William D. *Mounce's Complete Expository Dictionary of Old & New Testament Words.* Grand Rapids, MI: Zondervan, 2006.

Mounce, William D. *Basics of Biblical Greek Grammar.* Grand Rapids: Zonervan, 2009.

Myers, Allen C. *The Eerdmans Bible Dictionary .* Grand Rapids, Mich: Eerdmans, 1987.

Niessen, Richard. "The virginity of the `almah in Isaiah 7:14." *Bibliotheca Sacra 137 ,* 1980: 133-50.

Oden, Thomas C. *Ministry Through Word and Sacrament, Classic Pastoral Care.* New York: Crossroad, 1989.

Orchard, Bernard (Editor), Longstaff, Thomas R. W. (Editor). "J. J. Griesbach: Synoptic and Text - Critical Studies 1776-1976." *Society for New Testament Studies Monograph Series (Book 34),* 2005: xi.

Orchard, Bernard. *J. J. Griesbach: Synoptic and Text - Critical Studies* . Cambridge: Cambridge University Press, 1776-1976, 2005.

Oswalt, John N. *The NIV Application Commentary: Isaiah.* Grand Rapids, MI: Zondervan, 2003.

Outlaw, W. Stanley. *The Book of Hebrews* . Nashville, TN: Randall House, 2005.

Packer, J. I, and M. C Tenney. *Nelson Illustrated Manners and Customs of the Bible.* Nashville, TN: Thomas Nelson, 1980.

Packer, J. I. *Evangelism and the Sovereignty of God.* Downers Grove, IL: InterVarsity Press, 1979.

Parker, David C. *Codex Bezae: An Early Christian Manuscript and its Text.* Cambridge: Cambridge University Press, 1992.

Parker, David C. *The living Text of the Gospels.* Cambridge: Cambridge University Press, 1997.

Pink, Arthur Walkington. *An Exposition of Hebrews.* Swengel, PA: Bible Truth Depot, 1954.

Polhill, John B. *The New American Commentary 26: Acts.* Nashville: Broadman & Holman Publishers, 2001.

Pratt Jr, Richard L. *Holman New Testament Commentary: I & II Corinthians, vol. 7.* Nashville: Broadman & Holman Publishers, 2000.

Pressense, E. De. *The Early Years Of Christianity: A Comprehensive History Of The First Three Centuries Of The Christian Church; The Apostolic Age V1.* Whitefish, MT: Kessinger Publishing, LLC, 1860, 2007.

Price, Randall. *Searching for the Original Bible.* Eugene: Harvest House, 2007.

Ramsey, Boniface (Editor). *Manichean Debate (Works of Saint Augustine).* New City Press: Hyde Park, 2006.

Reinhartz, Adele ed. *Semeia 85: Gof the Father in the Gospel of John.* Atlanta: Society of Biblical Literature, 2001.

Richards, E. Randolph. *Paul And First-Century Letter Writing: Secretaries, Composition and Collection.* Downers Grove: InterVarsity Press, 2004.

—. *The Secretary in the Letters of Paul.* Tübingen: J.C.B. Mohr, 1990.

Roberts, C. H. *Books in the Graeco-Roman World and in the New Testament in the Cambridge History of the Bible, Vol. 1, From the Beginnings to Jerome* . Cambridge: Cambridge University Press, 1970.

Roberts, Colin H. *Manuscript, Society, and Belief in Early Christian Egypt.* London: Oxford University Press, 1979.

Roberts, Colin H., and Theodore C. Skeat. *The Birth of the Codex.* London: Oxford University Press, 1987.

Robertson, A. T. *An Introduction to the Textual Criticism of the New Testament.* London: Hodder & Stoughton, 1925.

Robinson, G. L., and R. K. Harrison. *The International Standard Bible Encyclopedia, vol. 2.* Grand Rapids: Eerdmans, 1982.

Rogers, Rick. "Theophilus of Antioch." *Expository Times*, Feburary 2009: 214-224.

Royse, James R. *Scribal Habits in Early Greek New Testament Papyri (New Testament Tools and Studies) (New Testament Tools, Studies and Documents).* Leiden & Boston: Brill Academic Pub, 2007.

Royse, James Ronald. *Scribal Habits in Early Greek New Testament Papyri.* Leidon, Boston: BRILL, 1981.

Schaff, Philip, and David Schley Schaff. *History of the Christian Church, vol. 2.* New York: Charles Scribner's Sons, 1910.

Schurer, Emil. *A HISTORY OF THE JEWISH PEOPLE IN THE TIME OF JESUS CHRIST (Volume II).* Edinburgh: T. & T. Clark, 1890.

Scott, Julius J. Jr. *Jewish Backgrounds of the New Testament.* Grand Rapids, MI: Baker Academic, 1995.

Smith, Gary. *The New American Commentary: Isaiah 1-39, Vol. 15a.* Nashville, TN: B & H Publishing Group, 2007.

—. *The New American Commentary: Isaiah 40-66, Vol. 15b.* Nashville, TN: B&H Publishing, 2009.

Souter, Alexander. *The Text and Canon of the New Testament.* New York: Charles Scribner's Sons, 1913.

Starr, Raymond J. "The Circulation of Literary Texts in the Roman World." *The Classical Quarterly*, 1987: 213-223.

Stein, Robert H. *A Basic Guide to Interpreting the Bible: Playing by the Rules.* Grand Rapids: Baker Books, 1994.

Stetzer, Ed, and David Putman. *Breaking the Missional Code: Your Church Can Become a Missionary in Your Community.* Nashville: Broadman & Holman, 2006.

Swanson, James. *A Dictionary of Biblical Languages - Greek.* Washington: Logos Research Systems, 1997.

Theophilus, of Antioch. "Theophilus to Autolycus." In *The Ante-Nicene Fathers, Vol II: Hermas, Tatian, Athenagoras, Theophilus, and Clement of Alexandria,* by Marcus Dods, 85-122. Buffalo, NY: Christian Literature Company, 1885.

Towns, Elmer L. *Concise Bible Dictrines: Clear, Simple, and Easy-to-Understand Explanations of Bible Doctrines.* Chattanooga: AMG Publishers, 2006.

Tregelles, Samuel Prideaux. *An Account of the Printed Text of the Greek New Testament: With Remarks on Its Revision Upon Critical Principles.* London: S. Bagster and Sons, 1854.

Tuckett, Christopher M. "P52 and Nomina Sacra." *New Testament Study,* 2001: 544-48.

Vine, W E. *Vine's Expository Dictionary of Old and New Testament Words.* Nashville: Thomas Nelson, 1996.

Wace, Henry. *A Dictionary of Christian Biography and Literature to the end of the sixth century.* Grand Rapids, MI: Christian Classics Ethereal Library, 1999.

Wachtel, Klaus, and Michael W Holmes. *The Textual History of the Greek New Testament: Changing Views in Contemporary Research, Text-Critical Studies.* Atlanta: Society of Biblical Literature, 2011.

Wallace, Daniel B. *Revisiting the Corruption of the New Testament: Manuscript, Patristic, and Apocryphal Evidence.* Grand Rapids, MI: Kregel Publications, 2011.

Wallace, Daniel. *The Reliability of the New Testament: Bart Ehrman and Daniel Wallace in Dialogue.* Minneapolis, MN: Fortress Press, 2011.

Walls, David, and Max Anders. *Holman New Testament Commentary: I & II Peter, I, II & III John, Jude.* Nashville: Broadman & Holman Publishers, 1996.

Walton, John H. *Zondervan Illustrated Bible Backgrounds Commentary (Old Testament) Volume 1: Genesis, Exodus, Leviticus, Numbers, Deuteronomy.* Grand Rapids, MI: Zondervan, 2009.

Walton, John H. "Isaiah 7:14: what's in a name?" *Journal of the Evangelical Theological Society 30*, 1987: 289-306.

—. *Zondervan Illustrated Bible Backgrounds Commentary (Old Testament) Volume 3: 1 & 2 Kings, 1 & 2 Chronicles, Ezra, Nehemiah, Esthe.* Grand Rapids, MI: Zondervan, 2009.

—. *Zondervan Illustrated Bible Backgrounds Commentary (Old Testament) Volume 5: The Minor Prophets, Job, Psalms, Proverbs, Ecclesiastes, Song of Songs.* Grand Rapids, M: Zondervan, 2009.

Weber, Stuart K. *Holman New Testament Commentary, vol. 1, Matthew.* Nashville, TN: Broadman & Holman Publishers, 2000.

Wegner, Paul D. *A Student's Guide to Textual Criticism of the Bible: Its History Methods & Results.* Downers Grove: InterVarsity Press, 2006.

—. *The Journey from Text to Translation.* Grand Rapids: Baker Academic, 1999.

Westcott, B. F., and F. J. A. Hort. *The New Testament in the Original Greek, Vol. 2: Introduction, Appendix.* London: Macmillan and Co., 1882.

Westcott, B. F., and Hort F. J. A. *The New Testament in the Original Greek, Vol. 2: Introduction, Appendix.* London: Macmillan and Co., 1882.

Whiston, William. *The Works of Josephus.* Peabody, MA: Hendrickson, 1987.

Whitney, Donald S. *Spiritual Disciplines for the Christian Life with Bonus Content (Pilgrimage Growth Guide).* Colorado Springs, CO: Navpress, 1991.

Wolf, Herbert M. "Solution to the Immanuel Prophecy in Isaiah 7:14-8:22." *Journal of Biblical Literature 91 ,* 1972: 449-56.

Wood, D R W. *New Bible Dictionary (Third Edition).* Downers Grove: InterVarsity Press, 1996.

Woodbridge, John D., and Frank A. James III. *CHURCH HISTORY VOLUME TWO From Pre-Reformation to the Present Day The Rise and Growth of the Church in Its Cultural, Intellectual, and Political Context .* Grand Rapids: Zondervan, 2013.

Wright, N. T. *Hebrews for Everyone.* London: Westminster John Knox Press, 2003.

Zodhiates, Spiros. *The Complete Word Study Dictionary: New Testament.* Chattanooga: AMG Publishers, 2000, c1992, c1993.

Zuntz, Gunther. *The Text of the Epistles: A Disquisition upon the Corpus Paulinum.* London: Oxford University Press, 1953.

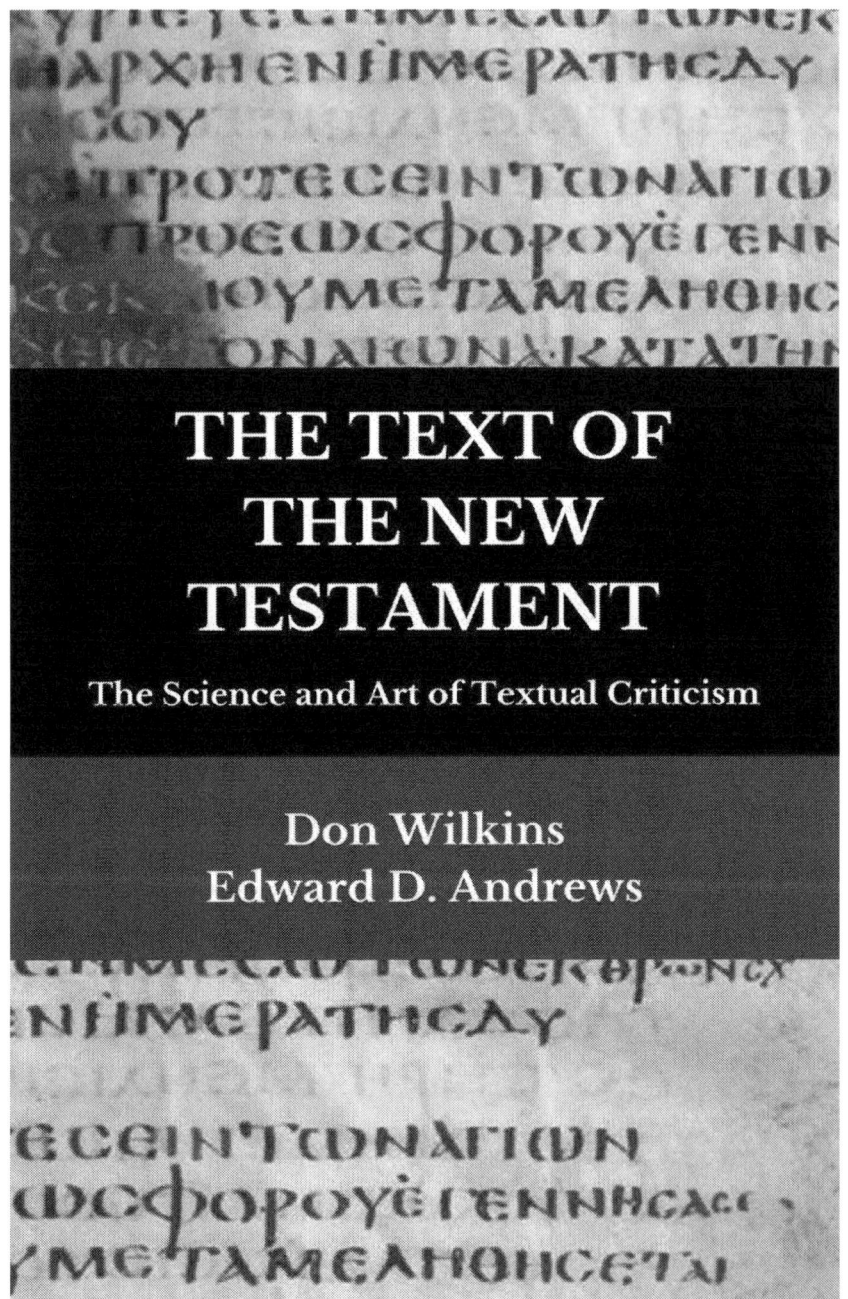

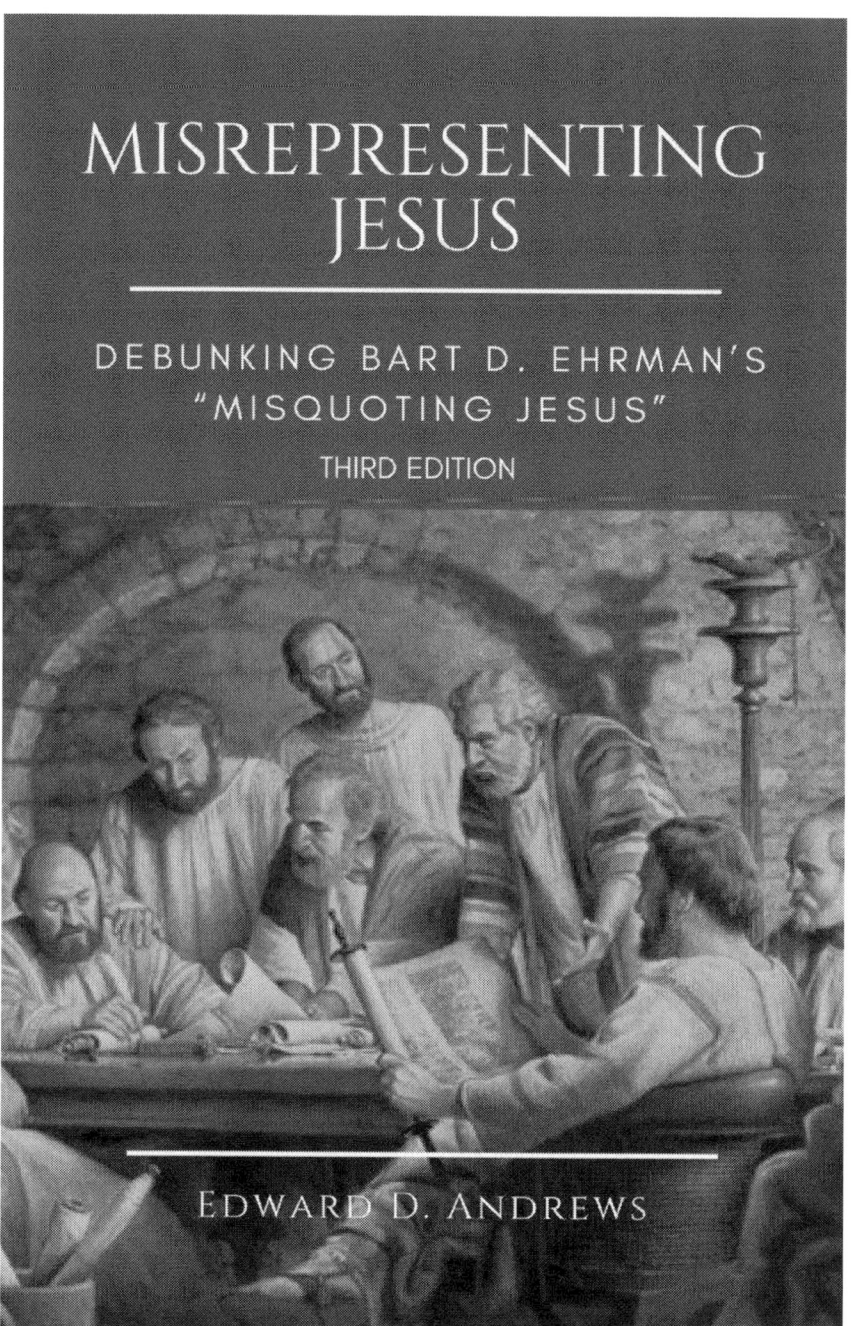

MISREPRESENTING JESUS

DEBUNKING BART D. EHRMAN'S "MISQUOTING JESUS"

THIRD EDITION

EDWARD D. ANDREWS

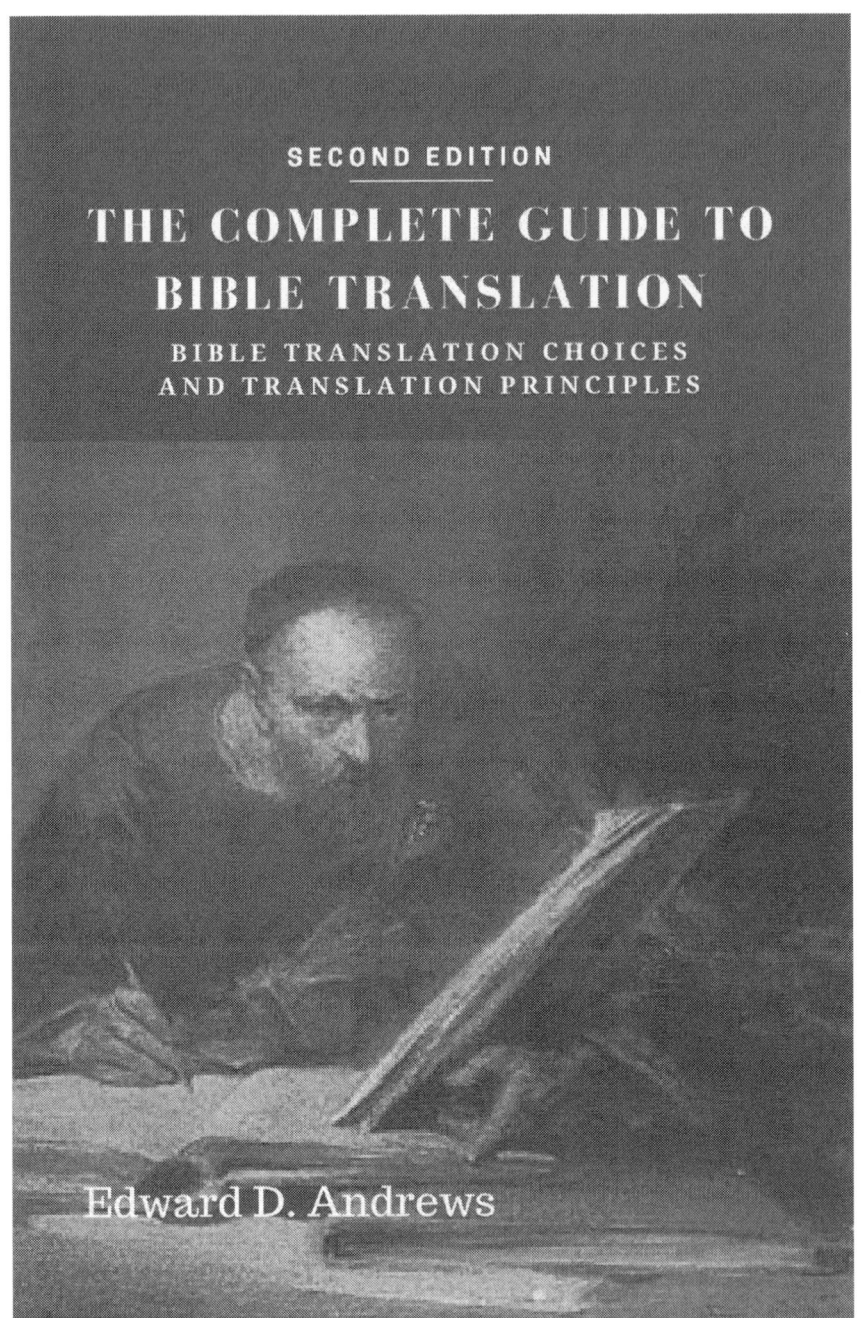

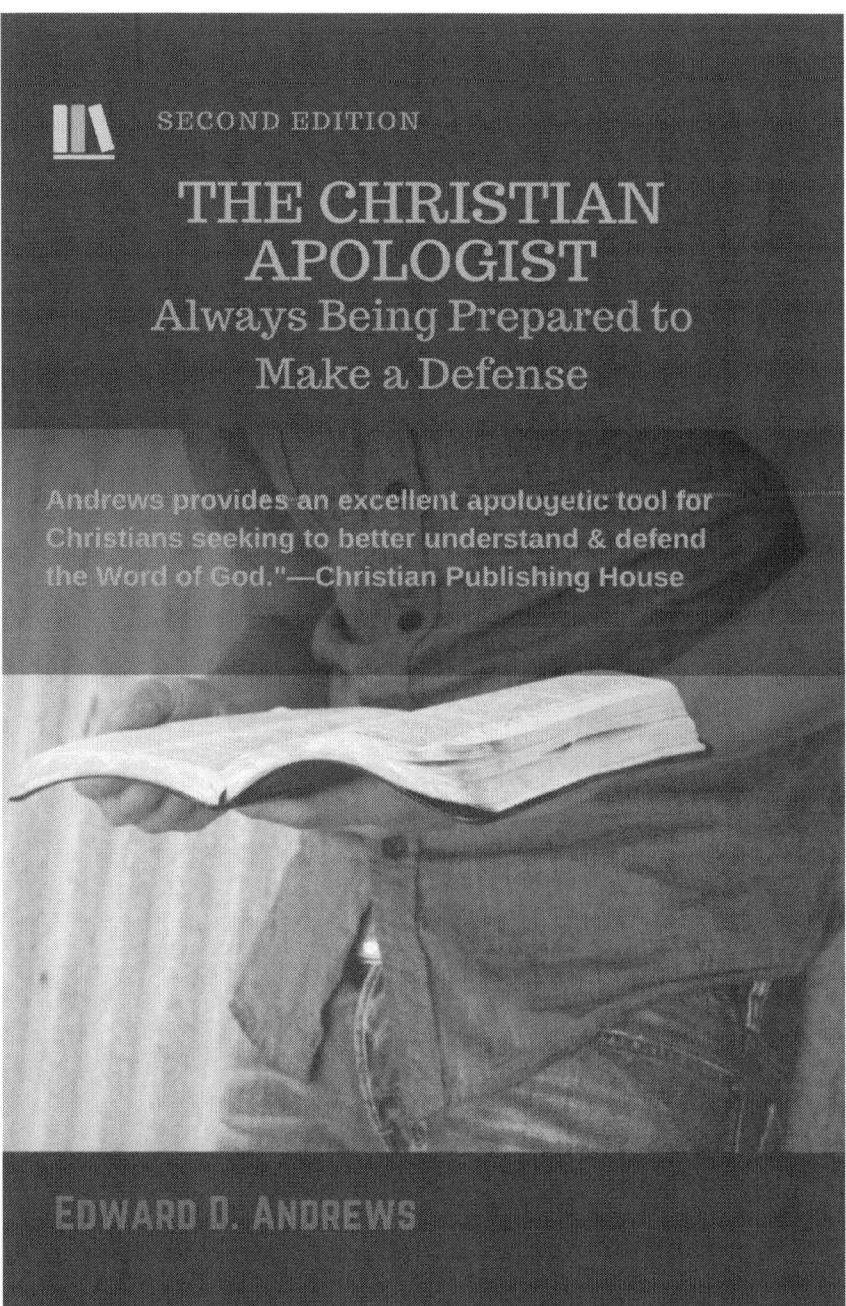

SECOND EDITION

THE CHRISTIAN APOLOGIST
Always Being Prepared to Make a Defense

Andrews provides an excellent apologetic tool for Christians seeking to better understand & defend the Word of God."—Christian Publishing House

EDWARD D. ANDREWS

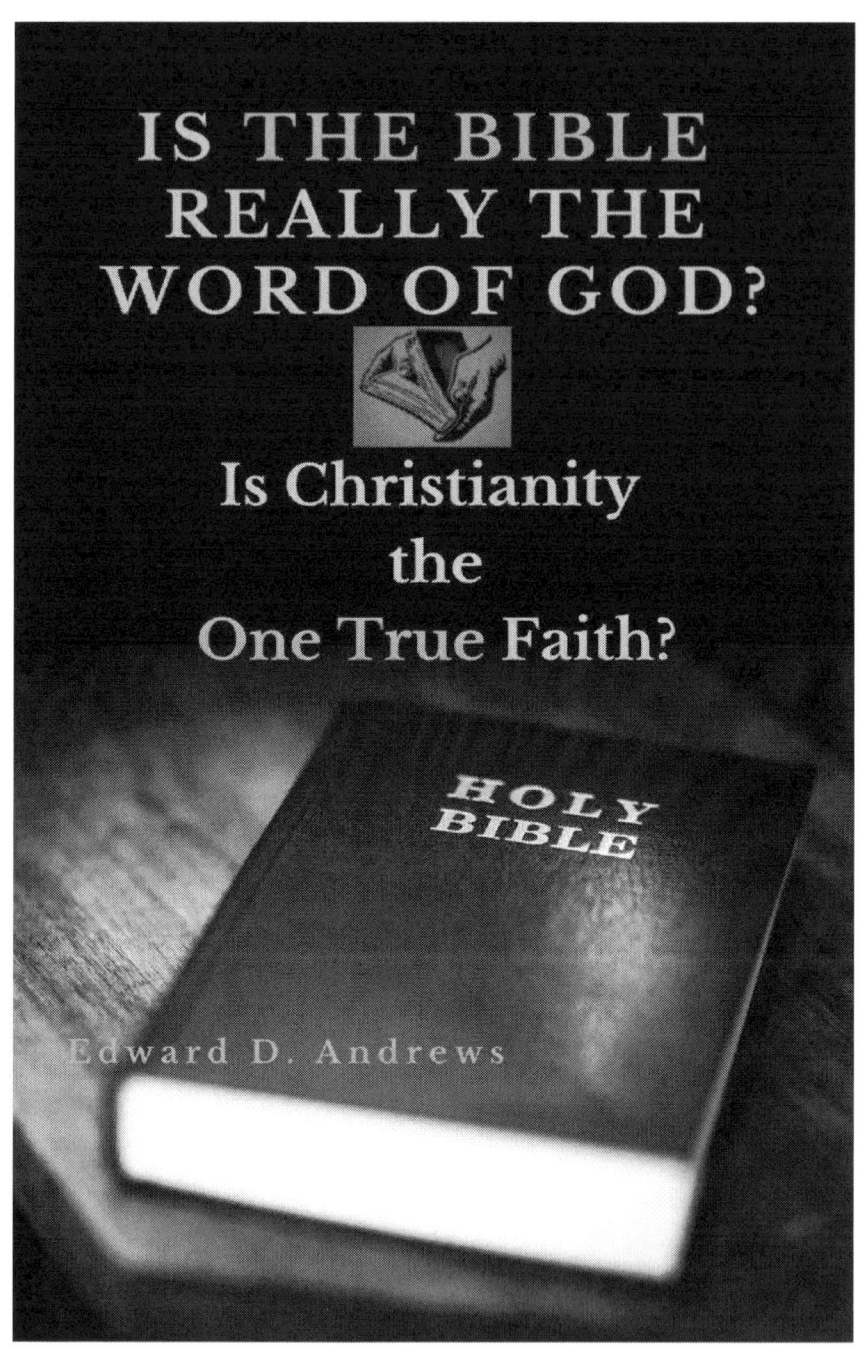

IS THE BIBLE REALLY THE WORD OF GOD?

Is Christianity the One True Faith?

Edward D. Andrews

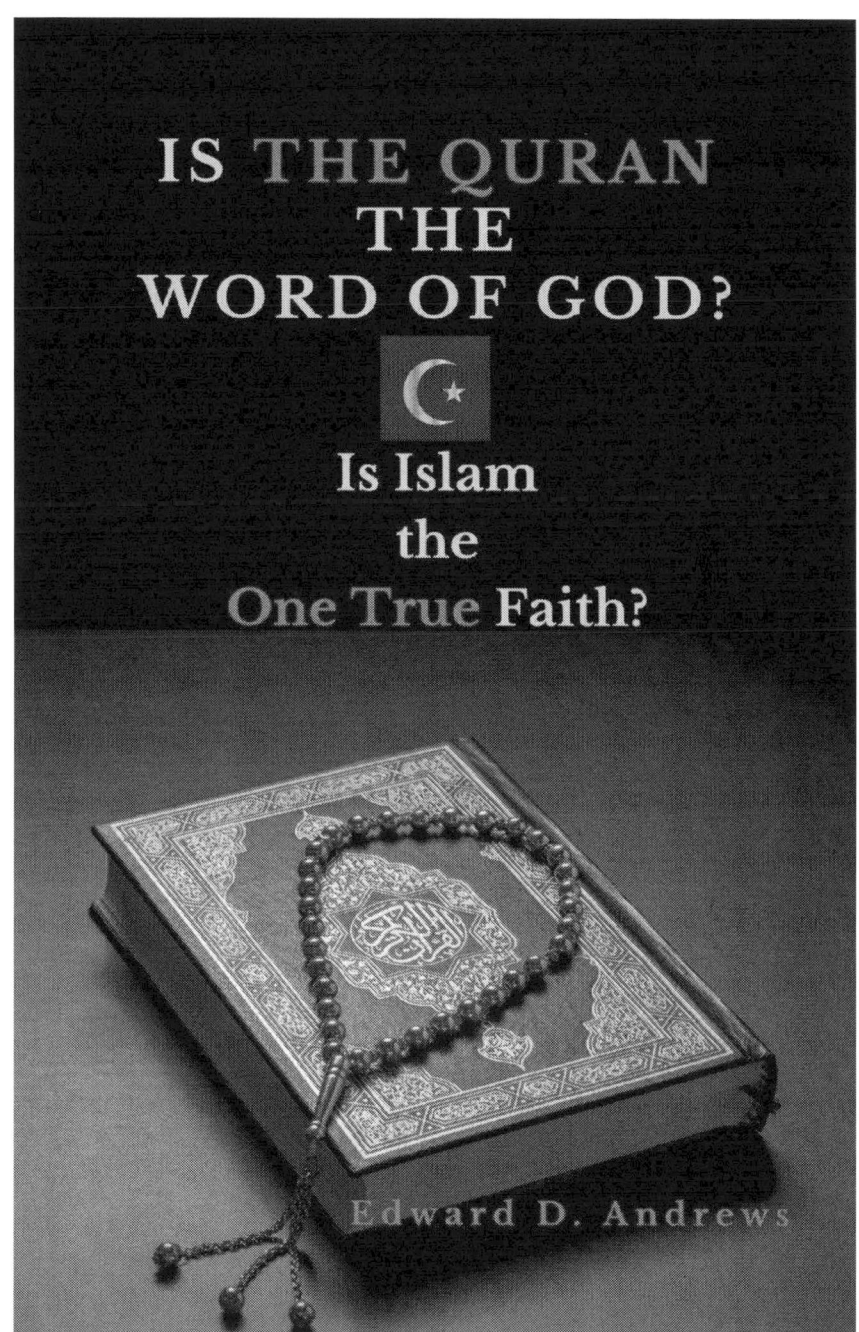

IS THE QURAN
THE
WORD OF GOD?

Is Islam
the
One True Faith?

Edward D. Andrews

SECOND EDITION

CONVERSATIONAL EVANGELISM

Defending the Faith, Reasoning from the
Scriptures, Explaining and Proving,
Instructing in Sound Doctrine, and
Overturning False Reasoning

Edward D. Andrews

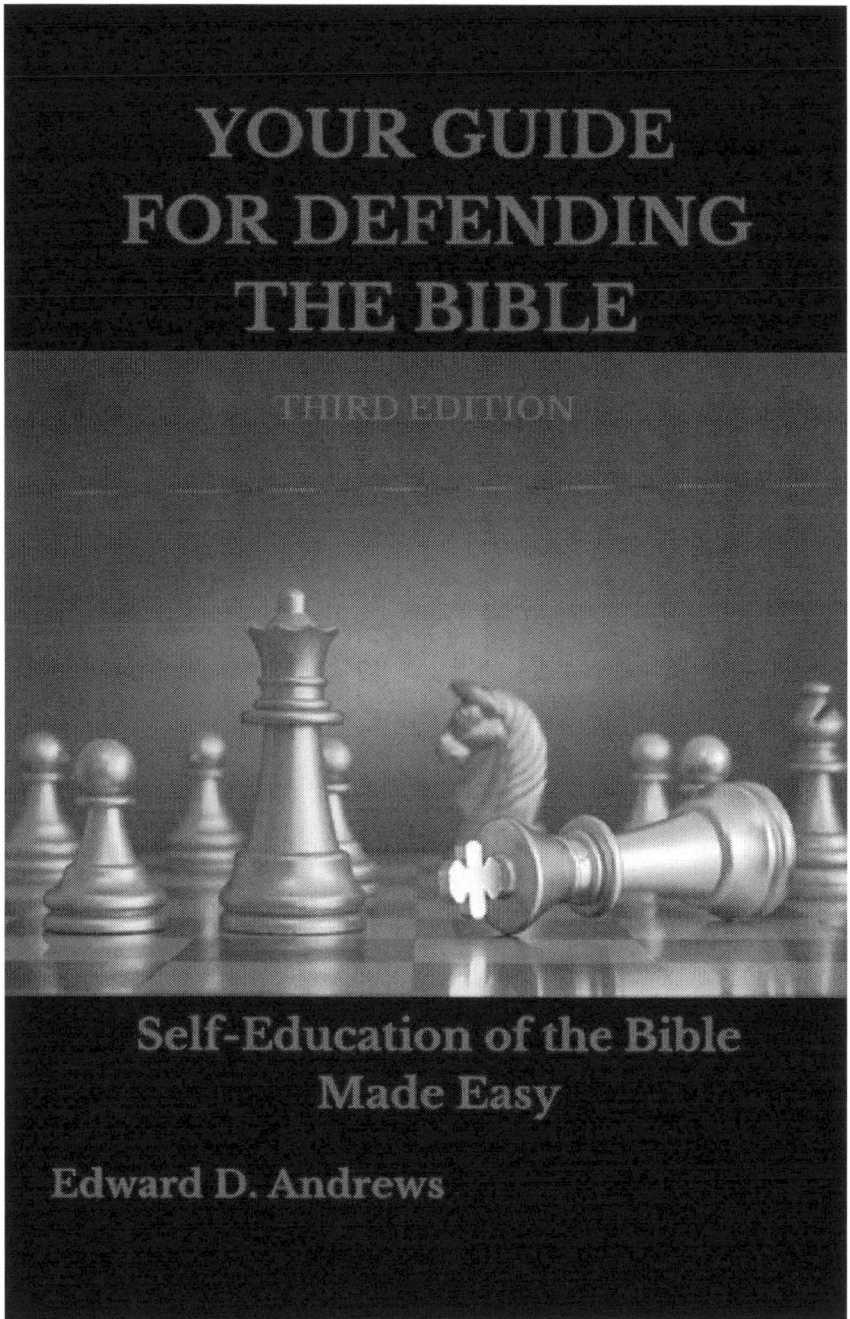

YOUR GUIDE FOR DEFENDING THE BIBLE

THIRD EDITION

Self-Education of the Bible Made Easy

Edward D. Andrews

SECOND EDITION

THE EVANGELISM HANDBOOK

How All Christians Can Effectively
Share God's Word in Their
Community

Matthew 9:37-38: Then he said to his disciples, "The harvest is
plentiful, but the laborers are few. Therefore beg the Master of the
harvest to send out workers into his harvest."

Matthew 24:14; 28:18-20: Jesus said, "this gospel of the kingdom will
be proclaimed in all the inhabited earth." "... Go therefore and make
disciples of all nations ... teaching them ..."

Edward D. Andrews

47379560R00132

Printed in Poland
by Amazon Fulfillment
Poland Sp. z o.o., Wrocław